PLACES FOR CHILDHOODS

MAKING QUALITY HAPPEN
IN THE REAL WORLD

by Jim Greenman

This book is a collection of Jim Greenman's
"Living in the Real World" columns, revised and updated,
originally published in *Child Care Information Exchange*.

Child Care Information Exchange is a bimonthly management magazine
for directors and owners of early childhood programs.
For more information about *Child Care Information Exchange*
and other *Exchange* publications, contact:

Child Care Information Exchange
PO Box 3249
Redmond, WA 98073-3249
(800) 221-2864
www.ccie.com

Production Department:
Bonnie Neugebauer
Carole White
Sandy Brown
Tami McNeal

Photographs:
Bonnie Neugebauer

ISBN 0-942702-25-5
Printed in the United States of America

REFLECTIONS AUTHORS

Paula Jorde Bloom is a professor of early childhood education and director of the Center for Early Childhood Leadership at National-Louis University in Wheeling, Illinois. She has taught preschool and kindergarten, designed and directed a child care center, and served as administrator of a campus laboratory school. She is the author of numerous journal articles and several widely read books including: *Avoiding Burnout: Strategies for Managing Time, Space, and People; Living and Learning with Children;* and *A Great Place to Work: Improving Conditions for Staff in Young Children's Programs.* Her most recent book, *Blueprint for Action: Achieving Center-Based Change Through Staff Development,* provides a framework for understanding child care centers as organizations and how staff development can serve as the vehicle for improving program effectiveness.

Lella Gandini is an author of children's books, books for parents and teachers, and a correspondent for the Italian early education magazine, *Bambini.* She serves as official liaison in the United States for the dissemination of the Reggio Emilia approach for children. She is adjunct professor in the School of Education at the University of Massachusetts, Amherst.

Karen Miller is the author of *Ages and Stages, Things to Do with Toddlers and Twos, More Things to Do with Toddlers and Twos, The Outside Play and Learning Book,* and *The Crisis Manual for Early Childhood Teachers* (Gryphon House). She is also the author of "Caring for the Little Ones," a regular column in *Child Care Information Exchange.*

Elizabeth Prescott is professor emeritus of Pacific Oaks College, Pasadena, California. She has had a series of research grants from DHEW to study child care environments. She is co-author of the NAEYC publications (now out of print), *The "Politics" of Day Care* and *Day Care As a Child-Rearing Environment.*

Diane Trister Dodge, founder and president of Teaching Strategies, Inc., is the author of more than 20 books on early childhood education. She is a well-known speaker and trainer and currently serves on the board of the National Center for the Early Childhood Work Force (NCECW).

Janet Gonzalez-Mena taught early childhood education at Napa Valley College in Northern California for 15 years. She is now a full-time consultant and writer. She has also been a child care director and a preschool teacher. She holds an MA in human development from Pacific Oaks College. She is co-producer of a video series for training child care teachers called "Diversity." Recent books include *Dragon Mom: Confessions of a Child Development Expert* and *Foundations: Early Childhood Education in a Diverse Society.* She is also the author of *Multicultural Issues in Child Care.* In addition, she writes a weekly parenting column for *The Napa Valley Register.*

Roger Neugebauer is publisher of *Child Care Information Exchange.* He is a current or former board member of the Association of Work/Life Professionals, the National Association of Child Care Resource and Referral Agencies, the High/Scope Educational Research Foundation, and the National Association for the Education of Young Children.

Anne Stonehouse is currently an associate professor of early childhood at Monash University and director of the Centre for Early Childhood Research and Professional Development. Her recent publications include: *How Does It Feel? A Parent's Perspective on Child Care, Trusting Toddlers, Not Just Nice Ladies, Ourselves in Their Shoes,* and *Opening the Doors: Child Care in a Multicultural Society,* as well as many articles. Her most recent book, *Prime Times: a Handbook for Excellence in Infant and Toddler Programs,* is co-authored with Jim Greenman. She has given numerous conference addresses, talks, workshops, and in-service training sessions for early childhood professionals over the years.

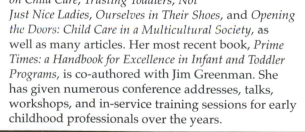

ABOUT THE AUTHOR

Jim Greenman is vice president for education and program development at Bright Horizons Family Solutions. His other books include **Caring Spaces, Learning Places: Children's Environments That Work** *(Exchange Press), and* **Prime Times: A Handbook for Excellence in Infant and Toddler Care** *with Anne Stonehouse (Redleaf Press).*

ABOUT THE BOOK

The material in this volume covers nearly 20 years of thinking about child care. Dated material was edited out or updated. The book is organized by topic and follows the logic of the content, not when the piece happened to be written. As with any book of columns, the thread that weaves throughout the content is the sensibility of the author. There has been no effort to tighten the weave with new material. Each section contains a guest reflection by a colleague whose work has served as a source of ideas and inspiration.

ACKNOWLEDGMENTS

The usual suspects made this possible. Emma, Anne, and Jan put up with the selfishness and neglect of a writer trying to hoard time to write on the side. They also served as ongoing inspiration and a daily reality check. Bob Lurie has been a colleague and critic for 20 years and never allowed me to descend into the depths of earnestness or self-importance. Anne Stonehouse has long been a source of ideas (mostly credited) and friendship. I have learned from Janet Gonzalez-Mena, Paula Jorde Bloom, Lella Gandini, Karen Miller, Elizabeth Prescott, and Diane Dodge, and appreciate their contributions to this volume. Child Care Information Exchange has also endured the flip side of the same time crunch: missed deadlines, submissions one or two drafts away from coherence. Bonnie Neugebauer, Sandy Brown, and Carole White have shown great patience for a long time (undoubtedly out of my sight — a sometimes prickly and rather worn patience) and deserve the credit for making this volume happen and look good.

PLACES FOR CHILDHOODS

MAKING QUALITY HAPPEN IN THE REAL WORLD

CHAPTER 4 — CREATING A WONDERFUL PLACE TO BE A CHILD

CHAPTER 5 — LIVING IN A VERY REAL CHILD CARE WORLD

CHAPTER 6 — ORGANIZATIONAL REALITY

CHAPTER 7 — PLACES FOR CHILDHOODS INCLUDE PARENTS, TOO

CHAPTER 8 — TRAINING AND CHANGE

FINAL THOUGHTS

INTRODUCTION:
I'VE BEEN HERE SO LONG IT FEELS LIKE THERE

I was 38 years old before I realized I was in child care — really in, not just in transit on my way to law school, or finishing my Ph.D., or writing novels. This epiphany was a bit peculiar because since college it was virtually all I had ever done. Now, ten years later, it startles me again to realize that child care is what I have done for 30 years. In that time I have played nearly every role but cook. My perspective is broadened by experience as an aide, teacher, parent, consultant, researcher, trainer, director, environmental designer, and corporate administrator (pretty much in that chronological order). Child care has given me the opportunity to continually, seriously, and mostly joyfully play — play with children and adults and play different roles, hoping the new skills would catch up with me: writer, researcher, videographer, speaker, critic.

Putting together this book of columns is an exercise in revisiting the architecture of that professional life. The first column dates back to 1980, the last from 1998. Throughout, there have been consistent themes that shadow nearly all the topics.

THE COMPLEXITY OF CHILD CARE

Child care is only easy when you don't know what you are doing. When I first began writing in 1977, the simple model of child care pretty much dominated the public consciousness:

$$\frac{\text{good people (AKA kindhearted women)} \\ \text{enough toys and materials} \\ +\ \text{pretty good space (renovated basement)}}{\text{good child care}}$$

Most of us in the field then had a more sophisticated view of good people (well trained, enough people to produce good ratios and small groups), and a more thoughtful and detailed view of what equipment and facility was required. But in the last 20 years I think we have grown by leaps and bounds to appreciate how inadequate the simple model really is, even as it lives on in the minds of most of the public and in the political world. Child care centers are complex organizations and engender complex relationships.

Quality is more about brains than warm laps and kind hearts. Quality flows from active brains daily solving the problems and making the trade-offs necessary to balance competing needs and priorities and scarce resources — the most precious resource being time to think and plan. Quality is also more than a "by the numbers" regulatory or accreditation criteria approach to those good people and space. It doesn't just flow from good ratios and group size, training, and a center designed for child care — but you certainly have to start there.

CHILD CARE IN ITS OWN RIGHT — DISTINCT FROM PART-DAY EDUCATION PROGRAMS

I was a young child care teacher in the 1970s between episodes of academia, and I lived the need to sort through the distinctiveness of child care (then day care). Nearly all the early education training and research was based on the kindergarten and nursery school (or preschool) experience. The world of research and training didn't seem to understand the enormity of the child care experience, compared to the part-day nursery school or newly emerging Head Start experience, or the complexity of the organization or the relationships. For kids, the nine and ten hour days, five days a week, 50 weeks a year was certainly enormous — 12,000 hours of their early life, as much time as they would spend in institutional life from kindergarten through high school. Instead of a brief slice of early childhood like the 500 to 1,000 hours of nursery school or Head Start, child care centers would, in essence, provide childhoods to these children.

Now if you ask most of us "What kind of childhood do you want for your child," we would give a very different and more complex answer than we would to the question "What should an early education program provide your child?" Few of us would conjure up a vision of a subterranean childhood of 12,000 hours under fluorescent lights, filled with easy to clean plastic toys, circle times, and tiny, arid playgrounds. In half-day programs — where children go from home to a few hours of "not home" (AKA the center), and back to home — the quality of life is far less important. A mediocre environment or program is unfortunate but much less debilitating in smaller doses.

In a good child care program, the relationships between caregiver and child and caregiver and parent also typically assumed a breadth and a depth beyond that of part-day educational programs. The weight of parental "day care guilt," combined with the quantity of time of parent-child separation and the high cost of care, set in motion dynamics never addressed in the world of lab schools or training programs.

In time, it became clear to me that child care's rightful institutional analog was more the good home than the good school; a good place to be a kid, a good place to learn, to be me (not just another kid), and a place that supports the values and goals of my family.

THE DIFFICULTY OF MAKING QUALITY HAPPEN IN THE REAL WORLD

I love conceptualizing what child care should be and then passionately speaking and writing about it — making the ideas come to life. But making an idea come to life is not quite the same as making the idea real — it is the difference between the mouth-watering picture on the menu and that bland taste in your mouth. The real world is so real and that reality grinds away at reformers, improvers, dreamers, and ideologues. Change is hard. It is never just enough money, or the need for training, or more energy, or new ideas (which are often good old ideas with new names). The ground is never smooth and the roots and cracks of daily life always trip up progress: the comings and goings of people and funding, the thorny tangle of personalities, and the sheer weight of "shoulds."

I have tried, not always successfully, to avoid the earnest litany of "shoulds" that are the staple of advice givers. They come either packaged in an upbeat, perky Martha Stewart like "I did it and you can too" sermonette; or the easy-to-follow list: "Ten steps to better supervision and cooking with baby root vegetables." Quality child care is not paint by the numbers.

CHILDHOODS ARE IMPORTANT

> *Childhood is the world of miracle and wonder: as if creating rose and bathed in light, out of the darkness, utterly new and fresh and astonishing. The end of childhood is when things cease to astonish us. When the world seems familiar, when we have gotten used to existence, one has become an adult.* — Eugene Ionesco

In every culture, childhood is a special time, the most powerful period in our lives. In a commercial sense, childhood in America is thriving; more attention than ever is focused on children and childhood as a market for products, services, and information. And childhood is lasting longer; some say extending into middle age, helped by Nike and Aaron Spelling. But in another more meaningful sense, the zone of mostly carefree childhoods abundant with natural life, a variety of real people and places, and time to mess about is shrinking like the rain forests: slashed and burned by the ravenous commercial marketplace, and paved over by the concrete web of our good intentions. Many children are increasingly cut off from the real and natural world. More children rarely have the chance to experience that "thrilling free feeling of feeling freewheeling" (Eve Merriman). Of course, many children of poverty never had carefree lives to lose. Their lives are all too real and never carefree. The institutional life I lament for more affluent children might provide some respite from frequent chaos that tyrannizes many children of the inner city.

But I do periodically wonder whether the vision of childhood I write about really is important or instead only a matter of taste or a nostalgic excuse for dramatic metaphor. Taste is, of course, an important part of the vision. Authenticity is subjective. My dislike of the Disneyfication and the malling of America — the shroud that the adult commercial world casts over childhoods — is both a matter of aesthetics and ideology, not child development or moral truth. But as my daughter periodically says, loaded with attitude: "So, what's your point?" Until proven otherwise, I think a childhood that brings out the human best in children is endangered.

The Institutionalization of Childhood Is Real and Needs to Be Fought

It is amazing to me, a mostly unrepentant enthusiastic participant of the '60s, that we have so thoroughly institutionalized middle American childhood. Each decade brings more scheduled, managed, packaged, purchased institutional life. Why? It is fueled by both a climate of fear for the safety of children, a two-parent work force, and an insecure drive to make sure that my kid has a leg up, has the best of things, and does not miss out on any potential formative experience. We are sacrificing the child's present under the guise of preparing for the perfect future.

In the early 1990s when I visited child care programs in Australia and Canada,, I was struck by how the best programs there had a different sense and sensibility, a sensibility common in the United States 20 years ago and far less evident today. There, and then, the approach was "Let's create a great place to be a kid, then we will figure out how to make it healthy and safe, and look good."

We are caught in the opposite approach. First, we create safe, healthy, risk and liability free functional environments for children, and then hopefully enough life and learning will be able to seep through. We certainly can't afford to be sued, cited, or misunderstood by customers. While I am firmly on the side of high standards, health, and safety (and truth and justice), the lesson of centers outside of America is that there are other ways to approach the doing of child care than our current approach.

There Are No New Ideas Under the Sun

Mark Twain said that originality is usually undetected plagiarism. I like it when people consider me an original thinker. "Pshaw," I mumble, and blush and look humble. I'm flattered, of course. But all I have to do is glance at my bookshelves to lose the false modesty, because I know that it isn't true. My original thoughts; new ideas for environments; bold new perspectives on education, children, or families all have traceable origins — although I probably have had original ideas that didn't work.

While I am cynical about all the renaming and repackaging of old ideas, creativity is about recognizing that important ideas come from a universe far wider than the spot occupied by early education and child care in America today. Whether the topic is child care environment or curriculum, parenting or teaching, politics or policy, wisdom inevitably comes from bringing to bear a perspective that includes historical experience and the thinking of artists and architects, social thinkers and educators, writers and philosophers.

I can easily trace my ideas to the following people: Millie Almy, Elizabeth Prescott, Gwen Morgan, Susan and Nathan Issacs, Sylvia Ashton-Warner, Betty Jones, Seymour Sarason, Lilian Katz, John Holt, James Herndon, Paolo Frere, Eric Ericson, David Elkind, Ellen Galinsky, Erving Goffman, E. B. White, Educational Facilities Lab, Robin Moore, and Christopher Alexander.

The other great source of ideas comes from the other direction: the day-to-day actions of teachers, children, and parents trying to make child care work for them. I have made a living trading off the ideas of countless teachers creating wonderful learning centers and watching and listening to the experience of children and parents living their child care lives.

CHAPTER 1

PLACES
FOR
CHILDHOODS

LOOK CAREFULLY AND YOU WILL HEAR . . .
(OR LISTEN CAREFULLY AND YOU WILL SEE . . .)

by Lella Gandini

My experience in the field of education in Italy and in the United States, as a continuous student and observer in the cities of Reggio Emilia and Pistoia and in places in this country that are working on innovation, convinces me that, as Jim Greenman suggests, we must work to deinstitutionalize institutions for young children and transform child care centers into a new kind of family center. These are essential directions to take.

Loris Malaguzzi, the founder and philosopher of the Reggio Emilia approach, wrote that programs for young children "distort and assault their own nature if they do not connect to the families, to the culture, to the local issues and if they are in some ways prevented from having a free and democratic dialogue with the environment in which they operate." And also, "We support a school where the educators realize how enriched is their work if they place their hands in the hands of families and in those of the people in the community." (Cited by S. Mantovani in "I cento Linguaggi dei bambini," 1995)

Educators in Italy have often taken stock, through years of laborious development of their programs, of the importance of communication at all levels. In their daily work they became aware of the power of observing, listening, speaking up, and supporting dialogues and discussions among children and adults. In fact, through time their interpretation and analyses of what observing, listening, dialoguing, and communicating can mean have become more attentive, and deeper (Carlina Rinaldi, Innovations 96). This has made it possible for their communication to be thoughtful, varied, respectful, and effective. How to improve communication is, in fact, a constant concern and commitment because the means, ways, and goals of communication have to be reexamined and readjusted as new children come into their programs along with new parents. Furthermore, changing societal needs and demands are brought continuously into the centers and schools.

Observing and listening to children is at the basis of their work, which is to create environments where those children will feel a sense of well-being, can feel accepted, and therefore are ready to explore, open to learn, and eager to enter in a dialogue with adults and peers. It is by observing the children and listening to those dialogues that educators will discuss first among each other choices that will form the basis of the educational content, rather than their arbitrarily imposing it. The teachers will return to the children the children's own words and thoughts with new questions and materials to explore that can sustain the continuation of the dialogue and the pleasure of discovering. In that way, the initiatives and strategies of the experience will be negotiated and constructed together by adults and children.

If parents are helped to notice how teachers carefully listen to and observe children, and how children's sense of well-being and developing interests are supported, they can form a sense of trust toward the educators, the center, or the school. The invitation to feel close to their children's experience away from home will come through the process of building this sense of trust.

It is not an easy task. Instead, it is a slow, patient construction and a continuous adjustment, even when good communication is in place. In too many situations, the life of a child in the center and the life of the child at home run a parallel, silent course. It is unknown to the parents and it is unknown to the teachers what happens in the other place where the child spends so much time, where small events and life-changing experiences accumulate and form the identity of the little girl or the little boy. The child's voice is too small to make that connection possible.

Teachers can use their voice to tell and to help parents understand what they have understood and heard; they can give strength and power to the voice of children. We have to find effective ways to communicate with parents in an ongoing way what is happening in the school. How can we make that communication readable, explicit, and inviting? What languages can we find to make our work interesting to parents so that they not only become involved in being helpful with the process of their children's learning and of the school organization, but they gradually become participants, protagonists in the life of all children in that class and in the school?

The goal is not for parents to become substitute teachers or helpers; in fact, their experience of being parents is invaluable for teachers to come to know, because it is part of what teachers do not know about the children's life. Parents should be gradually invited to be decisionmakers in collaboration with educators.

But what about the parents' voice? How many languages, real and metaphorical, do we have to learn and create to truly listen to them and communicate with them, so that they can feel safe and heard? They need our help to enter into a dialogue and into the conversation that is going on in the center. As educators, we can help to make the dialogue truly significant and respectful of the culture that each one of us brings. It is by working all together that we patiently construct, bit by bit, the particular culture of the small community in that particular school. That place, then, through the transformation, sheds the shell of "institution for children, do not enter unless authorized" (Jim Greenman).

AN AFTERTHOUGHT

Loris Malaguzzi told me the following story. In the late 1960s, many families from the south of Italy had immigrated to Reggio to find work. The cultural and linguistic differences between south and north in Italy are enormous, and so are the prejudices on both sides. The dealings between teachers and families were very cautious, with a great deal of apprehension and sense of inferiority, which can always be easily transformed into hostility, on the part of the families from the south. After some time, with the impression that the progress of understanding was too slow, Loris Malaguzzi had an idea. One day he gave the key to the school, which included the keys to the kitchen and provisions, to one mother who was in a way the leader of the group of new families. He asked her to prepare a big dinner for teachers, children, and all the other parents of the school with the dishes from the south she and her friends loved, so that all the parents could begin to understand and appreciate the different tastes and flavors.

That mother and the other parents were deeply impressed by the trust that Loris Malaguzzi, who was the revered head of the system of schools, was demonstrating. They prepared everything with the utmost care. The dinner was a great success and opened up the communication that had been missing, and that became a strong source of solidarity among all the adults and children.

RECONSIDERING OUR PART IN THE LIVES OF CHILDREN

As early childhood professionals, we think a lot about children in making our particular programs work. We focus on children's needs, development, and curriculum. But suppose we held our preoccupation with needs, development, curriculum, and like notions in suspension for a while; long enough for us to think about childhoods — children's lives in a broad context. Of course, childhood is made up of elements that fit into all of these boxes; but perhaps by shifting our focus we may gain new insight into what it is like to be a child today and our part in improving children's lives.

When we think of our own early childhoods — happy or unhappy, chaotic or relaxed — or perhaps even more powerful, the imagined childhoods we might have had or wish for our children, what images surface: what places, experiences with people, moments of pure pleasure, or wonder?

For most of us, images of fluorescently lit group times, worksheets, Legos, magic circles, easel time, and so on cannot hold their own with memories of secret places in the home or yard, moments with our friends unwatched (we thought) by adults, real conversations and physical intimacy with adults important to us.

Today we have institutionalized our children; there is no other word for it. Many children, almost from birth, are in a world of organized experiences in managed groups — child care, preschool, after-school programs, camps, swim/gym, and other classes.

We have done it for admirable reasons: to keep them safe while we work and go to school, to give them opportunities for learning and new experiences. Like it or not, trends in housing, work, leisure, crimes against children, and nearly all aspects of modern life seem to make institutionalization inevitable. It is hard to quarrel with any of the children's programs individually, but the net effect is disturbing.

We are a society perhaps more attentive to children than any other; but it is a limited attention, most often directed toward parents and children as consumers. Organized around children's *needs* and desires and parents' desires for their children, goods and experiences are packaged, bought, and sold — Cabbage Patch dolls, Suzuki violins, parent-child classes, computer camp.

Needs are defined or created and marketed; goods and services are rushed in to fill the gap.

While we may be in an *age of childhood*, Ivan Illich points out, "If society were to outgrow its age of childhood, it would have to become livable for the young." Rita Liljestrom, speaking of Swedish preschools, echoes Illich: "Let's admit there is something dubious about setting up special sanctuaries for children, about putting children in special preserves with adults who are specialized in looking after youngsters in a segregated child milieu with special furniture and toys for children, . . . in a very real sense the preschool can be seen as expressing a hostility to children in the social development."

What is missing? For many children, it is a sense of the variety of life — the real world of people and nature and machines and an opportunity to explore that world and be a part of it. In the past, children did not need special places for play. They had more free time in houses, backyards, fields, and streets. They lived amidst shops and trades people and mothers and fathers working in and around the home. And they had the time and freedom in their lives to *mess about*, captured beautifully by Kenneth Grahme in *The Wind in the Willows*:

"Nice? It's the only thing," said the Water Rat solemnly as he leaned forward for his stroke. "Believe me, my young friend, there is NOTHING — absolutely nothing — half so worth doing as simply messing about in boats. Simply messing," he went on dreamily, "messing — about — in — boats; messing —"

"Look ahead, Rat!" cried the Mole suddenly.

It was too late. The boat struck the bank full tilt. The dreamer, the joyous oarsman, lay on his back at the bottom of the boat, his heels in the air.

" — about in boats — or with boats," the Rat went on composedly, picking himself up with a pleasant laugh. "In or out of them, it doesn't matter. Nothing seems to really matter, that's the charm of it. Whether you get away, or whether you don't; whether you arrive at your destination, or whether you reach someplace else; or whether you never get anywhere at all, you are always busy and you never do anything in particular: and when you've done it there's always something else to do, and you can do it if you like, but you'd much better not."

It is not just that aspects of children's quality of life have changed, but their education as well. It is in messing about that children dream dreams and discover what they might be. Messing about is when children act

on the world and discover what it is made of and how it works.

Kenneth Eble, in *A Perfect Education*, describes a perfect education as one that "proceeds by surprises and the promise of other surprises, one that offers most opportunity for discovery." He observes that nature is the area in which our urban society is most lacking. "Even though our tremendously rich, tremendously mobile society gives far more people access to the more spectacular areas of nature than ever before, nature is not an important part of daily experience." He laments this loss because "it was nature, and it above all, that was to be discovered, bounteous, mysterious, unmindful, neither judging nor cautioning nor limiting, but mostly for children at least, infinitely inviting. . . . Zoos and public parks are wonderful as museums. . . . Yet for discovery one needs some things unmanaged, undesigned until a child's eye imposes a pattern."

Unmanaged, undesigned until a child imposes a pattern by his actions, here is precisely what is shrinking in the child's experience with both the physical and social world. EVERYTHING is managed and patterned and scheduled and governed by the patterns imposed by the sensible dictates of regulation, insurance, the bottom line, and the compromises of group living.

Cut off from the real world of society — a world of work and machines and production, unmanaged nature, social relationships with a wide variety of adults and children in different settings — and fewer and fewer opportunities to simply *mess about* following one's own inclinations, more and more children of each successive generation are losing opportunities for delight and wonder.

So what are we as early childhood professionals and advocates to do? We can lament the loss of the past, but it will not forestall the modern age. What we can do is think

Childhood is the world of miracle and wonder: as if creating rose and bathed in light, out of the darkness, utterly new and fresh and astonishing. The end of childhood is when things cease to astonish us. When the world seems familiar, when we have gotten used to existence, one has become an adult.

— Eugene Ionesco

critically about our roles, our places, and our programs in terms of the contexts of the lives that today's children are leading.

Perhaps if we thought more about childhoods and less about needs, some of our programs would look less like schools and more like homes and children's museums, or like fields and parks. We might develop varied places with a genuine sense of place — of beauty, variety, and elements of surprise and mystery; places where adults and children delight at times in simply being together, messing about, and working at the tasks that daily living requires.

If we thought about childhoods, we would notice that Joe's and Maria's and Emma's and Nguyen's childhoods are very different. Child care providers might accommodate to Joe's needs for sleep due to his 5:30 wake up time and parents' evening schedule, or recognize that Maria almost never leaves the barrio, that Emma has no contact with children of other ages, and that Nguyen is sorting through the strange ins and outs of American culture. There are needs here, as there are the strengths of Joe's adaptability, Maria's determination, Emma's charm with adults, and Nguyen's sense of responsibility far beyond her years.

If we periodically shifted our focus to childhoods, we might temper our clinical approach that views Joe and all the others as an assemblage of needs through the narrow lens of the tiny piece of Joe's life that we administer to. But it is difficult, because as we rightly tighten regulations, require credentials and specialized qualifications, develop accreditation, and *get our act together* in our programs — all the standardizing actions designed to improve general quality — a secondary effect is often an increased clinical approach (IEPs), more environmental management (no birds, bunnies, or lizards for health reasons),

The noticeable thing in New Zealand society is the body of people with their inner resources atrophied. Seldom have they had to reach inward to grasp the thing that they wanted. Everything, from material requirements to ideas, is available ready-made. . . . They can buy life itself from the film and radio-canned life. . . . They dried up. From babyhood they had shiny toys put in their hands, and in the kindergarten and infant rooms bright pictures and gay materials. Why conceive of anything of their own? They have not the need. The vast expanses of mind that could have been alive with creative activity are now no more than empty vaults that must for comfort's sake be filled with non-stop radio, and their conversation consists of a list of platitudes and clichés.

— Sylvia Ashton-Warner

less program flexibility to accommodate multi-age groups and to hire a diverse staff.

Perhaps all we can do here is to examine each issue from a broad perspective and at least recognize that some of our ostensibly sound decisions may form a mosaic that ultimately is not altogether positive.

Critiques like this do not lend themselves to easy solutions. Perhaps together with parents we can look at the quality of a child's life; and in the piece of childhood that we affect, look to establishing warm and flexible settings of space, time, and people that exist to expose children to the wonder and the magic of the world and allow them relatively unfettered opportunities to

discover the powers that they have within them to live and love and learn in the world.

REFERENCES

Ashton-Warner, Sylvia. *Teacher*. New York: Simon and Schuster, 1963.

Eble, Kenneth. *A Perfect Education*. New York: Collier, 1966.

Grahme, Kenneth. *The Wind in the Willows*. New York: Grosset and Dunlap, 1966.

Illich, Ivan. *Deschooling Society*. New York: Harper and Row, 1970.

Liljestrom, Rita. Quoted in *Report on Preschool Education*, November 8, 1977.

WHAT KIND OF PLACE IS THIS?

When I was a child, my brothers and sisters and I loved to visit my great aunt Meg — a tall, angular, elderly woman who is fixed in my memory as Babar's woman with the yellow hat. She would greet us at the door of her tiny Victorian house with the same words: "Come, children, we must find the fairies in the garden." Off we went to the small overgrown garden to find the fairies amidst the mushrooms and worms, lilies and lilacs. Each sparkle of dew was certainly a fairy, twinkling in and out of our lives with the power of van Goth's "Starry Night." Then we would wash off most of the mud and troop in for hot chocolate and stories on her velvet couch. We would be snuggled against the crook of her powdery arm, enveloped by the lemony smells of furniture polish, cats, and Aunt Meg (a scent of violet, cream, and an exotic smell we loved, later to discover it was the Ben-Gay ointment she used for her arthritis).

Is there a more secure place to be than drinking hot chocolate in the arms of a loved one? This security was essential as Aunt Meg read to us old Russian fairy tales — scary stories of witches and evil parents and the poor children, regularly subject to terrible predicaments. Our favorite was "Prince Ivan and the Witch Baby." At the climax of this tale, young Prince Ivan is chased through the countryside by his mountain-sized baby sister, who is grinning horribly with her huge iron teeth and chanting: "I've eaten my father, I've eaten my mother, and now I will eat my baby brother." (Looking at my younger sister, I identified completely.) We listened, delighted in our horror, waiting to be startled by the clock chimes on the hour or the raucous tea kettle.

Years later, we went to see Aunt Meg in the hospital just before she died. She slipped in and out of our reality, then suddenly appeared alert: "Do you still find the fairies?" she asked. We must have looked embarrassed because she quickly said in an impatient voice, "Oh, don't look like that, I'm dying, not demented — I know the house is gone (to make way for an apartment parking lot) — but the fairies are still there, only they've gone and buried most of them."

Childhood is about magic and wonder, of coming to terms with an inexplicable world of fairies and monstrous fears, of loved and feared adults, and a sensual world of sounds and smells and sensations. In an increasingly institutionalized world, are we bound to discover that we have buried all the fairies?

12,000 Hours: An Early Start on a Lifetime of Long Days

When children enter the world of child care, they may well spend up to 12,000 hours in child care before they reach the age parents decide it is no longer necessary — 12,000 hours, more time than they will log in elementary and secondary education. Almost from birth, eight to ten hour days, five days a week, 50 weeks a year. In contrast, children in nursery school, Head Start, or preschool usually spend no more than 15 hours a week, five days a week, 30 or so weeks a year, for two years of their lives — a total of less than 1,000 hours. Similar educational situations, vastly different experiences for children.

These profoundly different realities should have ramifications for nearly every aspect of child care program and facility design. Children in a part-day educational program go from home to a school (a *not-home,* an institution) and back to home where they spend most of their lives. What happens at the school may be an important and enriching experience, but it has relatively little overall influence on the quality of the child's day or childhood. If the program is too regimented and children spend too much time waiting, lining up, or following instructions, it is, after all, only for a few hours. The same is true if there is too little to do or the place is dreary, lacking natural light, or absent of charm. These programs provide only a small fraction of the child's experience.

However, in an all-day program, the quality of the child's day is determined by the program; indeed the quality of the child's childhood will be hugely influenced by his experience of child care people and places.

12,000 hours spent in a dark church basement, or sandwiched between gleaming vinyl floors and institutional uniform fluorescent lighting in small rooms based on 35 square feet per child, or being marched around with children the same age is not the childhood of which dreams are made, no matter how wonderful the teachers.

Whose Place Is It, Anyway?

Why has this huge difference between the child experience in a part-day and full-day setting been so little remarked upon in the literature and training? Why haven't we taken it into account in the design of facilities, and in licensing and accreditation guidelines about necessary space and experiences? The answer is egocentrism — ours. Because for us, the adults who inhabit the child care world, the difference between our days spent in child care, nursery school, and school are not so different. Our daily lives are not profoundly transformed as we move between the streams of early education.

Places for Childhoods

Given the time children spend in them, it is not an exaggeration to view child care programs as places for childhoods. Childhood is terribly perishable. It is a territory always under siege. Sometimes it is threatened by the forces of poverty or adult indifference. Other times it is threatened by an equally deadly onslaught of adult attention. Whether based on a view that childhood is primarily a no-nonsense time to prepare for future adulthood or a time to prolong innocence, well-intentioned adult attention can fence children off from the world and impoverish them with a benign, but sterile, existence.

When we institutionalize childhood, as we have certainly done, we risk doing what institutions nearly

always do — diminish the poetry of everyday life. We eliminate the highs and lows and wash out individual differences, trading predictability and security for the messy idiosyncrasies of individual lives. Is that what we want for the one childhood allocated to our children?

What Kind of Place?

"God is in the details," said the architect Mies Van de Rohe. The soul of the building was not in the impressiveness of the facade, nor in the ornamentation, but in how it all came together: the rightness of the door knobs and the vapor barrier, the color of the brick and the form against the sky, the flow of water and air, and the feeling of being together inside on a cold day — how it worked, how it felt, how it was lived. Similarly, when Mozart composed, he understood that God was in the notes and the rests — the sound and the silence.

In education, childhood, life, it is the richness of the **background** that creates value — focusing on the foreground distorts our perspective. Forever, educators (and parents) tend to forget that, for, indeed, we are the foreground. In our programs, perhaps it would be far better if we conceived ourselves as creators or, more modestly, orchestrators of the background, a greater role than simply being the teachers out in front.

Quality in early education and care is an accumulation of small transactions, between child and adult, child and child, child and objects and physical environment. The richness of place and the overall experience outweighs the value of teaching to a group, yet that is often where the bulk of planning is directed. Even in programs less group and school oriented, our focus is inevitably drawn and weighted toward our teaching and caregiving, and we lose sight of the learning and being cared for that may not take place.

It is in the laps and conversations, the side-by-side work and play, and the shared bouts of silliness and sadness that a child learns that he or she is somebody important. It is the bursts of energetic noise and the interludes of silence that punctuate reflection. Sunlight and breezes, frost on the window, and shadows descending on a corner of the room give daily life its fullness and sensuality.

The three R's can be present as well in the exuberant exploration of the world, if the awareness of the value of language and number infuse every experience. The sifting, kneading, and mixing on the table, and the digging and splashing are necessary precursors to laboratories of beakers and archaeological expeditions. The rhythm of the rain and the swing of the pendulum are both mathematical and musical experiences. Gazing at the crack on the ceiling that has the habit of looking like a rabbit, the row of dandelions at attention like an army of golden soldiers, and the flashing color from the angel fish or the canary enrich our sensibilities and inform our artistic vision.

It Ain't What You Do, It's How You Do It
(Charlie Parker)

Childhood, like sex, is dirty if you do it right (to paraphrase Woody Allen). It is also noisy, exuberant, and poignant. It requires liberal doses of freedom and mess to thrive. If we are to create places for childhoods, we have to deinstitutionalize our newly important institutions of childhood. We have to recognize and resist the ever-present tilt towards formality, uniformity, and blandness that legitimacy brings.

E. B. White once wrote to a reader of *Charlotte's Web* that "all that I hoped to say in books, all that I ever hope to say, is that I love the world. I guess that you can find it in there, if you dig around." That is what we need to find when we dig around our child care programs.

How Institutional Are YOU?

The notion that we are institutionalizing children in child care is not one that we like to hear. After all, we child care professionals are the good guys. We love children, childhood, primary colors, and cookies. And yet there is not another appropriate term for what we are doing. A child care center or home is an institution — a formal, established organization. It is the connotation we find hard to take: *institutionalize* conjures up, well, institutions, particularly those that sociologists call *total institutions* (asylums, hospitals, prisons, some schools) — places where uniformity, order, and rules are the primary values.

Sociologist Erving Goffman studied institutions and noted that while every institution captures something of the time, space, and interests of its members, some are far more encompassing or total than others as to their control and impact on the lives of their members. In total institutions:

All aspects of life are conducted in the same place and under the same authority (eating, sleep, play, work, social life, etc.). Second, each phase of the member's daily activity is carried on in the immediate company of others, all of whom are treated alike and required to do the same thing together. Third, all phases of the day's activities are tightly scheduled, with one activity leading at a pre-arranged time into the next, the whole sequence of activities being imposed from above. . . . Finally, the various enforced activities are brought together into a single rational plan purportedly designed to fulfill the official aims to the next. (Goffman, 1961)

In total institutions, there are inherent tendencies that work in concert to dehumanize all the members, including staff. Child care centers have many of the defining characteristics of total institutions. That isn't bad, it's just the nature of the beast. But total institutions can be bad, very bad; and those inherent tendencies are present in child care. To avoid becoming the sort of institution that we find far removed from a good place for a childhood, it is helpful to consider some of the typical characteristics of total institutions:

Room

Total institutions rarely allow much space per individual, justified by cost. Large group life is thus predominant, and comes to be considered acceptable. In child care, 35 square feet per child (25 in some states) and limited outdoor space has become standard, without many objections.

Time

Institutions always control time and parcel it out in time blocks based on institutional needs, creating an institutional rhythm that renders the rhythm of the individual or the task irrelevant. There is hospital time — change the sheets at 6:00 AM; school time — bells and buzzers mark lunch at 11:00; recess at 2:00 before a departure at 3:00; and child care time

OF SQUARE PEGS AND ROUND HOLES

Kyle was the epicenter of chaos. His enthusiasms worked on him like tectonic plates, grinding and shifting until the air around him was vibrating in a state of anticipation. He could no more portion out his interests and passions into 19 and 42 minute time slots than use his four year old body to drive a truck. He could, however, be a truck, a dog, an airplane, or his pièce de résistance — a dinosaur.

And when he was taken over by his dinosauritis, he didn't want to put down the dinosaurs and read about them at story time like the teacher suggested; he wanted to continue his play because at that moment he WAS a dinosaur. He needed to sound like one, move like one, eat like one. Watching him try to sit with the group and involve himself in the teacher's words that hazily floated toward him and focus on the small two-dimensional images of dinosaurs on the pages between the heads of the other children, you could see the very thin veneer of civilization slipping away from his four year old body as he began reverting to the dinosaur he truly was only minutes ago. And, of course, his devolution carried Julian and Katie along with him. "TIME OUT, KYLE!," again.

The pressure to shape up and fly right was not occasional, but continual, and often led to frustration. The tragedy was that it was Kyle's wonderful qualities that brought down the institutional wrath. His enthusiasm, his charisma, his attention span, and his devotion to HIS task created problems, whether the task was dinosaurology or being engrossed in a book or building a fort. In the institutional context, it was hard for the staff not to see Kyle as a disruptive troublemaker, which he was, but only because of the context over which he had no control. Trouble was not *badness* but enthusiasm. Staff rarely saw the person in Kyle, the person who is present now and will emerge in various incarnations as the nine year old, the teenager, the adult. Looking at Kyle that way, one sees an inquisitive person with a huge appetite for experience and an ability to focus on the experience. His inability to apportion his appetite to the child care context at four years old is unfortunate for the staff, but hardly a signal of future socio-pathic behavior.

— diapering at 9:30, outdoor play from 11:00 to 11:30, nap from 1:00 to 3:00 ("I don't want to tell you again, back on your cot!").

PRIVACY

Institutions allow little privacy, justified by the lack of space and the need for order and security to protect members from themselves and each other. There is a very small personal zone, the area surrounding an individual, that the individual can claim ("get outta my face"). There is often no way to own time or space, except perhaps during punishment.

The child care equivalent is limited, secluded, or *cozy* areas. There is now an unfortunate, near universal, simplistic tendency to confuse supervision with surveillance; the children must be under the observation of adults every second — thus large open spaces and no seclusion. This replaces the more sophisticated concept that supervision also includes a safe, planned "yes" environment,

shared expectations, socialized children, and adults who are aware about what is happening without needing to become omniscient wardens.

PERSONAL PROPERTY

Institutions limit personal property, for the protection of the property and maintenance of order. In a child care context, this means little security for the child's art or treasures and restrictions: "Park your blankee at the door, buster."

MEANING AND RESPONSIBILITY

In institutions, there is little activity that has much meaning outside the institution. There is a tendency to be insulated from the outside world. Occupants have little responsibility for anything meaningful, including meeting their own needs for care. You are usually dependent on others for meeting basic needs, either for permission, or timing, or access. The child care equivalent is no indepen-

dent bathroom access, portioned-out food, sleep and wake up when told, and no responsibilities for the tasks of daily life.

EXUBERANCE AND SPONTANEITY

Institutions rarely tolerate exuberance or spontaneity. These qualities are usually viewed as impulsive or immature. They disrupt routines and raise the terrifying specter of chaos. Institutions do not suffer gladly life-enhancing individuals — those characters whose "joie de vivre" leads to exuberance and spontaneity.

These troublemakers make magic and stir things up. We may love them in literature and film — McMurphy in "One Flew Over the Cuckoo's Nest," Robin Williams' characters in "Good Morning Vietnam" and "The Dead Poet's Society," Pippi Longstocking, Mary Poppins, Peter Pan — but supervising them or working with them is another story.

SECURITY, SAFETY, AND ORDER

Institutions are preoccupied with safety, security, and order, usually justified for the good of the inmates. If in doubt, restrict. If the overall effect is a contained, lifeless atmosphere, c'est la vie (or le mort).

SIGNIFICANT OTHERS IN THE OUTSIDE WORLD

Institutions take pains to limit the power and influence of others, specifically family (e.g., parents). There is rarely an accommodation to the context of others to allow them to participate or have influence on the institution. In schools and some child care, closed classroom doors, professional assertions of expertise and jargon, and PTAs channel parents away from raising questions and influencing their children's experience.

STAFF

Institutions are hard on the staff, who often feel the only power they have is ruling over the inhabitants. Low salaries, limited autonomy, virtual confinement within the institution during work, and lack of professional respect place them only a notch above their charges.

INDIVIDUALITY

Individuality is a casualty of all the other dimensions. The reality is that the important defining characteristics are not individual, but relative to the group and context. The whole person within is rarely considered. For child care and schools, it is age. The more age-graded the situation, and the more parents are kept at an arm's length, the less the individual child is recognized.

DIGNITY AND RESPECT

Institutions rarely leave much room (literally) for dignity and respect. Simple kindness is not enough to overcome the loss of individuality, privacy, and responsibility. Total institutions are not places where life is to be lived in all of its joy and drama. Joy and drama are too unwieldy. It is easier to turn day-to-day life into mostly pageant-ritual doings and observations. Drama has fire, the hint of chaos, sensuality, intense moments of concentration, and the intricate mini-plays of social life. It is engagement with life. Thomas Merton commented once that civilization was heading toward lives of low definition with little to decide, an apt description of institutional living.

Total institutions arise not because of evil or ignorance, but out of legitimate concerns for order, smooth standard operations, and the well-being of the inhabitants as a group. They become mindless as they lose sight of the individual and the real goals, the end goals, as they concentrate on the means. Order takes precedence over mental health in asylums, education in schools, rehabilitation in prisons, and childhood in those child care centers that fit the description.

Childhood depends on some precious formula of freedom and mess. Until institutionalized through child care, children in the most structured homes could usually break through the concrete web of good intentions and find the cracks, alive with possibilities for movement, exploration, and discovery — in the room, under the bed, in the backyard, on the stoop, alone or with friends. These were times when adult sanctions were weakened, allowing exploration of forbidden words with delicious hard consonant syllables and intriguing substances. These were times when space opened up rather than contained; and jumps, shouts, and giggles pierced the air. More centers can have the same feel by being alert to the dehumanizing tendencies that are ever-present.

REFERENCE

Goffman, Erving. ASYLUMS: Essays on the Social Situation of Mental Patients and Other Inmates. New York: Anchor Books, 1961.

ACTUARIALLY CORRECT

There is a school of thought that argues we should teach children the right way to go down the slide — erect, with hand on railing, body poised for a safe landing — and a right way to swing — erect again, the chain fully grasped on each side, eyes straight ahead. There are also licensing requirements in some states that require children to have shoes on at all times, in spite of the well-established primal need of a toddler to have one shoe on and one lost. No one is in favor of playground injuries or harm to feet or foot-borne disease; but a world of erect, shod children is hardly the stuff of childhood dreams.

MY BABY

Caitlin came with a raft of accessories every day: a photograph, a cookie, a necklace, and a stuffed animal. It was a struggle to enforce the policy of discouraging toys from home. Her first day back from vacation she appeared with a new baby doll. Despite gently being told she already had her authorized "lovey" at the center, she demanded admittance for her new baby, "Ashley." "Babies do not belong at home alone," she sniffed. "MY BABY will not be home alone," she bellowed with her maternal instinct aflame. Quick-witted, the teacher (to the dismay of some of the staff) admitted Ashley and began a baby doll day care. There was never a more ferociously protective group of mothers than those four year olds looking out for the interests of their babies.

IT'S THE REAL THING

We are growing used to shopping malls replacing city downtowns. The civilized world, as we like to think of ourselves, is increasingly fastidious and cautious. In the mall, trees flourish without visible water or dirt. Autumn leaves do not fall because there is no real autumn in a mall, only Halloween displays and Thanksgiving sales.

Life is carefully measured. Bird sounds may be piped in, amidst the safe cheery music bearing no chords of ethnicity or individual style. Seasons are signalled by sales, holiday music, and commercial art. There is food, magically produced through invisible deliveries, and garbage pick up. There are no shadows, no discordant noises, few signs of age or wear.

People are measured, too. The *streets and lanes* of the mall are private property. Not bound by strict requirements of free speech, they don't have to accept the rowdy or those in pain engaged in dialogues with their tormented inner selves. No one has a right to be there, least of all those who may assert their struggling or divergent reality upon us. Malls are *cool* settings, teeming with neutrality — smooth, lacking edges or ideas that delight us or jar us. Heat comes from consumption. Life outside the mall is an adventure because of chance encounters of sight, sound, smell, and people. In a mall, adventure is restricted to the buffet of abundant goods and services to be consumed.

CANNED CHILDHOODS?

What has this to do with child care? Shopping malls are cities turned outside in. Child care centers are homes and yards turned inside out. The issues in all our common spaces of how to balance life — with its joyful but frequently messy and sometimes disturbing realities — and our desire for a safe existence — with its seductively numbing sterility — are played out in both malls and child care programs. Critics call malls *canned life*. Can we afford to have canned childhoods?

We are well on our way to the *malling* of childhood. The shadow world is losing ground to fluorescent light. The child's laboratory is shrinking. Unmanaged experiences that children shape and give meaning to through their investigations require some exposure to fields and streams, or vacant lots and rainy streets. Time available for child science and freedom from the eyes of solicitous and restricting adults shrinks as child care and organized activities fill the child's day. We are tightening our concrete web of good intentions and driving out the flowers growing in the cracks.

Children have become increasingly valuable objects of consumption — clothes, classes, coiffures. The tolerance for allowing these natural but inherently messy scientists the opportunity for vigorous investigation into the world about them is dropping. An opportunistic insurance industry and a litigious fashion sweeping the culture have banished the notion of accidents from life; there is only negligence and liability.

Perhaps we can do little to reorient a culture bent on inauthenticity. But a little may be a lot for young children who require much experience to fuel their learning.

11 SMALL WAYS TO BRING LIFE IN

1. Open the windows. Outside is life in all its sensory richness. Unless your center is an oasis amidst the pollution and uproar of modern life, opening windows frequently allows valuable real life to seep in.

2. Turn off the lights. Many center classrooms are lit like school classrooms with banks of fluorescent lights that have the virtue of lighting every inch of the room uniformly. Turn off the lights occasionally and let shadows flourish. Let the day have a rhythm based on natural light.

3. Smell the roses — or the garlic. What are the smells of your childhood? *Our* places, those we treasure, have smells that trigger our affections: the smell of baking or freshly oiled wood; flowers or newly mowed grass; or the smell of people and their perfumes, powders, and layers of work smells. The aesthetic feel of a center or home is enhanced if the aromas are varied and pleasant.

4. Grow, baby, grow. Plants add smell, color, texture, change. They don't require walks, just a little sun and water. Dried flowers and leaves don't even require that.

5. Get real. The business of life includes cooking, cleaning, and laundry in regular sequences. To children, it is play. To good teachers, involving children in work is valuable.

6. Get out of there. Going outside is the real thing — nature. Outside is a natural world and a world of people and commerce and industry to be understood. Inside we often are only able to offer pale imitations of that world (granted imitations that often we are able to make safe and sensible to young children).

7. Everything is relative. Life is people and for children especially — people we love. Photographs of parents, grandparents, siblings, and families easily connect the center to life outside. Visits and celebrations add to the connections.

8. The patter of little feet. "Fluffy was murdered," the TV-influenced small set chorused as we encountered the less-than-lifelike guinea pig. Small animals, birds, reptiles, fish, and other living things bring the life cycle into the classroom: life and death, aging, decay, sounds and smells, and motion.

9. Earthly delights. The unexpected sunlit alcove in a new house, a patch of wild flowers on a trail, the sound of appealing music on a city street — delightful surprises that bring smiles and sometimes take our breath away. In a child care center, fresh flowers on a table, a child's eye hallway exhibit of prints, textured sculpture in unexpected corners, or a ceiling display — such delights may enliven one out of the 12,000 hours of childhood spent in child care.

10. Who was that guy? Institutions desperately require some life enhancers to drive away greyness: Pippi Longstocking, Mary Poppins, or Madeline. When Bev Bos or Ella Jenkins or any other life enthusiasts enter a classroom, the world shifts and new forms of adventure and learning are possible. Life enhancers are often difficult and trouble our safe routine existence, but how else are we certain we are actually alive?

11. Who's that knocking? Surprise and spontaneity shake up our days. In reasonable doses, they put steam in our stride. Unexpected visits, trips, food, or changes in routine that upset the order without sowing insecurity activate our potential.

AND THREE MAJOR CHANGES

1. More room. It is hard to provide life in many of its lively vagaries having only 35 square feet per child. Life pulsates. The smells, visions, and sounds of life need room to be appreciated or else they merge into a whirling, noisy, indistinct mess.

2. More time. Appreciation of life follows no straight lines. Its pleasures and mysteries unfold in bits and pieces. Life fit into 20 minute slots regulated by others removes the edges of experience that provide the interest and the depth.

3. More freedom. We all need to be free to actively *engage* the world and to step back and quietly make sense of it. Children (and teachers) in regimented programs are marching through life with their heads down too much of the time.

We have fenced children off from the world, and society may suffer. Childhood experience forms the core of our being. It is the stuff of dreams and futures.

> *The purpose of life, after all, is to live it, to taste experience to the utmost, to reach out eagerly and without fear for newer and richer experience.*
>
> — Eleanor Roosevelt

> *Gimme an L! Gimme an I! Gimme a V! Gimme an E! L-I-V-E! Otherwise you got nothing to talk about in the locker room.*
>
> — Ruth Gordon to Bud Cort in "Harold and Maude"

CHILDREN NEED TO LIVE IN THE REAL WORLD

At what point did childhood become so driven? Children have a lot to learn. We can fill them up, busy their days, keep them occupied and industrious in all manner of ways. There can be singing and dancing, books and computers. It can all look good — it can even be good. But unless we can connect them to the real world of nature and people outside the walls of our children's world, unless within our walls we can give them time and place to simply be and find themselves, it is not enough.

There are melodies in the waves and poetry in the wind that blows the leaves off trees. There is art in the anthills and the strands of seaweed on the beach. Thoughts lay dormant without stillness and solitude. Reality is difficult. It is messy and loud and profane. There are people with warts and frowns, and decidedly mixed virtues. But childhood is a time when we help children begin to live in the world and *love the world*, and we can't do that fenced off from it in a world of two-dimensional glowing screens and plastic balls and slides.

Nature was there before the Nature Company, before playgrounds, before parks. An infinite laboratory, a stage and concert hall, the natural world is a school for young children.

Nature is unpredictable. It is the uneven, the changing and evolving, the glorious untidiness of it all that provides such contrast with life inside. The ground under our feet

B eing born is a messy thing, the first time and every time. There's always a lot of screaming and crying and bodily fluids. But there are also hoots of laughter and tears of pure pleasure. It doesn't take long to get cleaned up, and there are lots of smiles and touching. But we are never too far away from the screaming and the crying and the bodily fluids.

At what point did caution become dominant? When did we surrender our children's lives to tabloid-induced fear and the sacred order of risk managers? "The purpose of life, after all, is to live it, to taste experience to the utmost, to reach out eagerly and without fear for newer and richer experience," said Eleanor Roosevelt, who overcame crippling shyness and a love-starved childhood.

may slope or buckle. The air may be heavy and weigh us down or be so light that time has fallen asleep in the sunshine. Nothing falls from the sky inside — but outside there are leaves and snowflakes, rain and hail. Inside, nothing flies (except flies) or burrows or leaps from tree to tree. Many of us age and forget the joy of the small, unstaged event — the sudden dark cloud, the bird at the feeder, the toad in the garden.

Nature is bountiful. There are shapes and sizes, colors and textures, smells and tastes — an enormous variety of substances. In a world of catalogs and consumable objects, designed spaces, and programmed areas, sometimes it helps to remember that the natural world is full of multi-dimensional, unassailingly educational experiences for children. Nature is hard, soft, fragile, heavy, light, smooth, and rough. Armed with our five senses, we explore the world and call the adventure science — or, if you prefer, cognitive development, classification, sensory development, or perceptual-motor learning.

Nature is beautiful. The rainbow in the oily water or the rainbow in the sky, the dandelion or the apple blossom; there is so much loveliness we grow slack and leave the awe to artists. But **look** at those towering cliffs of clouds and the light streaking through the pine needles. **See** the silvery birch leaves and the swirls in the bark, the rain dripping from the roof, and delicate, lace-like etchings in the leaf.

Nature is alive with sounds. It is not only Maxwell House coffee makers that make music, so do the wind and rain, and, of course, birds and crickets; even dogs make music. The world is full of natural and man-made rhythms that children experience and imitate.

Nature creates a multitude of places. Lie out in the open on that hill, or under that willow. Sit on that rock or in that high grass. Squeeze under the hedge or march through that puddle. A small strand of trees makes a forest if you are small.

Nature is real. Everything dies — the ant, the baby bird that fell from the nest, the flower, the leaf. Thistles have stickers, and roots trip unsuspecting feet. It is our world, not Gilligan's Island.

Nature lives inside and out. Any room is enlivened by plants and animals, birds and reptiles, flowers and dried plants, stone and wood. Open a window, turn off a light.

LET THEM BE — SOMETIMES.

Anne was having a long conversation with her best friend Kassie, trying to find a time to get together for a "play date." The two six year olds kept running into conflicts of swim/gym, soccer, music lessons, and other play dates as they checked the calendars kept by their mothers. Listening to them, I fully expected the conversation to end with: "Well, Kassie, I'll have my people call your people and we'll take lunch real soon." I wonder if there are any six year olds with beepers or their own cellular phones?

It's not just that most children don't have the lives of Tom Sawyer or Opie in Mayberry anymore, they don't even have the freedom of the Brady Bunch. Many lead scheduled week-at-a-glance lives, managed by parents and punctuated by television. The neighborhood, the park, even the yard plays less of a role in the lives of many children.

Children need time to mess around, literally, without direction of any kind, and with *stuff* of their choosing, in places of their making, where they can make their weird sounds and faces. Between idleness and industry lie other states — of experimentation (alias play), reflection, or joy.

IT'S NOT JUST WHAT YOU DO, IT'S WHO YOU ARE.

"What's that yucky stuff on the water?" I don't know. Don't touch it.

NATURE

There is a pleasure in the pathless woods,
There is rapture on the lonely shore,
There is a society where none intrudes,
By the deep sea, and music in its roar;
I love not man the less, but Nature more,
From these our interviews, in which I steal
From all I may be, or have been before,
To mingle with the Universe and feel
What can ne'er express, yet cannot all
conceal.

— Lord Byron, from *Childe Harold*

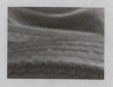

He not busy being born is busy dying

— Bob Dylan,
"It's Alright Ma (I'm Only Bleeding)"

"What is that flower?"
I don't know. But don't eat it.

"Why doesn't the vacuum work?"
I don't know, it's broken, said the teacher.

There are few things more depressing than to be in the classroom of the incurious (except the classroom of the uncaring) — rooms staffed with people who fail to ask "why" and "how," not to stimulate the children's thinking and answer their questions, but to answer their own. Not knowing is certainly no sin in the classroom. Not being interested, not having questions, not seeking answers, not showing an enthusiasm for discovery is a sin, because intellectual lethargy is contagious.

The *failure to wonder* shrinks the universe and begins to dampen the child's marvelous spirit of inquiry.

One does not have to be interested in everything, or exist in a constant state of childlike awe. However, a passionate interest in something, as well as delight and appreciation for a child's sense of wonder, brings a classroom to life.

JUST DO IT!

"It's all right, dad, I'm only crying."
— Emma Greenman, age 4
(when life was a little too real)

The drive to protect our children is profound and easily can extend to scotchguarding their lives. Scrubbing and polishing every raw experience in the name of health and safety or protecting innocence scrapes away the natural luster of childhood. Some of the wonders and joys of childhood that fuel the best in our adult selves are unavoidedly birthed in bumps and bruises and tears.

WHAT ARE FRIENDS FOR?
REFLECTIONS OF A NEW-AGE PARENT

Childhood is changing for many children. Where lives in the past were bound into neighborhoods, family, and friends of the family, today the landscape of a young child's life is stretched every which way by the realities of modern life. When I was a child, friends came from the neighborhood, the neighborhood school, the children of relatives, and family friends. As I neared junior high age, the swimming pool and tennis courts widened my range slightly. I don't remember many external forces (parents) impinging on my early social life. I could spend time with whomever I chose (perhaps whoever would have me), occasionally, however, getting thrown together with other children by parent doings ("Come on, you'll love playing with Marcia.").

My seven year old child's life is very different She spends time in her dad's house and her mom's house, in two different neighborhoods. She is bussed to school in a different neighborhood and goes to a school-age child care program. On the weekend, she goes to Hebrew school; in the summer, she goes to day camp. The way Emma is currently talking, there are music lessons and the like on the horizon. Her mother's friends have children that she sees, and my friends have children. Her world is rich in people, many of whom I don't know. Since she was three, she has lived in three neighborhoods and attended two child care programs. My childhood had two hubs, three if you separate the neighborhood school from the neighborhood; Emma's has at least seven, with relatively little overlap.

For the most part, whom I played with out of school required no adult involvement. Emma is constrained by both time and space; and she often needs one or both parent's assistance to see friends. If she wants to see friends in the neighborhood in which she is staying (mom's or dad's), she has to get picked up early from latch-key on a weekday. If she wants to play with school friends or friends from the other parent's neighborhood, or latch-key friends on weekends, permission and transportation are required. This dependence will last until she is old enough to maneuver city streets by herself.

Emma is a sturdy, plucky kid. At present, she seems to be living her life as an opera, filled with on-the-spot arias, laughter, and occasional fury. Despite bouts of shyness and insecurity, she would adapt to Hari Krishna or the Marine Corp with the same aplomb. Her good-natured, plunging enthusiasm seems to carry her into and out of her settings. This may be a lucky accident of nature or a learned adaptation to her life, but it seems to fit her surroundings. As someone whose limit of being a joiner is holding a library card, I am often impressed with this child of mine.

Emma's life may not be typical, nor perhaps was mine. There have always been mobile families that changed neighborhoods frequently and children spread thin with camps, lessons, even work who have been bussed or driven to school as well.

And today, many children of intact families do attend neighborhood child care, neighborhood schools, and life in neighborhoods peopled with relatives and family friends. But there seems to be little question that for most children, and adults, life is more complicated, more hurried, and potentially more superficial.

Child care centers have spread to all socio-economic strata and are an integral aspect of child rearing. Shared parenting, blended families, and housing mobility will continue to stretch the social landscape of childhood.

WHAT'S BEST FOR CHILDREN?

What does this all mean for children? For parents struggling to do the *right thing*? As a parent, I often feel unsure. Here is another aspect of Emma's life where I face issues of sacrifice (arranging my life to become a chauffeur) and, more important, issues of parental social engineering. What role should I play in shaping Emma's social life? The idea of parents structuring their children's social lives appalls me. It conjures up images of social climbing, debutante balls, narrow prejudices, or simply a suffocating parental presence. I like the knowing laissez-faire tolerance of Ward and June Cleaver as Beaver and Wally socialized with their odd assortment of Sancho Panzas and Lagos.

But I find myself without design in a pivotal position. It is not an issue of whether to be involved. I am involved because Emma needs me as a driver, or she needs my consent to go along with sleep-overs (popular among children with full daytime calendars), or my acquiescence so that she can redistribute the time she spends with one parent or the other. The temptation is not to judge her choice of friends but to help her establish relationships. I can encourage relationships that are likely to last over time (perhaps children of family friends) because I believe that is important, particularly for children

without siblings. Best friends right now are also important, and these are often drawn from children available day in and day out. But there is also a need for balance, seeing children often enough so that they do not slide in and out of her life. Emma's social landscape will probably always be complex and spread out. The ability to develop friends in every setting is clearly a positive adaptation. But we all need more than a friend in each port.

When Emma and I discuss these matters, she sees no problem. Her friends are all equal. She has no best friend. "They are all best friends," this sage, egalitarian, seven year old reassures her dad. But she is only seven; I think *what does she know*?

Although there is no shortage of experts in advice or social science willing to guide us toward the right and true, I expect that each parent has to come to their own conclusions about what is right for their child and struggle the best they can. Much of the time Emma makes the choice. But I do admit to making suggestions and influencing choices at times.

WHAT ABOUT THE ISSUE OF PROTECTION?

The families that make up Emma's social world are far more diverse than that of my childhood. They range across the socio-economic spectrum, from different cultures, lifestyles, and values. Our gregarious children bring us into contact as they plead to eat over, sleep over, or go together on an outing. Often the parental contact is as disembodied voices on a phone, or two minute drop-off and pick-up vestibule pleasantries. The adults know little about these others — these strangers — to whom they entrust their children.

As a male, single parent, apartment dweller not easily fit into a niche (to say nothing of bearded and rumpled), I often feel the need to work into the short encounter some

indication of my social acceptability — "I've got to go frame my master's degree." These encounters sometimes resemble flirting, five minutes of small talk establishing affinity and the absence of any striking deviance.

Another difference from my childhood seems to be the climate of concern, even fear, that shadows child rearing. "What do I know about these people?" The specter of sex, drugs, alcohol, or permissive indifference is omnipresent, at least in many minds. The thought to somehow seek the equivalent references of some families is not uncommon among parents that I know.

A decidedly non-rumpled friend of mine, a respectably married suburban stalwart with her child in a good nursery school, called the parent of her child's preschool sidekick to invite the child over to play. "But we don't know you," the child's mother replied, which stopped the conversation and, for a time, the budding friendship. *Knowing* was achieved by a very brief, polite, and inane conversation at a T-ball game.

WHAT ARE THE IMPLICATIONS FOR CHILDREN'S PROGRAMS?

As a child care provider, I have just begun to consider what this changing social picture means for programs. It is possible that a focused concern on the fragmenting social world of children may argue for neighborhood child care, if not for neighborhood schools. Reducing the geographical spread, with school-age child care based near or at schools that also serve as the base for enrichment classes, would simplify the lives of some children and parents.

There are some things that programs can do to help parents and children. Many programs hold meetings, potlucks, and fundraising events which serve to bring parents together. For some parents, these events are a chance to possibly make friends — for others, an obligation, a chance to talk to staff, or to be involved in their children's lives. But all these events can be consciously structured to allow parents to *check each other out*. Children can determine seating at a potluck; pairings for work days could take into account children's friendship patterns. Simply having staff view part of their role at parent events as bringing together parents in their children's social circle who do not know each other, like hosts at a party, would be helpful. Often at these events, we all — parents and staff — talk mostly to those people we already know. Perhaps our busy acquaintance-rich children will be different.

Parents differ considerably in their interest in parent events and in their free time. There are other ways for a program to serve as a broker of information that acquaints parents with the households of their children's friends. Children can put together biography books that include information about where the family lives, what work the parents do, what the family does for fun — a family history. Family photographs in a photo album or on bulletin board displays convey information that reassures us that we are not turning our children over to strangers.

What seems most important is that professionals who work with or study children pay attention to the totality of the lives of children and parents and make decisions reflecting the broader context. As children's lives become more fully *institutionalized* through child care, schools, camps, and so on, we should consider deinstitutionalizing the institutions. As the child's social landscape grows in territory and complexity, we should either behave so as to simplify the landscape or help children and parents better navigate. Doing either will require more thought and study, but most of all acceptance of the role and experimentation. Meanwhile, as a parent, I will, like all parents, muddle through.

Don't Happy, Be Worried: Connecting Up the Dots

better paying early childhood, early elementary, or family education programs will accelerate the talent drain. One implication: generally preschool staff without good training in early childhood tend to adopt school and school teachers as their models. Yet, at the same time, they lack the training to plan and implement a teacher-directed classroom that is developmentally appropriate in care or learning.

3. "Excuse me, do you have a cap and gown in size 2-T?" There will be increased pressure, mostly from parents, to be "educational" — structured and school-like, not only for threes and fours, but infants and toddlers as well. In some programs, pressure will take the form of heavier doses of special enrichment classes.

4. "Look over yonder and what do you see?" There will be more building and renovating of child care programs. The recognition that child care is here to stay and worthy of tailored space is widespread.

5. "Eat your sushi, Brooke, and don't touch the mural on the wall." For many upscale programs, there will be pressure to "look good." This may take the form of looking expensive, new, in vogue (e.g., the right colors, wicker), or educational (computers, serious art, touted curriculums). Simply the newness of buildings will add to a tendency to metaphorically leave the "plastic on the furniture." The result is often lifeless "good-looking" classrooms.

There are some clear trends that are setting the context within which child care centers continue to operate for at least the next decade:

1. "So long, it's been good to know you." There is going to be a *labor shortage* for the foreseeable future. The rate of growth of workers entering the labor force will continue to decline for at least the next 10 to 15 years. It will be harder to recruit staff, and turnover is more likely as the competition for staff increases.

2. "No, Virginia, Piaget is not a watch." Child care will also experience a *talent shortage* for the indefinite future. The number of motivated, talented, trained in early childhood staff willing to work in child care will continue to decline at a faster rate than the overall decline in the labor force. Any increase in other,

6. "Just say *no* to flashcards." There (hopefully) will also be increased countervailing pressure on programs to be *good* child care and early education — developmentally appropriate learning, personalized and individualized care, parents as respected partners, and simply good places to *be*, to spend a childhood. For this to happen, accreditation will have to be marketed more aggressively as a *necessary* standard for good programs.

What are directors to do in an age when they cannot find staff, are under pressure from some parents and staff to create pseudo-school classrooms, and yet know that good child care is not teaching numbers and letters and spending the day in two straight lines? The secret to thriving *and* producing quality child care will be clear, innovative thinking to maximize resources, good center design, and an ability to articulate and sell a vision of quality. A good director will more than once rethink the doing of child care and be prepared for change.

Sell, Sell, Sell

When we are swimming upstream in the waters of general opinion, we can't afford the gentility of *raising consciousness*. We have to sell our ideas to aggressively market our view of the good life in child care.

1. Sell childhood. Even the fastest track parents want their children to have happy childhoods. Reminding them of their childhoods and the learning and pleasure derived from "messing about" with people and things and drawing out the child still lodged inside them rarely fails to bring a response. Quality of daily life

---

> *It doesn't take a weatherman to know which way the wind blows.*
>
> — Bob Dylan

---

and opportunities for delight and wonder are issues schools have ignored and are issues less central to limited hour nursery schools. But they are central to child care where a child may spend 12,000 hours of his life, in effect a childhood — more time than in all public schooling.

2. Sell education and learning, but not school. We need to be able to help parents delight in the educational value of their child's developmentally appropriate play. If we are not able to articulate the serious intellectual content of what is happening — the infant exploring motorically the concepts of under and through, the toddler collecting and dumping, preschool dramatic and block play, and kindergarten classification — and if we are unable to explain how that content is far more likely to pave the road to a good university than the fraudulent numbers and letters recitations, then parents struggling to do the best for their children will buy sad imitations of schools. Why can't we help parents to see their children as delightful little scientists, architects, explorers, acrobats, and scholars who use all their senses, their whole bodies, and their own behavior as the tools for astonishingly thorough, albeit messy, investigations in the world of people and things?

Computers and enrichment classes have some real value to children as a complement to other elements of the program. But beyond that, they signal serious educational purpose. If the strength of that signal allows leeway for more messy and active sensory and motor play, they are worth it for the symbolism alone.

3. Sell beauty and taste. Children need beauty in their lives. We may be able to avoid the home-beautiful/architectural digest syndrome in upscale programs with expensive buildings, if we accept both the need for taste and beauty and the need for exuberant, sensory, child-ordered settings — in short, lived-in places. If nicely appointed facades, foyers, offices, common spaces with fresh flowers, art, wicker, or whatever signals taste in the community buys active, lived-in classrooms (also with fresh flowers), those features are not frills.

DESIGN FOR LEARNING

For decades, the National Association for the Education of Young Children and others have fought against the insulting and debilitating view that "anybody can teach." Yet it is true today — and will become even more true in the future — "anybody" **is** teaching. Many centers have had to fill teaching roles with "anybody." Hopefully, though, most programs are not using *just* anybody, but gentle, kind people who appreciate and know children and enjoy caring for them. Some — perhaps many of these people (given the chance) — help children learn and make an effort to help them develop a positive sense of self.

If we are not going to have many teachers to choose from, how do we promote education? The answer is not to create teacher-proof curriculum. Nothing is worse than the *teaching* at children in teacher-directed

formats by low-skilled *teachers*. It dulls everyone's intellect — adults and children — and leads to oppressive child management practices. Unfortunately, a great many centers throw marginally trained people into the ring as teachers, as if the title and the large print activity guide will act as Dumbo's magic feather. Other centers fortunate to have a few well trained staff in a few classrooms agonize over quality differences from room to room and fluctuations in quality as these teachers come and go during the day, week, and year.

Teaching environments only work with teachers. In fact, teaching environments in early childhood only work with *very* skilled teachers. It is not easy to create a place for individual young children in classroom groups to live and learn over a ten hour day. It is hard to cater to so many different interests, abilities, rhythms, and personalities.

What's the alternative? We can create *learning* environments, designed to work with staff with few teaching skills. If we can find people who are *good* with children, we can design learning environments that work with those people. In the wilds of homes, backyards, and streets, children play and learn, developmentally appropriately. It is only when we place them in institutional group settings under adult direction that this becomes an issue.

Designing learning environments that are less dependent on teaching requires searching for new models and drawing from old ones. Children's museums, some nature centers, and playgrounds represent settings designed for teacherless learning environments. Open classrooms and Montessori environments

were designed for independent learning with less teacher direction.

What then to expect from most staff? Staff value the ability to treat children with respect and gentleness, a willingness to converse with children — listen to them, ask questions based on their activities. With training and experience, perhaps those who stay will develop the skill to ask those questions that will nudge the child toward greater understanding and new challenge.

A learning environment approach can maximize the human talent available to the program because those who do have early childhood training and experience can put that to use in supervision and in developing classrooms — building learning into the environment, designing learning centers and self-directed activities, organizing storage and staff orientation materials.

DESIGN FOR LIVING

For centers to work as non-institutional settings where children (and adults) reside for up to ten hours a day, they have to be conceived as places to live — places with sufficient room and character and built-in supports for competent and comfortable daily living.

DESIGN FOR WORKING

With a shortage of talent, designing centers that are easy places in which to do the work of child care is a key to quality — places which are easy to keep clean, plan effectively, re-store the classroom order; places where it is easy to help kids with toileting; have meetings; and involve parents.

What's reality got to do with it?

— Tina Turner

CHAPTER 2

A GREAT PLACE FOR BABIES

It's an Art to Create
Quality Infant and Toddler Care —
You Are the Artist

by Karen Miller

I have a conviction that truly fine quality infant and toddler group care is an art form. There's taste, talent, and, yes, passion involved. Some of the art comes from the subconscious — instincts for caring and compassion. This is what makes caregivers respond warmly and appropriately to children and parents. The artist also draws consciously on training and is constantly striving to sharpen skills.

Creating good care for infants and toddlers is a *living* art form. Every day the provider of care is faced with innumerable judgment calls, deciding such things as what materials to put out and where to put them, how to entice the interest of children so they can exercise their new skills, how to remain accessible to parents, when and how to interact with children, and when to stand back and observe.

The environment is the starting point. It provides the frame and the background for quality care. Without a well-designed environment, it's almost impossible to provide care where children and adults can be relaxed and natural, and where children can grow and learn, because the adults will be too busy compensating for environment flaws. That takes time away from nurturing.

When the lucky artist is offered the opportunity to be part of the ground-up planning and design team for a new child care facility, the true joy of creativity can come forth. Most often, however, the artist/caregiver is faced with a *make-do* challenge. Confronted with an indoor and outdoor space, the question is voiced, "What can I do to make this setting beautiful and functional?" The variables of space, natural and artificial light, surface textures, color, and moveable materials are explored and adjusted until the composition pleases the artist.

As Jim Greenman emphasizes, when you design work and living spaces for babies, you must ask yourself how it feels to be that little individual in this space and what you can do to make it feel right. We should always evaluate our programs from the point of view of the child.

The space has to be designed for exploration. Too often what one sees in infant rooms is rows — rows of cribs, rows of swings, rows of infant seats, rows of walkers. Contraptions. *Trap-tions*. Things that literally trap babies and keep them from exploring. In toddler rooms, one often sees empty shelves, or shelves turned to the wall, and toys stored inaccessible to children, so that it is easier for caregivers to keep things neat — an adult value. In our drive to keep babies and the space clean and prevent them from hurting themselves and each other, it can be easy to forget that a critical part of cognitive development comes from exploring space and objects. The focus of attention should be on creating easy-to-supervise spaces that are safe for children to explore, and finding lots of interesting objects — *stuff* — to have there that is fun for children to manipulate and act upon.

The space has to be designed for interactions as well. Another critical part of cognitive development comes from interacting with other human beings. The child learns from watching others, especially other children, and by playful give and take with peers and adults. So the environment and routine must have adequate space and time for the adult to be comfortable at the child's level, either observing or interacting with the child in a playful way, following the child's lead.

Try practicing some positive imaging for your environment. Start by imagining your own environment — make it as perfect as possible. Draw it. Cut out images from magazines and catalogs. Put yourself and your children in it. Anything goes! As you do this, it will become easier to see in your mind the changes that need to be made and how to make them. It may not happen all at once, and you may never reach the goal. But if you create and maintain that mental image, reality will inch close and closer to that idea. If it is possible to do so safely, make your changes while the children are present, so they can see the transformation process.

When it comes to examining your outdoor space, the first commitment is to get the babies outside each day, weather permitting. Too often infants are kept inside in the *clean* environment and caregivers fail to appreciate the benefits of fresh air, sunshine, and nature. Babies love being outside because it is such a sensory rich place. There are many different fragrances. The visual field is constantly changing with light and shadow and moving things. There are rich textures to explore and interesting sounds of all types. Again, challenge yourself to look at the variables of space, textures, and equipment as you make this area right for babies. How many textures can you add? How can you make it safe with natural and built barriers so non-mobile and mobile infants can enjoy the same space? The fence offers an interesting surface. Can you hang objects for children to examine on it? How about creating a *sound garden* with objects that make interesting noises — wind chimes, things to hit with a small mallet suspended nearby, different types of shakers.

When it comes to dealing with the issue of biting, the caregiver/artist must become a *dramatic artist* — one who uses words, gestures, and actions to convey information and emotion as you shepherd children, and their parents, *through* this process. Again, positive imaging helps immensely. Imagine this child in control with new strategies under his belt — strategies you have taught and modeled.

Art reflects values. How you arrange your space is an outward reflection of your philosophy. It tells people what you value and how you feel about babies.

- If you value children's play, your environment should provide ample, safe play space and materials.

- If you value warm interactions between children and caregivers, your environment should offer places that are comfortable and welcoming for adults and children to be together.

- If you value cleanliness and health, your environment should be easy to keep clean, safe, and organized.

- If you value close relationships with parents, your environment should be welcoming, comfortable, convenient, and organized to facilitate good written and oral communication.

I came across this quote about the nature of *art* by Evelyn Waugh:

> "A work of art is not a matter of thinking beautiful thoughts or experiencing tender emotions (though those are its raw materials) but of intelligence, skill, taste, proportion, knowledge, discipline and industry: especially discipline."

In child care, many people have wishes, or *beautiful thoughts*, and lots of tender emotions when it comes to caring for babies. But it takes intelligence, skill, taste . . . all of these things to do it well. Be proud of your art!

WORLDS OF INFANTS AND TODDLERS

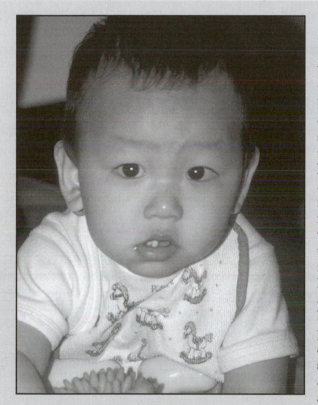

Our surroundings affect our behavior. As adults, we whisper in libraries, we feel lost on the streets of strange cities, we relax in our own homes. Exactly like adults, children's feelings and behaviors are shaped by the physical situation in which they find themselves. Even children who are too young to know about rules or possible dangers are affected by physical space: think about an infant's surprise at being laid down on a cold changing table, the way a two year old runs when faced with a ramp, the shyness of many four year olds entering a new classroom.

But, for many years, people have argued that while young children react to their environments, they are most strongly affected by the immediate qualities of their surroundings: cold air or bath water, wet diapers, rough edges, lost balance, or loud noises. This view of children's relationships to the physical world is meeting considerable challenge.

INFANTS: WHAT DO THEY KNOW?

For a number of years, researchers argued that the vision of infants is hazy. Consequently, people believed that infants react to skin sensations more than to the *world out there*. Over the last 20 years, researchers like T. G. R. Bower and Robert Fantz have shown that even young infants make sense of their physical surroundings in clear and highly organized ways. Infants can recognize an object from the front, the side, or the bottom. Similarly, infants are distressed when they see a videotape of their mother in one location and hear her voice coming from a different location.

Until very recently, people believed that since young children are limited to personal or body sensations, they understand very little about the actual geography of objects, rooms, and larger spaces. This description turns out to be harsh. Research by Susan Rose and Holly Ruff at Einstein College of Medicine shows that as early as six to twelve months babies work at piecing together separate kinds of spatial information. Infants who mouth objects without seeing them can later recognize those same objects by sight.

Research from the laboratories of Herbert Pick at the University of Minnesota and Linda Acredolo at the University of California at Davis shows that infants do realize how large spaces are organized. They have been able to demonstrate that infants think in terms of landmarks, not just bodily cues. If a window is on an infant's left on a trip down a hall, the baby will look for it on her right side during the return trip.

Clearly, the physical environment is not at all a distant blur or a bundle of immediate sensations for infants. Beyond worrying about the temperature and texture of surfaces, we have to recognize that very young children are sensitive to the organization and appearance of their surroundings.

TODDLERS: HOW DOES THEIR WORLD SHIFT?

If infants are already beginning to have a sense for the world's geography, then what, if anything, changes between the ages of one and three years? In this period, children go from sitting to crawling to walking to running. With the shift away from *armchair* life, children begin to cover increasing amounts of territory. They have to figure out not only how to get from here to there but how to get back. They may try to follow a ball as it rolls out of sight and bounces off different objects. They learn to use someone's voice to guide their way back to *home base*.

Once children lie, squat, walk, and run, they are faced with solving a whole new set of spatial problems. Children who can be at all these levels live in a very complex spatial world. When such a child hunts for an object, he has to take into consideration not just where but from what point of view he last recalls seeing it.

During these years, the social world of children is often reorganized. Many children are increasingly able to separate from their parents. Once they give up clinging to familiar knees, they wander and explore. A two year old can easily follow a peer behind a bush in a playground. From that vantage point the whole world looks different. At a moment like that, a child may have to cope with confusion, even fear. She will also have to call on all kinds of alternative cues for navigating: taller landmarks like roof lines and trees, or quite different clues such as noises and voices.

Work by Jerome Kagan and his colleagues shows that during their second and third years, children develop an initial set of standards. Two and three year olds realize that certain behaviors are *right*, whereas

other behaviors are *wrong* in particular situations. In that way, children may cease to think about all physical spaces as being the same. Even though they could not put it into words, two year olds know the difference between what is expected in a nap room and what is expected on the playground. In other words, even though toddlers may not follow out their understandings, they have sense for the social messages carried by different spaces.

ENVIRONMENTS MADE FOR INFANTS AND TODDLERS

Despite this changing picture of young children's understanding of space, we lack good models for thinking about the design of infant and toddler environments. One mistake is to create bedroom-like settings which are limiting and lack challenge. The other mistake is to borrow familiar plans for preschool spaces and add cribs and changing tables. In this case, the scale is too large and the organization much too formal to make sense for younger children.

In place of borrowing, we need original designs meant specifically for infants and toddlers. These kind of designs are based on observing *babies in the wild*. A keen sense of how babies or toddlers act at home, in parks, or in group care is probably the most important tool. The best training is to watch an infant or a two year old and to observe such things as:

- how they move through space

- how they explore the surface and objects they meet

- what captures their attention

- the level of their gaze and reach

- what disturbs or frustrates their activity

Once you have a *feel* for the way that an infant or toddler interacts with

space, you have to take the basic qualities of good environments and ask: "How does this apply to infants?" or "What would this mean for toddlers?"

HEALTH AND SAFETY

Of course it is important that an environment be safe and healthy. This means that there must be careful control of temperatures and ventilation (especially at the low levels where children will be). There must be sanitation precautions that are thorough but easy for caregivers to follow out. The setting must be inspected for sharp edges, dark corners, uneven flooring. Materials must contain no toxic substances. Toys should be examined so that no baby can choke, suffocate, or be cut — even when playing with the toys in unorthodox ways.

At the same time, an environment which is overprotective is unhealthy in its own way. It stifles movement and exploration; it hurts children's ability to trust themselves and the physical world. Children are smart about their own safety when it comes to motor skills; they simply do not make the same errors over and over. They learn how to handle steps and how to protect themselves if they roll off a riser. The job is to learn not to patrol children or to limit the kinds of equipment but to set up the environment.

Crowding is often overlooked as a basic safety problem. There must be clear spaces for large motor activity, but spaces should be small enough to prevent children from bunching up. Until children are older, they lack much clear sense of other children's space needs; more than three or four children may lead to a fair amount of accidental bumping and knocking. Also, small numbers permit children to concentrate. If a child is alone on a ramp or a ladder, she can think about where she puts her feet. If there are large numbers of other children around, she is likely to be distracted.

If a child's fingers are pinched by a rocker, don't ban the rocker. Look for a new place to put it where it won't be in the flow of traffic. Think about padding and carpeting risers and lofts. Don't do away with drawers if a child's hands get closed in one. Instead, realize that two year olds are fascinated by opening and closing; build alternative sources for that experience into the room.

In boring rooms, children end up exploring each other. That leads to poking, pushing, even biting. In restrictive rooms, adults are constantly pulling children away from items or areas that interest them. Being turned into a police person makes teachers tense, even angry. It wastes valuable teaching and caring time.

VARIETY

One of the biggest challenges of group care lies in avoiding the institutional qualities of the experience: everyone doing the same thing at the same time. This *factory* atmosphere has high costs: boredom, frustration, loss of individuality for both caregivers and children. In hospitals and nursing homes, just as much as in child care, staff members have to work to avoid this kind of dulling routine.

The actual layout of physical spaces and facilities can be extremely important. If the spaces are individual and small enough, babies won't be moving in *packs*. Because of the size of the children, there should be something interesting every two feet. That way, within a small area two will be playing hide-and-seek behind a pillow, one will be collecting blocks, another will be in a lap looking at a book. In this type of space, babies and toddlers move at their own pace. Consequently, their active, quiet, and sleeping periods will become individual.

Personal or individual activity schedules can be accentuated by the kinds of furniture in the room. If the room contains large motor equip-

ment as well as low mattresses and groups of pillows, one child can be very active while another infant takes a cat nap. The variety of possibilities also answers to the fact that in any single day individual children will feel energetic or quiet, sociable or crabby, needy or independent.

A second issue in providing individualized care comes from thinking about infants or toddlers in age groups. *Infants like . . . ; Infants can . . . .* Anyone with child care experience knows that no two infants are alike at nine months. Spaces must reflect the individual rates of development and the spectrum of interests or skills likely to show up in any group of children. Basically this means there must be considerable variety. The same room must work for babies who sit or walk, who like books or ramps.

A final problem with group care comes from age segregation. Usually infants and toddlers are restricted to their own company and their own spaces. Many teachers and directors are concerned that older children will mow down babies. But infants and toddlers need the variety of walking to other rooms in a center — even playing in baby-proofed regions of other rooms. It is not positive for younger children (or their teachers) to be walled off from the three to five year olds.

Programs should consider ways of integrating babies into the larger community. Five year olds can help feed babies or they can come to play with individual toddlers in the late afternoons. Perhaps there can be a loft or a window which permits two year olds to observe older children in another room or to watch traffic through a hallway.

FLEXIBILITY

At no other time in their lives are children changing in quite so many ways at once. Yet it is rare that we think about what this rapid rate of development means for the way we design and furnish spaces. Infant

and toddler spaces have to be set up *flexibly* so that the environment can *keep in step* with children's shifting needs but stay within what is often a very modest budget.

Take the instance of providing seating and surfaces. High chairs take up precious space. Low chairs with trays and "sassy seats" that attach to a table provide more flexibility. An extended top over a water table turns a very usable learning center table into a lunch table.

Another form of flexibility comes from rethinking the usual, like a couch. For infants, a couch provides a perfect space for two caregivers to sit and hold babies. As children learn to crawl, the couch can be moved out from the wall to create an interesting path. When children want to practice walking, the same couch provides a soft walking rail. Once toddlers become fascinated by more complex kinds of spatial games like hide-and-seek, the couch can become the base for a slide or for tunnels made from blankets. This process of designing and redesigning an environment creates a caring and a working space which keeps pace with changes in children.

SCALE AND PERSPECTIVE

It is easy to forget how small infants and toddlers are. Almost everything in their lives goes on under 30 inches. This requires that designers and teachers turn their normal expectations upside down — beneath three feet is the *active zone* (where the curriculum happens), above three feet is the *passive zone* (storage, wall-mounted cradles, bulletin boards).

The body size of infants and toddlers has implications for laying out spaces and distances within a play-room. What is a small space for an adult may feel like a baseball diamond to an infant. A fiberboard drum, a cardboard box, a pillow leaning up to a couch are all rooms large enough for two babies. Play spaces much larger than that may lead to overcrowding. What is a short distance for an adult to cross may be too great a span for a young child. As children become self-assured walkers, these distances and spaces should change.

In planning environments for very young children, adults also have to think about adjusting their perspective. While older children and adults spend almost no time looking at the ceiling or the undersides of furniture, babies see quite a lot of this kind of scenery. The challenge is to find ways of making these spaces interesting and functional. As people plan infant and toddler rooms, they should consider mobiles above changing tables, ceiling displays in nap rooms, textures along baseboards.

SOFTNESS AND RESPONSIVENESS

Infant and toddler rooms should spark the response: *What a neat place to be a little kid! What a neat place to be WITH a little kid!* There are two major ingredients in producing this type of response: softness and responsiveness.

Softness is created by masking the sterile, efficient side of child care settings with the qualities of a living room: soft light, plants, nooks and corners, comfortable furniture, easily moveable props like blankets and pillows. The point is not to create some *House and Garden* setting. The point is to design a place where babies will know how to find privacy and intimacy and where adults will find it easy to provide these same things.

Responsiveness is a slightly different quality. It is the way in which a room speaks back to a child who acts on it. A room has to be sensitive to the way that children of different ages are likely to act. Infants and toddlers provide a good contrast in this respect. For infants, a room has to be a fine space in which to sit, crawl, or walk short distances. It is full of pillows, low mattresses, barely raised

platforms, and changes in textured surfaces.

The materials in an infant room should react to light touch and chance motions, because that is what babies produce spontaneously. In a playroom for babies, you want mobiles that respond to air currents; mirrors that reflect simple changes in position; easily grasped items such as soft balls, foam blocks, or books with cardboard pages. An ideal item is a plastic swimming pool containing scarves, strips of cloth or paper. A baby can crawl directly into the pool and sit in the middle, where the smallest change of position creates interesting noises and visual changes.

But toddlers enjoy an environment which responds to quite different kinds of action. By the age of two, most children enjoy interacting with materials that demand more focus, work, and planning. Storage shelves that have compartments with some doors, shutters, and drawers would frustrate infants, but they can fascinate toddlers. Similarly, the furnishings in a toddler room can be more challenging. Possibilities include ladders to lofts, slides down from raised areas, light moveable cubes which permit children to create their own novel spaces.

The toys in such a setting should also change. An infant should be interested by a mirror in a busy box, but a similar display would be boring for two to three year olds. Instead, they need a mirror with a set of colored plexiglass covers mounted nearby or a mirror covered with all different kinds of latches and catches.

HARMONY AND ORDER

An environment for young children has its own brand of attractiveness. It is beautiful if it works well for the children who spend their hours there. More often than not this means that the setting is harmonious and well ordered, rather than cute or pretty. A mural of Mickey Mouse

may amuse adult visitors, but it is unlikely to mean much to small children. From a child's vantage point, it may just be *visual noise* — lots of complexity which doesn't help the child to understand the way the room works.

A child care center contains huge amounts of details and motion because of the sheer number of people in the same room. Walls and surfaces should provide a background against which the items that children use stand out. Plain wooden shelves show off toys and materials well. Against that kind of simple background, picture labels showing where items belong stand out. With a backdrop of neutral walls and fabrics, people stand out sharply. This makes it easier for infants and toddlers to find them, move toward them, and focus communications.

A COMMUNITY OF ADULTS AND CHILDREN

As much as it is important to take a *child's eye view*, it is critical to consider the needs of adults working in infant and toddler rooms. An environment which is exclusively child centered will be tiring and stressful for teachers. Hidden nooks delight infants, but if a room contains any number of invisible hideouts, teachers will be distraught in no time.

Infant and toddler rooms must be highly organized. Items which are used together must occur in the same space. A diapering area must contain not just the changing table, but the sink with toweling and plastic bags mounted on the wall and storage for clean clothes. This kind of thoughtful centralization means that teachers spend their time with children, not on hunts for equipment. It also means that parent helpers, substitutes, or extra help at lunch time can step in and be helpful immediately. This kind of organization also promotes safety. Adults are not constantly darting back and forth; they can focus their attention on what children are doing.

Materials and spaces should not promote a false sense of security. Changing tables with straps or rails are dangerous in their own way. Sooner or later a baby will escape, and there will be an accident. Better no such gimmicks, then it is clear that no child can be left alone.

Finally, rooms for young children must have easily *restorable* order. Infants have no rules against spilling. No two year old can resist seeing if popcorn will float in the water table or what happens if poker chips are mixed in with the play dough. If adults are going to last whole days (never mind years), child care settings have to contain built-in limits on the amount of dirt and chaos. Surfaces must be easily wiped off. Different types of messy materials can be rotated through an area of the room that is especially set up for handling drippy, dirty stuff. In that way, children can experience water, play dough, and paint without adults being run ragged with mopping and changing.

Activities involving small pieces such as tabletop blocks, Legos, or poker chips can be carried out in small, more contained spaces. Toddlers love dumping, sorting, and collecting. In order to answer to this fascination and preserve staff sanity, build a sorting pit which is separated from the rest of the room by pillows, shelves, or a carpeted bump.

Spaces can be designed so that the order is visible and clear even to young children. Items are less likely to get scattered wildly around the room if children have defined spaces for play: raised platforms, trays, mats, areas marked off with tape, changes in flooring, or circles of hosing. Even young children can become responsible for maintaining order if the clues are sharp and clear. If the play phones are stored on a shelf with a picture to label the space, toddlers have adequate clues for putting them back. Two year olds can easily grasp this kind of simple space-to-item matching. Teachers can be flexible in what they think of as worthwhile activities. For example, toddlers can be given empty buckets labeled with pictures of toy cars, Legos, or chips. They can be asked to hunt for all the stray bits scattered throughout the room. The basic idea is to create a setting in which learning and nurturance, not maintenance, consumes the most attention and interest.

This article is based on an interview with Jim Greenman by Dennie Wolf.

Places for Babies:
Infants and Toddlers in Groups

Imagine a room with light streaming in the windows, shadows dancing on the floors and walls, and a richly textured world of different shapes and sizes of furniture to climb on, over, around, and in — with places to just sit, places to snuggle. It is a room where you can sometimes make wild messes as you discover the mysteries of sensuous substances that often end up on you. It is a room with different *places to be*, just like your house — places that look, feel, sound, and smell different. There are lilacs here and baskets of ivy hanging by the window. There is a door to the outside, that wonderful place with grass and sun and shade. Out there the messes can be even wilder, and you are free to kick up your heels — sorry, you can't do that — let's say instead bounce and waddle with abandon, roll and swing, twist and shout.

It is NOT a room dominated by cribs, nor are you sandwiched between the glare of fluorescent lights and gleaming tile. It is NOT a tiny cell-like space where the day is divided into time on the crowded rug, the bounce chair, and the crib — nor is it a room filled with tables and chairs and a random assortment of toys, where activities are put out to keep the group busy.

In the room are large and small people interacting; the interactions are warm and relaxed and frequent. There are real conversations between adults and children. Adults listen to children and respond to their vocalizations.

Look closely and see — it is a room filled with individuals. There is Stephen, striding into the room like Louis the Sun King, expecting to be loved, his good nature surrounding him like a bumper. There is Alexander, always a worried man who likes to be held. And Alicia, who likes to sample everything, and JoAnna, who needs a morning nap.

Children are trying to "do it myself" — infants holding spoons and cups, toddlers pouring milk and wrestling with zippers.

Parents clearly belong in the room; one feels their presence through photographs and the information directed toward their eyes. The warmth with which they are welcomed and their familiarity with the life occurring within leaves little doubt that it is their place as well.

There is a sense of **security**: both the security that comes from knowing that this is a safe place for children, beyond the normal bumps and bruises that go with active learning, and the child's security that she is truly known, understood, and accepted for who she is.

There is a sense of **engagement**: when adults interact with children, they give them their full human presence. When children are exploring the world and their emerging powers, they are intent.

There is a sense of **active learning**: children are genuinely INTO things, and ALL OVER things, as befits creatures that learn with all of their senses and through whole body action.

Unfortunately, it is not easy to find programs with these characteristics. Probably fewer than one in ten centers are truly *good places for babies*. Quality does not come easily or inexpensively.

Quality care for babies is not brandishing an infant curriculum or *infant stimulation*. It is not spic-and-span tile and formica, or attractive lofts, or a bump-free environment, or even low ratios and smiley, warm people. Quality is each and every child experiencing warm, personal care and developmentally appropriate opportunities for sensory, motor, and language learning. Quality is parents feeling in control.

How Does Quality Happen?

Without infant ratios of no worse than one adult to four children, toddler ratios of one adult to five children, it will not happen, or at least happen for all of the children all of the time. And quality depends on people who genuinely appreciate babies for who they are, for what they can do right now, not just what they will be able to do or are in the process of becoming. But good ratios and good people don't guarantee quality.

Quality happens because the environment — time and space — is designed and planned to support care and learning. The setting is furnished, equipped, and organized to maximize the caregiver's time. Quality is a result of considerable

thought and planning: maximizing resources, adjusting to individual needs and changing circumstances.

The Importance of Built-In Learning

An essential quality of good infant and toddler programs is moving away from a traditional early childhood focus on activities and building learning into the environment. When learning is built in, it frees caregivers to BE WITH children and focus on the child: to take the time to slowly diaper a child, or to help a child through the agony of separation, or to appreciate the joy of newfound discoveries. These are the PRIME TIMES, the important times. It is upside down priorities to rush through these times to get back to *teaching* or managing children.

While teacher-directed activities may take place, there are always other opportunities for those toddling to a different drummer. Activities take place individually and with small groups within an environment rich with opportunities for vigorous motor and sensory exploration.

The Importance of an Organized Convenient Environment for Staff

Convenience and organization buy time for staff to spend precious minutes with a child. Poor storage and inadequate equipment result in lower quality.

What Kind of Place for Babies?

A Safe and Healthy Place

Good places for babies follow the National Health and Safety Performance Standards: Guidelines for Out-of-Home Child Care Programs in *Caring for Our Children*, developed by the American Public Health Association and the American Academy of Pediatrics standards for group care.

But there are also two important understandings: (1) Learning

involves the risk of acquiring the normal bumps and bruises of childhood, the natural result of learning to explore the world with a developing body. (2) *Sanitary* and *clean* are not the same thing and are usually confused. A good program has a vigilant concern for avoiding the spread of germs and disease, but not a preoccupation with cleanliness that gets in the way of sensory exploration and other active learning.

A Good Place to "Be"

A good place to be a baby and be with a baby for long days and weeks includes:

- sufficient room for adults (including a few parents) and children

- windows and doors to the outside

QUICK EVALUATION OF AN INFANT OR TODDLER LEARNING/CARING ENVIRONMENT

If infants or toddlers could choose their own setting, they might ask:

How many places are there where I can:

climb up?	_____	climb in?	_____	climb over?	_____	climb on?	_____
go through?	_____	go under?	_____	go in and out?	_____	jump?	_____
pull myself up?	_____	reach?	_____	kick?	_____		

How many semi-enclosed places are there?

How many different places to be are there for me, places that feel different because of light, texture, sound, smell, enclosure, and sight lines?

When you put me in an infant swing or bounce chair, am I only there for a short time and can I get out when I want to get out?

How often do I get out of the room?

How often do I go for stroller or cart rides?

How often do I get to get out of the stroller/cart and walk/crawl around?

How often do I get to play with messy things — water, sand, dough, paint?

What is there to transport?

   push/pull?

   collect/dump?

   throw?

Do I get to feed myself as soon as I can hold a spoon, bottle, or cup?

Do I have to wait to be changed or use the toilet?

When I talk my talk, will someone listen and respond?

When you talk to me, will you look at me and use words I am learning to understand?

Will someone read to me?

Permission granted to copy for personal use. *Places for Childhood* by Jim Greenman. Redmond, WA: Child Care Information Exchange, 1998.

- home-like lighting that allows a variety of lighting conditions

- multiple *places to be* — that feel different when you are there

- *places to pause* that allow you to step back from the action

- soft places and more soft places — pillows, couches, futons

- enough tile surface for eating and the rest carpet

- a separate crib room or area that accommodates individual schedules

- plants and multi-textured decor

- an outdoors of shade and sun, grass and deck, hills and flats, things to climb on, and loose parts to collect

A Good Place to Learn

Nearly all the important learning in the first two years of life is sensory, motor, language, and self-knowledge: "I am important, competent, powerful, and connected to others." A good place to learn is filled with challenge and exploration:

- large motor learning: climbing, pushing, grabbing, and motor opportunities of all kinds

- sensory learning: a *world at their fingertips* to touch, taste, smell, see, and hear

- language: conversations, listening to children, reading

- expression and accomplishment: opportunities to express yourself in motion and mess (art), solve problems, and *do it yourself*

- loose parts to inspect, collect, dump, and sort

A Good Place to Work

A good place to work needs:

- water and toilets, where they are needed

- ample storage, close to the point of use

- ample information space, close to the point of use

- clear organization and signage

- cleaning supplies, right there

A Good Place for Parents to Be

Parents are welcome, greeted, and helped to understand how the room works. There is storage for their things.

A FINAL NOTE: BABIES IN THE REAL WORLD

Babies deserve more than they usually get from group care. Too many programs are too hard, inflexible, over and understimulating, and tolerate too much child distress. But it is not really the people involved who are to blame. Many programs for babies are the equivalent of shanty towns, makeshift creations put together out of the wonderful stuff we can find and keep, the found and purchased spaces and materials barely adequate for the task, and all the energy and love and commitment that can be mustered. It is easy to accept what is and avoid criticism of programs doing the best they can. But at what cost to children? It is our job to assert what quality is and to push for the resources for all programs to achieve it.

Babies Get Out:
Outdoor Settings for
Infant/Toddler Care

Imagine a playground for babies.* A what? Probably few images are conjured up. Playgrounds are rough and tumble places where running, jumping, hurling, and the traffic of miniature speeding vehicles and general wild abandon flourish. Life in the fast lane is no place for a baby. Okay, instead imagine an infant/toddler park. Again, it probably seems strange to think of an outdoor place for children under two.

Let's start over. Imagine outdoor places that would be wonderful to be in with a baby, that would enable you to enjoy the world outside the walls of your daily place of work, while taking pleasure in the growing power and competence of the child — parks with sun and shade, flowers, gentle breezes, grassy hills, winding pathways, and places to relax and talk and appreciate the sounds of birds and water and crickets and babies.

Now return to the idea of a baby playground. Imagine an outdoor arena for baby play: a setting that encourages the visual exploration of a four month old; the reaching and grasping, rolling and leaning of a nine month old; and the stepping and toddling, pulling and pushing, hauling and dumping, exuberant exploration of older babies. If we begin with the idea of somehow adapting playgrounds for older children, we may get nowhere, or a somewhere that doesn't work. If, instead, we begin thinking about what we want to experience outdoors and what we want babies to experience, we may end up with something entirely different.

DESIGN CONSIDERATIONS

What is the value of the outdoors? Why go outside at all? What does the outdoors offer that the indoor setting cannot?

Climate. The outdoors has weather: wind, sun, rain, fog, clouds, snow, and warmth and cold.

Landscape. Outside we can have hills and knolls, hedges, ruts, holes, streams, surfaces of all sorts of textures and descriptions and levels, and vegetation with varying colors, smells, textures, and growing characteristics.

Openness. Outside there is a vastness, a sense of infinite boundaries, even if only in one direction — up.

Messiness. Outdoors we can be much freer to be messy (or, perhaps more appropriately, earthy).

Wildlife. The world of uncaged birds and squirrels, bugs, worms, and other life forms is outside our windows.

People. Outdoors there are people in their natural habitat: working, living, playing, traveling.

All of the above is, of course, not news. Yet I think it is important to begin here if one of our criteria for design is to take advantage of what the outdoors has to offer. If we look at some outdoor settings for children (traditional school playgrounds come to mind), it is clear that this criteria may not have been taken into account.

THE NATURE OF INFANTS AND TODDLERS

In the first two and a half years of life "children go all the way from complete helplessness to autonomy and assertiveness without any moral responsibility" (Ferguson). A baby actually thinks and acts through his gross motor abilities. Babies experience a very different world than we do, one dominated by senses and bounded by the here and now: their own body, this moment's feelings, the limits of their physical control. They are also very small and "have tiny little hands and tiny little feet" (Randy Newman), and the scale of settings they find themselves in is rarely accommodating. Imagine what it is like to investigate predominantly with your eyes, mouth, and entire body (and not your mind and hands), to store knowledge in your physical reactions. An understanding of the way babies are and how they learn is critical to planning quality outdoor space.

Infants and toddlers have a drive to explore, to discover, to comprehend — in Piaget's terms to "construct" reality, in Montessori's terms to "absorb" their environment, in Susan Issacs' words to "realize themselves." The more an infant sees and is able to make comprehensible, the more he wants to see. Vision becomes coordinated with hearing and other senses and with growing motor skills. The baby is constructing, piece by piece, "the world as we know it" — more accurately to a Piagetian, "as I know it." As a toddler begins to master her body and extend her field of action, her will to achieve greater and more sophisticated mobility is joyfully insistent.

Outdoors, as well as in, the baby needs a safe world where above all else, in Jerome Bruner's words, he is "encouraged to venture, rewarded for venturing his own acts, and sustained against distraction or premature interferences in carrying them out" — a world that doesn't make them ill, frighten them, or inordinately bang them up. Columbus would not have made his second voyage if he fell off the edge, or even if he just had a close call. Babies also come equipped with parents who have a quotient for cleanliness, scrapes, and bruises.

Because the outdoors presents countless threats to life and limb of the hardiest baby, it may be tempting to just keep them inside. (They do eat worms, after all, and have not heard Frank Zappa's caution about yellow snow.) Danger lurks with ingestion, falls, the effects of sun and wind on sensitive skin, and, not least, those sturdy classmates bereft of moral responsibility. "When you have an infant of three months lying on his back watching tree patterns together with a two and a half year old who is learning to pour sand, it can be a disastrous combination" (Ferguson). Yet good design and thoughtful adults can overcome these obstacles.

THE NATURE OF CAREGIVERS

Because we do not customarily approve of babies on the loose by themselves, infant toddler playgrounds are also places for adults, and the design must take this into account. If there is no shade or wind break, if access to the outdoors is inconvenient, if keeping the children safe and healthy appears to require considerable effort, if there is no comfortable place to sit or lie down with a baby — in short, if it feels like a hassle to get out and an unpleasant experience to be out — use of the outdoors will be minimal.

The act of going out and being out with a baby is very different than with older children. **Going** out usually requires more forethought — change diapers? bring which bottles? sunscreen? whose nap times are coming up? — and preparation —
stuff into snowsuits, fill the diaper bags, find the strollers.

Being out requires a level of grounds keeping found elsewhere only on putting greens, a watchfulness associated with the Secret Service, and a tolerance for periodic inactivity similar to that of Ferdinand the Bull. Appreciating a six month old's grooving on the sounds and sight of water dripping from the gutter only lasts so long. It is also important to note that adults, of course, vary considerably in their appreciation of the outdoors.

THE LANDSCAPE

The basic dilemma: The infant/toddler landscape has to be safe to eat. Shrubs, flowers, and trees in all stages of growth cannot be toxic and should be checked with the local poison control center (nurseries probably won't know in enough depth since the question of children sucking on shrubs rarely comes up). Sand areas that attract cats, wooden objects that grow moss and mushrooms, and gravel areas all present problems that need to be thought through.

Ideally, outdoor spaces for babies would have a variety of:

Surfaces: Grass, sand, wood. There should be gentle inclines to roll down and toddle up, grassy knolls to feel secluded in, and flat surfaces to strut and wobble upon.

Textures: Smooth round boulders, coarse bark and smooth sensual wood, soft and not-so-soft pine needles, and other vegetation to feel and rub up against.

Color and scent as seasons change: Trees and shrubs that complement each other and transform themselves as seasons change with falling leaves, cones, and blossoms, and peeling bark (all certified by Euell Gibbons as edible).

Places to be: Round boulders and shrubs to create miniature grottos and secluded baby-size groves to go in and out, over and around; shady spots and sunny spots; open areas and tight hideaways.

Pathways: A pathway not only structures traffic patterns but in itself can be a central site for learning and exploration. Changing surfaces from dirt to cobblestone, wobbly planks, half logs, wood rounds, patterned rock, colored brick, and so on provides motor challenges and sensory exploration for babies as they crawl, toddle, push, or haul. Varying railings to include poles, chain, rope, and iron again changes the experience. (Remember how your hands were drawn to exploring railings as a child?) Pathways are exciting because they go somewhere; meandering pathways invite stopping along the way.

Barriers: Barriers, like pathways, direct the traffic flow and enclose activity areas. A creative use of barriers, restricting children to developmentally appropriate areas by requiring certain skills to surmount them, allows self-regulation. Jerry Ferguson at Pacific Oaks used tunnels, slatted wooden surfaces, shrubs, and other means to naturally regulate the whereabouts of crawlers and freewheeling toddlers. Tiny retaining walls of rock or wood that babies can lean against, scale, and explore with fingers and bellies and gates that open and close combine learning and crowd control.

STRUCTURES ON THE LANDSCAPE

Canopies, umbrella mounts: Shade is essential; and without trees, canopies, lawn umbrellas, and awnings become prime alternatives.

Swings: Opportunities to move in space, alone or with a trusted adult, are provided by swings with baby seats, porch swings, hammocks, and cradles.

Skeletal structures: Set in the ground ladders, hurdles, and bench-like structures are in themselves motor structures for climbing on, over, under. Skeletons can become even more by adding planks, ladders, fabric, and so on.

Fabric and flapping things: Banners, parachutes, wind chimes, and branches make wind visible and audible.

Decks or platforms: Wooden flooring outside offers a flat surface that drains easily, providing a good place for water play and outdoor play when the ground is wet. Raised, a platform offers a baby a chance to *get high* and to see the world from a new vantage point.

Slides: A slide inset in a hill eliminates most of the risk and leaves the thrills and spills.

Half-buried tires: Tires provide mini tunnels, places to sit or lean, and pathway railings. They can be painted to reduce surface heat.

Lean-tos, houses: Anything with a roof is a playhouse.

Young infant area: An enclosed area that encourages reaching, grasping, kicking, and so on as well as a variety of visual, auditory, and other sensory experiences (using fabric, branches, falling water, and so on).

Sound structures: Miniature shrines with materials that react to wind or touch with sound and motion.

Elevated waterways: Wooden, metal, or stone troughs off the ground that provide water in motion.

Diaper tables: In warm climates, outdoor diapering will maximize outdoor play.

Climbers, dead trees: Anything to pull up on, straddle, climb.

Wobbly structures: Boards on springs or tires, logs or planks barely off the ground fastened to a frame with chains, anything with a slight wobble.

Logs, benches: Places for adults to sit or lean while observing or nurturing babies.

Stored equipment and materials: Planks, ladders, parachutes and other fabric, wagons, wheel toys, wheelbarrows, pillows, balls, sand/water toys, and creative *junk*.

The success of infant/toddler outdoor time ultimately depends on the adults in the setting — adults who recognize and encourage the scientist and explorer in each baby, accept the ups and literal downs that ensue, and at the same time maintain a watchful eye and nurturant presence for long periods of relatively uneventful action. A good playground design can make the outdoor experience a delight for adults and babies.

REFERENCES

Bruner, Jerome S. "Organization of Early Skilled Action." *Child Development*, 44:1-111, p. 8, 1973.

Ferguson, Jerry. In Elizabeth Jones (editor), *Supporting the Growth of Infants, Toddlers and Parents.* Pasadena, CA: Pacific Oaks, 1979.

*The term *babies* is out of fashion but using it reminds us that infants *and* toddlers are indeed babies. The automatic tendency toward jargon-irrelevant precision can be harmful, e.g., are you pre-middle age?

REALITY BITES:
BITING AT THE CENTER — PART 1

Y ou can see it in the eyes of staff and parents when an epidemic of biting breaks out. A tension hangs over the room like smog, a demoralizing haze of fear and anger and anticipation: when will it strike again?

Children biting other children is at once the most common and the most difficult repercussion of group child care, especially with toddlers. It happens even in the best of programs (but it happens more in lousy programs). When it happens, it is often scary, very frustrating, and very stressful for children, parents, and teachers.

Group living is hard — people rub up against each other. Children in child care need and want attention from adults, and (sadly) negative attention is more desirable than being ignored. A bite is powerful and primal: quick and effective, usually inspiring immediate and dramatic reactions. Size and strength are not required, even a baby can inflict a painful bite. Once present, it is hard to get rid of quickly. The child often bites again, another child imitates, and soon it's an epidemic. Parents become very upset about biting, and the problem escalates.

WHY DO THEY DO IT?

Biting is a horrifying stage some children go through and a major problem or crisis for the group while it is happening. Yet at the same time, for the biting child, it's a natural phenomena that has virtually no lasting developmental significance. It derives its significance from the group care setting. **It is not something to blame on children or parents (or teachers).** A child who bites is not on a path towards being a discipline problem, a bad person, or a cannibal. Yes, it is an anti-social act, but an act of an individual not yet equipped to be fully social, just beginning life as a citizen.

So why does this child bite and that child not? We make all sorts of guesses but don't really know. There are a number of possible reasons that children under age three bite, none of them the fault of a bad home, bad parents, or bad teachers. Sometimes we think we have a good idea of what's causing the biting but most of the time it is hard to guess what is going on in the child's head. Some of the likely reasons suggest ways of handling the biting:

• **Teething.** When teeth are coming through, applying pressure to the gums is comforting, and babies will use anything available to bite. Obviously, if this is a likely cause, then a teething ring or objects to bite will lessen the baby's need to bite other people.

- **Impulsiveness and lack of self-control.** Babies sometimes bite because there is something there to bite. This biting is not intentional in any way, but just a way of exploring the world.

- **Make an impact.** Young children like to make things happen, and the reaction when someone is bitten is usually pretty dramatic.

- **Excitement and overstimulation.** When some very young children are very excited, even happily so, they may behave in an out-of-control fashion. Natasha loved moving to music and, after a session in care with music and scarves and everyone twirling and enjoying themselves, it was very predictable that Natasha would bite someone if an adult did not help her calm down.

- **Frustration.** Too many challenges, too many demands, too many wants, too little space, too many obstacles may lead a child to bite, especially before they have the capability to express frustration through using language.

WHO'S TO BLAME?

We have to blame somebody. If it isn't the child or the parents, it has to be the program, right? There is no blame, but **a good program should accept responsibility for biting** because it recognizes biting as a natural phenomena — like toileting accidents, tantrums, and separation trauma. It is the center's job to provide a safe setting where no child needs to hurt another to achieve his or her ends and where the normal range of behavior (including biting) is managed. In the dire case where all attempts to extinguish the biting

behavior are working too little or too slowly and the child has to leave the program, it is as much the program's setback as the child's or the parents'.

When a child has become *stuck* for a while in a biting syndrome and it is frustrating for the parents of victims that the caregivers are unable to *fix* the child quickly or terminate care, empathizing with their feelings of helplessness and their concern for their children is essential, while you let parents know all your efforts to try to extinguish the behavior quickly. It is important to articulate how you are struggling to balance your commitment to the family of the biting child with that of the other families.

The name of a child who bites another should not be released because it serves no useful purpose and can make a difficult situation even more difficult. PUNISHMENT DOESN'T WORK TO CHANGE THE CHILD — either delayed punishment at home which a child totally will not understand or punishment at the center which may make the situation worse.

MANAGING THE CRISIS

No other situation requires as much perspective, thoughtful responsiveness, and careful communication as an epidemic of biting. Doing the following are important:

- Prepare parents for the possibility of their child being either a biter or a victim **before** the fact, as early as the intake into the center. If it is not unlikely to happen, then let's not hide it.

- Empathize with all the children and parents involved, and the staff. It's a difficult situation for all.

- Make sure parents are aware of all the steps that you are taking to minimize biting and end the crisis before they become upset. They

---

MEMOIRS OF THE PARENT OF "THAT CHILD!"

"I still have vivid memories of that horrible period that began when she was 19 months old. It was so awful, every day walking into her room and waiting to find out who Jenny had bitten. Four bites in one day, 14 in a week, 25 for all of June. Life was hell. We slunk in and out like the parents of a criminal. Was it us — some flaw in our home or some mutant gene?

Jenny was such fun as a toddler — this tiny red-haired mop top, with a great smile and bouncy enthusiasm. Even at her biting worst, she was happy. We never saw the biting at home, there weren't very young kids around.

We'd have these meetings with her teachers and the director. We were all desperate, and even though we all were doing everything we could, we became defensive, sometimes disbelieving each other. Maybe she was bored (their fault), troubled (our fault), immature (her fault).

I knew other parents were upset. After all, their children were coming home with Jenny's imprint (thankfully this was before AIDS). I saw them look at Jenny, at us. Finally one mother began yelling at me, shoving her son's arm in my face with the incriminating two red half circles.

And then, at about 22 months, Jenny stopped. Part of it was all the stuff the staff was doing and we were doing at home. But probably she just outgrew it. Now I look at Jenny and see this high school kid — good student, lots of friends, never in trouble — and I can laugh about what Sheila and I went through. But I remember wondering how she would ever have a normal life."

CHART BITING AND OTHER INCIDENTS

Homebase — Toddler Unit

When?		Where?	Who?		Who?		Surroundings?		Why?
Date	Time	Location	Aggressor(s)	Behavior	Target(s)	Behavior	Activities	Circumstances	Comments/Analysis
6/2	4:45	Big Room	Jake	Attempted to bite face	Haley	Crawling under bear blocks together	Crawling/ jumping under/off bear blocks	Small space	Jake may have needed more space
6/3	11:15	Play Room	Jake	Attempted to bite shoulder	Audrey	Cooking in kitchen area	Dramatic play in kitchen — dollies to sleep with, books	Small group 3:1 quiet, after lunch — Jake alone in kitchen area — 2 kids in small wooden cubby	Jake may have wanted to be where Audrey was

THE OTHER SIDE OF THE MIRROR: MY CHILD THE VICTIM

"If I can't keep my baby safe, keep him from being some other kid's snack substitute, what kind of mother am I? One day there is a bite on his cheek, then on his arm, two days later another one, and then even a bite on his bottom. The teachers would empathize with me and say, 'Biting is normal at this age.' Yeah, I know that toddlers bite, but mothers protect and I couldn't protect my kid. It may be normal to bite, but it's not normal to be gnawed on every day.

'We're doing all we can,' they said. So? Was I supposed to live with that? I wanted those biters out. How long was I supposed to let my child suffer, at 14 months old? I was told, 'Stevie is so curious and friendly that he is the most common victim.' I blew up. So it's his fault?

I left the center with hard feelings. Not because it was the center's fault, or even that they wouldn't throw out the biters. They were trying so hard to solve the problem, they didn't seem to understand what it was like to be in my shoes. We had to leave."

need to know that our understanding biting as a natural and common phenomena does not mean we throw up our hands in resignation.

• Have a sense of how long you will stick with a child *stuck* in a biting pattern, and communicate that to the child's parents right away. Fear of a sudden loss of child care adds to the tension. Again, it is better if parents know this before a crisis occurs.

This article was co-authored with Anne Stonehouse.

Anne Stonehouse is an associate professor of early childhood at Monash University in Frankston, Victoria (Australia) and director of the Centre for Early Childhood Research and Professional Development.

REALITY BITES (FREQUENTLY): BITING AT THE CENTER — PART 2

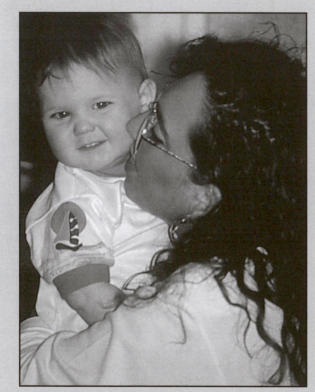

Knowing that infants and toddlers bite in group care is one thing. Doing anything about it is quite another. Even understanding why the biting is occurring doesn't necessarily lead to a "cure."

WHEN A CHILD IS BITTEN

■ Avoid any immediate response that reinforces the biting, including dramatic negative attention. The biter is immediately removed with no emotion, using words such as "biting is not okay — biting hurts." The caring attention is focused on the victim.

The biter is not allowed to return to the play and is talked to on a level that she can understand. You communicate that you understand the child's frustration (or needs for exploration or teething relief with an infant) and are willing to help her achieve self-control: "When you feel like biting, use words, I'll help you not bite." (Don't assert "I won't let you bite" unless you can deliver on that promise.)

■ Redirect the child to other play.

■ Look intensively at the context of each biting incident and look for patterns based on past incidents. Was there crowding, overstimulation, too few toys, too much waiting, other frustration? Is the biting child getting enough attention, care, and appropriate positive reinforcement for not biting? Does he need help engaging in play?

■ Work with each biting child on resolving conflict or frustration in an appropriate manner. Notice and reinforce all the occasions that the child does not bite.

■ Adapt the environment, and work with parents to reduce any child stress.

■ Make special efforts to protect potential victims.

CHANGES TO THE ROOM ENVIRONMENT

■ Analyze the room environment, schedule, routines, and expectations of children and staff to minimize:

• Congestion.

• Confusion and disorder.

• Child waiting.

• Child frustration.

• Child boredom.

• Commotion.

• Competition for toys and materials.

• Competition for adult attention.

■ Avoid large groups and break into small groups:

• Use other spaces in the center, the playground, and walks.

• Within the room, spread out the activities and the staff to avoid bunching up (also use the nap area).

■ Look for ways to increase the promotion of the children's sense of security and stability:

- "No surprises" — maintain a predictable schedule and ensure that children understand and anticipate the progression of the day.

- Ensure prime times with the child's primary caregiver.

- Ensure warm, cozy, semi-secluded *places to be*.

- Avoid staffing changes. Develop and maintain individual and group rituals.

■ Look for ways to engage children more effectively in the environment:

- Analyze choices perceived by children.

- Analyze the developmental appropriateness of choices.

- Provide duplications and multiple options.

- Consider whether to increase the motor and sensory choices available.

■ Look for ways to calm children after periods of excitement:

- Relaxed transactions.

- Calming music.

- Calming physical contact with caregivers.

■ Analyze grouping of children to avoid combinations that might lead to conflict or biting:

- Avoid grouping biters and likely *victims* together.

- Avoid grouping children who will compete for toys.

EPIDEMIC RESPONSE

When biting changes from a relatively unusual occurrence of a couple times a week to a frequent and expected occurrence, it should be considered an epidemic or health emergency, a serious threat to the well-being of the children in the room (including the biter). What happens in health emergencies? We apply extraordinary resources to the crisis.

Do the following:

■ Room staff meet with the director and/or assistant director on a daily basis throughout the crisis for advice, support, and to maintain a perspective devoid of blame (children, parents, or staff).

■ Chart every occurrence, including attempted bites, and indicate location, time, participants, behaviors, staff present, and circumstances.

■ Evaluate the immediate staff response to each biting situation to ensure appropriate intervention that includes:

- Comforting the injured child and treating the injury.

- Cool, firm, disapproving response to the biter that does not inadvertently provide reinforcement to the biter.

■ Analyze the chart and profile the behavior patterns and the environmental context of frequent biters and frequent victims.

■ *Shadow* children who indicate a tendency **to bite** and:

- Anticipate biting situations.

- Teach non-biting responses to situations and reinforce appropriate behavior in potential biting situations.

- Adapt the program to better fit the individual child's needs.

■ *Shadow* children who have a tendency **to be bitten**:

- Anticipate biting situations.

- Teach responses to potential biting situations that minimize the chance of becoming a victim.

■ Consider early transition of children *stuck* in a biting behavior pattern for a change of environment, if developmentally appropriate (and allowed by licensing).

■ If necessary, bring in outside observers to help you analyze the entire situation (not just the biter).

MAINTAIN POSITIVE RELATIONSHIPS WITH PARENTS

■ Let all the parents know that there is a problem and tell them everything that you are doing to stay on top of it.

CHART BITING AND OTHER INCIDENTS

Homebase — Toddler Unit

When?		Where?	Who?		Who?		Surroundings?		Why?
Date	Time	Location	Aggressor(s)	Behavior	Target(s)	Behavior	Activities	Circumstances	Comments/Analysis
7/1	9:50	Block Area	Hannah	Bite on right cheek	Clarissa	Trying to play with Clarissa	Block play, trucks	Waiting for breakfast — noisy	Clarissa surprised Hannah — she was hungry

■ Remind them of your philosophy regarding working with children in crisis — like a child stuck in a biting mode.

■ Work together as partners with the parents of both biting children and frequent *victims* to keep them informed and develop a joint strategy for change.

■ Prepare the parents of the biting child for the worst if suspension or termination from the program is possible and suggest they make contingency plans. Having to leave the program is a terrible consequence, having to leave with little warning is even worse.

HANGING ON

There are no magic feathers to *solve* a biting crisis. Sometimes nothing works and children grow out of it or leave the program. Doing all of the above should help alleviate or shorten the crisis.

Maintaining good relationships with parents during a biting epidemic requires all the trust and good will built up by good program practice. Because it is a *natural* and inevitable occurrence — like illness, earthquakes, and floods — all we can do is prepare for biting and maintain perspective while it is happening. It is the time when our expertise, professionalism, and character are put to the test.

CHAPTER 3

A GREAT PLACE TO LEARN

ACHIEVING BALANCE BETWEEN STRUCTURE AND WONDER

by Diane Trister Dodge

A great place to learn has to meet two criteria. First, it must be well organized and have a clear structure. Second, it should inspire and spark children's creativity and sense of wonder. While these two critical components of effective learning environments may appear to be contradictory, actually an organized and structured setting makes it possible for children to explore and be creative. Unfortunately, we tend to be better at achieving the first criteria than we are at creating environments that inspire wonder and imagination in young children. It is possible, however, to achieve more of a balance once we appreciate the critical role each plays in an early childhood program.

WHY STRUCTURE IS IMPORTANT

Most of us need structure in order to work efficiently. We may be reluctant to take the time to create the systems that are required; but once we do, the benefits are immediately obvious, thus inspiring us to maintain those systems. For example, how do you organize your kitchen? Have you identified spaces for different utensils, pots and pans, baking ingredients, and so on? Are spices organized alphabetically or do you have to hunt through your collection to find what you need? Knowing exactly where you can find things enables you to prepare a meal efficiently. If the order of your kitchen is logical and clear to others, someone unfamiliar with your arrangement could quickly learn to work efficiently in your kitchen as well.

Because teachers are creating spaces for children and for other adults, there are obvious benefits to having a well-organized and logical order to where things go. A well-organized, consistent arrangement of the classroom environment and materials helps children to feel safe and secure. They know where to find what they need and they can take responsibility for returning materials when they are finished. Thoughtful room arrangement can help us address common behavior problems in a positive way. Are children running in the classroom? Use shelves and furniture to divide up the space and make running impossible. Are you finding it difficult to get children to clean up? Label materials so children know where to find and return the materials they need. In this way, clean up becomes a matching game. Do children fight over materials? Provide duplicates of popular items and set up systems for taking turns such as waiting lists or a sand timer.

While "storage is not a glamorous or gripping topic," as Jim acknowledges, it can certainly make our lives easier. Two of my favorite ideas are using clear plastic containers for toys with small parts so that young children don't have to dump everything out to see what's inside and buckets with handles as storage containers which allows children to transport materials, thus promoting motor skills and creative use of materials.

BUILDING WONDER INTO THE ENVIRONMENT

I will always remember hearing Elizabeth Jones from Pacific Oaks caution us that "Teaching young children every day can be a very daily experience." Indeed, if the curriculum tells teachers what to teach, when, and how, and the environment is the same from day to day, teaching can become a very "daily experience" rather than an experience that continually emerges and holds interest and excitement. Wonderful experiences are more likely to happen if the environment itself is engaging, and teachers take the time to look at experiences through the eyes of the children. Adults need environments that nurture wonder as much as children do.

Jim's story of the mother and her four year old at the zoo (in "Just Wondering: Building Wonder Into the Environment") is a classic example of how wonder is killed by our tendency to teach through closed questions. How different this experience would have been for Johnny if instead of asking, "What color are they?" and "How many are there?" his mother had asked instead, "What do you notice about the flamingos?" or said, "Let's watch those giraffes and see what they do." Because it is difficult for all of us to recall open-ended questions, I often suggest to teachers that they make a list of open-ended questions and post them in the classrooms as a reminder.

To nurture a sense of wonder in ourselves as well as children, we should regularly ask ourselves, "What's new here for me? What do I see that I didn't notice before? What connections is this child making in attempting to understand the world?" Here is an incident that underscores how important it is to have living things in our classrooms so that children can make their own scientific discoveries:

One day in my kindergarten class a child said to me, "Look, we have to add more water to the fish tank because the fish are drinking the water." Focusing on his experience rather than what I wanted to teach, I asked, "How do you know the fish are drinking the water?" He pointed to the waterline mark and explained, "See, the water used to be up here and now it's down to here. So, the fish are drinking it." I took his explanation to the next logical step: "You mean if we filled a bowl with water the water would stay the same?" He answered, "Sure, because there would be no fish to drink it!" This led to a scientific experiment and more discoveries.

WHY WE NEED THE OUTDOORS

When was the last time you saw a child lying on the grass watching the clouds move and change shape, simply enjoying nature and having unhurried time to do so? It's unfortunate that nature and open spaces in which to explore are two important aspects of life that are too often missing for children. Can we afford not to offer all children this connection to nature? Is it possible in our inner cities with asphalt playgrounds surrounded by metal fences? We can do better and we must.

THE VALUE OF AN ENVIRONMENTAL APPROACH TO CURRICULUM

An environmental approach is very comfortable for me. It is the organizing framework for *The Creative Curriculum for Early Childhood*. We view the environment as the *textbook* of the curriculum and show how interest areas invite children to make choices, try out ideas, explore materials, and learn through their interactions with materials and others. Children can function in a structured environment more independently, thus freeing teachers to be with children, talk to them, and use the spontaneous moments that arise to promote learning and growth.

Creating an appropriate environment is the first step in planning curriculum. Once established, new teachers can be helped to appreciate the different kinds of experiences and discoveries children are making each day. A knowledgeable trainer/director can use these observations to highlight the teacher's role in guiding learning: knowing when to intervene and when to hold back; asking questions that extend children's ideas and spark new thinking; making suggestions and adding props that take children's play in new directions. A well-planned environment makes this kind of teaching possible — for new as well as for experienced teachers.

A well-organized learning environment is an important component of all quality early childhood programs. We must work to transcend the limitations of our environment to rediscover and reconnect with the wonders of the world.

Just Wondering: Building Wonder Into the Environment

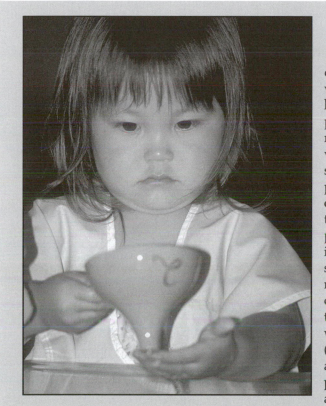

Children come to us stuffed with wonder, eyes lit bright with projects. Their hands are eager to pull apart life's mysteries, their voices ready to shout out accomplishments, each echo adding shape to their being. The primal urge to investigate does not stop there. The mouths of young children are there to taste and chew the world around them (admittedly, not always a pretty picture). Children are native sensualists, sucking up experience with genetically programmed gusto. Enthusiasm and curiosity race through the veins of children unless clotted by the form adults impose on their lives.

To wonder is to question, to imagine and speculate on what is and what isn't. To be full of wonder is to approach life with an openness, an eagerness to know and experience. When something is **wonderful**, it is something we take delight in — better than good and on the road to awesome.

What sort of environments support wonder and wonderful things and experience? Wonder is not hard to do; group living is hard to do, particularly with children. Group living leads to institutionalization which drives wonder underground.

For most of us, the wonder of life easily drifts into the background; it is the province of artists and children to throw light into the shadows of daily life and enliven our sensibilities. Children naturally poke into the corners and cracks of dreary common-place reality. WOULD YOU PLEASE PAY ATTENTION, LIFE IS HAPPENING HERE!, they tell us with their enthusiasms and their questions.

A classroom filled with wonder is not necessarily full of spectacle or rare and dramatic events or fancy equipment. Wonder is more often found in a collection of small moments when reality crystallizes and experience heightens.

There are the "I did it!" moments of wonder. The powers of "me" produce a sense of wonder in all of us that fuels striding on into the world: genuine accomplishment, real responsibilities carried out well.

In one small center, five year olds are occasionally entrusted with the responsibility of answering the phone. In another, children as young as two years old trek to the kitchen as waiters for second helpings.

There are the "this world is amazing and mysterious" moments that come with the discovery of how life works — birth, death, growth, love — and the moments of discovery of "how things work and happen" — machines, gravity, physics. Perhaps best of all are those "ain't life grand" moments of pure pleasure or beauty.

What Kills Wonder?

Wonder is easily diminished in children's programs by:

The weight and volume of daily life in groups. The energy it takes children to fit in, to carve out relationships and zones of privacy, and to take care of the mechanics of life may force wonder into the shadows. Group life often rations wonder by imposing restrictions (no "running feet," "outside voices," "keep it clean," "wait your turn") that flatten experience to keep the forces of chaos at bay.

The unbearable lightness of cuteness. Cuteness robs wonder of its evocative power, pasteurizing awe and delight into one dimensional chuckles and fuzzy glows.

Seriousness. Early childhood is far too serious to take seriously — that is, the seriousness that leads to earnest and passionate discussion on "Johnny's motivation," or two pages devoted to peekaboo in an infant curriculum, or a Ph.D. thesis on the developmental progression of skills involved with using scissors. Wonder often invokes the imperative to be silly, in both children and adults. Silliness in turn knocks down the formal structures that sometimes hold too rigid the shape of our straight and narrow orientation to task and routine and self-importance. Without periodic silliness, life becomes dreary and inspiration dims.

Blandness and lack of standards. Experience is not equal. In decidedly unwonderful programs, one gets the feeling that "a book is a book is a book," "a record is a record is a record," something taken from the shelf without much thought or enthusiasm. There is no sense of quality, of connection to the moment and the participants: that what is being heard or read has value and evocative power right now. One might hear Raffi in the background calling for movement as children, bemused and immobilized, sit at a table waiting for lunch, that album chosen because it was there. Or a listless reading of a long Disney Golden Book, a book with pictures too small to engage the increasingly restive large group. The joy of language and music fades in instances like this.

Gratuitous or unsought instruction. I watched as a mother and her four year old shared a moment at the zoo:

"Look, Johnny, flamingos!" the mother exclaimed. "What are they?"

"Birds," said Johnny.

"What color are they?"

"Pink," said Johnny.

"How many are there?"

"Three," said Johnny.

Two giraffes lumbered into view. Before Johnny's determined mom could open her mouth, Johnny called

---

*from **Sometimes Life Is Not A Literary Experience**
by Eugene Lesser*

*Tonight I sat on my back porch
and drank a bowl of
Campbell's chicken vegetable soup.
All that time watching the moon
and feeling absolutely great.*

*
---

out: "Giraffes, yellow, two." Johnny had overdosed on teachable moments. Wonder comes from a child's search and discovery, not from our dutiful prodding.

False engagement. Falsity diminishes wonder, and false engagement is probably worse than no engagement at all. An environment of "that's nice (pretty, good)" diminishes the child's quest.

Egocentrism, fatigue, and stress (ours). Teachers are egocentric the minute they focus on teaching (not learning) and caring (not care). Teacher fatigue and stress leaves little energy for real engagement with children.

Unbridled tidiness. Group living requires order, but an excess of tidi-

ness sweeps life into narrow bins and tiny corners.

Disorder and chaos. Chaos is scary and makes us insecure. We withdraw. Clarity is lost when chaos rules, and choices become random, beauty a blur. Without order, wonder is submerged and goes unrecognized.

Fear. In many programs, there is a low-level current of fear that bumps and bruises, stains and tears will lead to recriminations against the staff. Fear of risk, challenge, and mess suffocates wonder. Safety is a real issue, but often blown to grotesque proportions by fear of liability in a litigious society that refuses to see that "accidents happen." Parents' real concerns about wear and tear on children and clothes is lessened in programs where mutual respect between parents and staff leads to discussions on how best to create a sensible environment of wonder and discovery.

Censorship and political correctness. Wonder is diluted by political correctness of all stripes. Yes, all sorts of behavior are not acceptable and some have to be sanctioned because they hurt others or create problems in group life. But to wonder is to imagine and pretend, to explore the world of "what if" — a world that includes cross dressing, the immense power of imaginary weapons, and witches and monsters.

TALES OF WONDER

Five year old Anita and I were discussing wonderful things. We had rounded up the usual suspects of puppies and chocolate, puddles and Grandma's house, fishing with Dad, and riding her bike. Getting ready to go, Anita looked at me shyly and (slyly) and said, "And, you know, there's always poop." Take your epiphanies as they come.

FURNITURE AND EQUIPMENT TO PROMOTE WONDER

THE MIRACLE OF LIFE:

Incubators
Bird cages
Aquariums
Animal cages
Ant farms
Butterfly gardens
Bird feeders and bird baths
Baby carriers and furniture that creates laps
    (heartbeats and human contact)
Magnifying glasses

ALCHEMY AND CHEMISTRY:

Sinks
Plastic tubs
Water tables
Electric skillets
Microscopes
Toilets (unauthorized)

THE MAGIC OF CAUSE AND EFFECT:

Motors
Fans
Pulleys, levers, block and tackle
Computers

THE MAGIC OF VISION:

Lamps
Flashlights

Prisms
Stained glass
Canopies
Mobiles, hangings

THE WONDER OF LANGUAGE:

Tape recorders and headphones
Good books that value art and language
Typewriters
Computers

THE JOY OF INVENTED PLACES:

Lofts and platforms
Blankets, parachutes, and other fabric
Boxes and crates
Planks and blocks

THE WONDER OF CONSTRUCTION:

Blocks of all kinds, and more blocks
Planks
Mirrors
Connectors of all kinds —
    tape, string, nails, paste, glue

THE WONDER OF CARING ADULTS:

Adult furniture and the support to create
    good places
Ample storage

ENVIRONMENTS THAT SUPPORT WONDER

There is no mystery here. Wonder thrives in environments that embrace childhood and support the adults that live and work with them.

A child seeking active exploration would ask of a place:

- Can I be messy?

- Can I be alone?

- Can I move?

- Can I be outside — a lot?

- Can I spread out over space and time?

- Can I be noisy?

- Can I get some quiet?

- Can I be still?

- Can I do MY thing?

- Where's the stuff, the loose parts: the raw material of discovery?

A teacher might ask:

- Is there enough room?

- Can we keep it clean?

- Is there a place for me?

- Is there enough storage?

- Can we keep it safe?

- Will I get the support of staff and parents?

REMEMBRANCE OF THINGS PAST: A CAUTIONARY TALE

One can get carried away with the romance of childhood and forget that children are quickly acculturated. They, too, live in the real world — like it or not — the world of miracle, wonder, Macys, and Madonna. When

How Wonderful Is Your Classroom?

Walk into the child's place and create a sensory snapshot. Check with a + or − what you find.

The Smell of Wonder

_____ Flowers and plants

_____ Baking

_____ Herbs and spices

Subtract if you smell:

_____ Disinfectant

The Sounds of Wonder

_____ Child laughter

_____ Adult laughter

_____ Silly voices

_____ The sounds of birds, animals, fish tanks

_____ Rapt silence

_____ Music that creates a mood or sets bodies in motion

_____ "Wow," "I love it," "Look, look," "I did it"

Subtract if you hear:

_____ Baby talk

_____ Random background music (even Raffi)

_____ The silence of boredom or enforced stillness

_____ "That's nice" (yawn), "Do we have to?," "Sit still"

The Touch of Wonder

_____ Natural materials: wood, stone, and grass

_____ Sand, water, mud, clay

_____ Slimy, slippery, squishy, squeezy things

_____ Fragile things that require gentleness

Subtract if nearly all you touch is:

_____ Laps and hugs

_____ Plastic, formica, polyurethane, or metal

The Sights of Wonder

_____ Smiles on children's faces

_____ Smiles on adult's faces

_____ Looks of intense concentration

_____ "Faraway" dreamy looks of cabbages and kings

_____ "I did it" grins, maniacal grins of pleasure

_____ Living things — plants, animals, birds, fish

_____ Beautiful things — respectfully displayed

Subtract if you see:

_____ Vacant stares

_____ Commercial images and an abundance of *cute*

Which of these words apply to your classroom?

_____ Astonishment

_____ Lovely

_____ Sight to behold

_____ Mysterious

_____ Transformations

_____ Thrilling

_____ Ecstatic

_____ Intense

_____ Joyful

_____ Concentration

Permission granted to copy for personal use. *Places for Childhood* by Jim Greenman.
Redmond, WA: Child Care Information Exchange, 1998.

my daughter Emma was four, we spent a day together that I remember with intoxicating clarity — a warm summer day of picking wildflowers amid clouds of butterflies, paddling down a creek past baby ducks and egrets, and later being enveloped by grandparental pride. When I asked her about this day of wonder years later, she remembered it well. "Oh yeah, that's when I got my new red two-piece bathing suit." Proust would have kicked her. The moral here is not to diminish the importance of the natural world, only to note that a new red two-piece bathing suit is a pretty wonderful thing, too.

RESOURCES FOR WONDER

InsectLore
PO Box 1535
Shafter, CA 93263
(800) 548-3284
A unique company that sells butterflies, tadpoles, and all sorts of science-nature products.

This world, after all our science and knowledge, is still a miracle; wonderful, inscrutable, magical, and more, to whosoever will think it.

— Thomas Carlyle

Edmund Scientific
101 East Gloucester Pike
Barrington, NJ 08007
(609) 547-8880
All sorts of science and discovery equipment.

Bear Blocks
1132 School Street
Mansfield, MA 02048
(800) 424-2327
Carpeted planks and blocks to create ever-changing spaces.

Fancy Foote-Works
549 Moscow Road
Hamlin, NY 14464
(716) 964-8260
Custom-built environments, lofts, and play equipment.

* Every effort has been made to trace owners of copyright material, but in some cases this has not proved possible.

LEARNING ENVIRONMENTS FOR TODAY — PART 1

For most programs, we are entering a time when trained, talented teachers are hard to come by, yet the pressure to be educational will (appropriately) increase. Teaching environments for young children only work with good teachers who stay with the program. In a learning environment approach, a director can apply the knowledge and expertise of trained staff to create built-in learning and to plan learning centers so that less skilled staff can do what they do best — *be* with the children: listen to them, ask them questions, guide them toward self-control in the difficult waters of group living. Thus they can function, not simply as aides helping with care activities but more like museum volunteers, working off the learning they and others have *built in* to the setting.

THE LOGIC OF LEARNING ENVIRONMENTS

• **Children learn from the entire experience the day provides.** The way time and space are structured, the furnishings arranged, the equipment and materials provided, and all the ways adults and children behave *teach* the child what the world is like, how it works, what he is capable of, and his place in it.

All-day settings are not *schools* but places where adults and children live together for 8-10 hours a day. Education is one part of living. Learning and care are inseparable and both occur non-stop throughout the day. An all-day program has the entire day to build learning experiences into the program. There is no need for concentrated experiences as there is in programs with limited hours.

• **Young children do not benefit particularly from large groups**; but then who does? A good learning environment allows simultaneous, developmentally appropriate play individually, in pairs, and in small groups.

• **A rich, responsive learning environment**, set up to allow children to independently plan and explore, allows the staff to focus on *prime times*, those moments of one-to-one care and learning that lie at the heart of healthy development. Having to rush through one-to-one care and learning experiences, such as diapering, consoling a child in distress, or listening to a child's questions, to get back to teaching or managing children is the opposite of what should happen. Those are the times to draw out, to talk and listen and touch and reassure.

Planning the Learning Environment

- **Develop a room arrangement that regulates behavior.** A divided space with clear boundaries, traffic patterns, spaces of different sizes and with different functions will regulate crowding and wandering. Include spaces that are semi-secluded, protected from other children, small spaces for 1-4 children, small tables for 1-4 children, and open spaces. Bounded and contained learning spaces will help control the flow of loose parts — all the smaller materials and equipment pieces that may wander. Space can be divided by shelving units or curtains. Spaces can be found behind couches or chairs, under cabinets, or on top of low cubes or furniture.

- **Build sensory learning into the environment.** Within a coordinated tasteful aesthetic, use different textures, lighting, colors, temperatures or breezes, views or angles of vision. Use carpeting and rugs, fabric and materials that feel different or respond differently to light. Include mirrors, reflective glass and metal, open windows, lights on and off, and fans to provide air currents.

- **Build motor learning into the environment.** Furniture and equipment that encourages or allows climbing up or over, moving around, through, over, under, etc. — couches, pillows, stairs, ramps, planks and crates, small platforms, and cubes.

- **Create learning centers (interest areas) where materials are stored** and used to facilitate child-directed, autonomous play. Learning centers may be large (block area, housekeeping) or small one or two person learning stations (an individual clay area, a computer, a reaching area for infants). Some centers are really "take-out areas" with props for use throughout the space (costumes or science equipment like magnifiers). Interest areas may be flexible. In limited space, a "wet" or "messy" area may encompass art, sensory play, and projects. Teacher-managed activities *may* happen in learning centers.

- **Create ample, convenient, *labeled* storage.** Wall storage, cabinets, open and closed shelves, duffle bags, toy boxes all have their place, easily available *close* to the point of use.

- **Create ample, convenient communication space.** Clip boards, chalk or marker boards, post-it notes on a wall, *and* writing implements. Written systems ensure clear communication between staff and from staff to parents.

Some Keys to Effective Learning Centers

- **The right size and scale.** Think small as well as large. Learning areas can be as small as a 2 foot by 2 foot space on the wall and a 4 square foot rug or as large as a whole room. The size of the area should depend on what is to happen there and how many children are to be involved.

- **Good boundaries.** Defining where the actions will take place — a pit, rug, dividers, tape (any defining boundary) helps contain materials. Boundaries that require children to make a physical decision to enter or exit — open a gate, step up or over, etc. — result in children spending longer times in the area.

- **The right amount of seclusion.** Some visual and noise seclusion is important because wandering and distractions are primary problems in group care.

- **Zoning.** Locate messy areas away from carpets, active areas away from quiet areas.

- **Sufficient number of areas and choices.** The more areas (not necessarily always open), the more engaged the child will be.

- **Clear expectations, *visible for staff and children.*** Use signs and posters (with pictures) to express the limits of how the material can be used, how staff are expected to behave (e.g., get down on the floor, closely supervise the use of particular materials).

- **Open storage** that clearly displays materials and is picture, outline, color coded, or symbol labeled encourages children to return materials. Clear display means only a few items per shelf, clearly separated from each other.

- **Adult closed storage** should be convenient and close to the learning center.

LEARNING ENVIRONMENTS FOR TODAY — PART 2

Teaching environments depends on skilled teachers to daily design and implement activities and experiences that work for each child. Teachers *teach* and most or all of the planning goes into the teaching time, usually small and large group times. Curriculum depends on the teacher's presence.

In a **learning environment**, teachers plan for children to explore independently, to discover, and to learn through developmentally appropriate play. A playground, a museum, a Montessori or open classroom, or a park are learning environments where adults are facilitators, not instructors.

Good learning environments are individualized because they are rich with experiences children can access that fit their interests and developmental needs. How can you tell a good learning environment? Walk into the setting when teachers are **not** present and you should see learning built in or easily accessible to the children.

A good learning environment **empowers** children to become confident learners. The fundamental premise is that children are **active learners** who learn best from activities **they** plan and carry out themselves. Children are recognized as little scientists and builders, acrobats and artisans, who need active experience with the world of people and things, who need opportunities to plan and set goals and take responsibility.

Throughout much of the day, children make choices about which aspects of the learning environment to focus on; they participate in small groups and **short** times with the whole group. A typical day for a preschooler might include time at the listening center or reading books with a teacher, investigating the world of bugs outside, acting as an architect and builder with blocks or crates and wheelbarrows, group singing, making cookies for snack, digging and measuring and pouring indoors or out, and creating various costumed social worlds of home or business with friends.

THE ROLE OF TEACHERS

Teachers have two key roles in the learning environment:

1 With support staff, teachers prepare and maintain the environment for free and structured choice play, providing the necessary range of choices in activities and experiences, asking questions, and, of course, thinking ahead to the next transition. It is the watching and conversations that enables the teacher to plan experiences that *emerge* from the child's interests. Good planning of the environment makes conversation and observations possible.

2 Teachers facilitate the child's exploration of the environment to maximize her learning. The most important teaching happens when adults play and work alongside the children, not simply manage and teach. Good teachers are with the children — on the floor, on the grass, at the child's level participating alongside, listening, conversing, touching, observing, and paying attention when to engage the child and when to simply watch. At the same time, good teachers are keeping the flow of interest alive, recognizing efforts, finding the novel experience, asking questions, and thinking ahead to the next transition. Good planning of the environment makes this possible.

PLANNING THE LEARNING ENVIRONMENT

There are five parts to planning a learning environment:

■ Knowing and understanding the body of developmentally appropriate content:

- What developmentally important experiences are necessary for maximizing individual development?

- What experiences are necessary for each child to experience relaxed, happy days?

■ Planning the environment on a monthly basis:

- What interest areas are available?

- What props or loose parts are regularly available?

- What learning is built into the setting or routines?

■ Planning daily experiences and activities:

- What activities and projects are emerging from the interests of the children?

- What experiences are offered through rotation of materials in the learning centers?

- What activities are planned by teachers?

■ Monthly experience review:

- Are the experiences developmentally appropriate for the entire range of children?

- Are the experiences offered in the right balance? Curriculum area (motor, art, dramatic, construction, etc.) individual and group new challenge and practice/mastery

- Are the experiences multicultural, actively non-sexist?

■ Planning for individual children:

- Is the primary teacher/caregiver aware of the child's current interest, needs, and strengths?

- Does the teacher have a list of goals and desirable experiences based on the child's experiences in the group?

BUILDING IN LEARNING

The advantage of attaching things either permanently (with screws or bolts) or temporarily (with duct tape) is, of course, that they will stay put. This reduces the number of things that have to be reassembled or put back. Learning materials can be attached to almost any surface: walls, floors, benches, tables, backs of storage units, doors, fences, rugs, ceilings, windows, the inside of cabinets, and pillars.

Some of the many things that can be attached:

- toy steering wheels, other wheels.

- beads on wire or string.

- pounding benches or mallets.

- doors with latches, locks, hinges.

- fabric with zipper, velcro.

- cardboard or plastic tubes to look through, make noises with, put things in.

- metal surface for magnets.

- easel, linoleum for markers, with markers or crayons on strings.

- real or play telephones.

- mirrors; polished, smoked, or colored plexiglass; prisms; cellophane.

- clear, wire, opaque, woven containers for drop boxes and collection points.

- pulleys and levers.

LEARNING CENTERS AND LEARNING STATIONS

Many good learning environments organize the classrooms into these areas: construction/blocks, dramatic play, small motor, science, language, reading, water/sand, large motor, and sensory. But many others are possible, often taking up very little space.

Some examples:

Infant reaching/grasping/kicking area: Various materials attached on rope or fabric to hang.

Infant peek-a-boo/object permanence: Divider with holes in it, curtained area. Objects on a string that swing in and out of sight.

Infant walking/pulling up: Hand rails attached to the wall.

Communication center: Bulletin or marker boards, magnetic letters, tape recorders, newsprint, typewriter, a self-service writing station.

Electronics: Speak and Spells, computer, electronic games.

Playpit, plastic wading pool: A programmed, protected, contained space in which a child chooses to play.

Vehicles: Trucks, cars, trains, props like Fisher-Price people, houses, trees, small rocks and wood, blocks, ramps.

Hauling/transporting: (Contents to be used throughout the room with collection points) wagons, shopping carts, baskets, bins, buckets, cardboard boxes, toy boxes, mail slots, tubes.

Stuffed animal center: All sorts of stuffed animals.

Action center: Switches, zippers, velcro, locks and latches, doors, pounding benches, ramps, tubes, containers to drop or roll materials into, things to take apart.

Sound area: Chimes, whistles, instruments, strings to pluck and plunk, shakers, record player or tapes.

Animal area: Rubber or wooden animals, pictures, animal masks or noses, puppets, places for animals to live, props to fence, posters.

Cozy areas, places to pause (note plural areas): All sorts of pillows — couch, bed, throw, bean bag; inner tubes, throw rugs, bolsters, futons, blankets, parachutes, sheets, canopies, boxes, plastic wading pools.

Tiny areas: Spaces to squeeze into.

Body-image space: An area that responds to the child's whole body movement — a space filled with beach balls, paper, hanging fabric, etc.

Surprise area: A place where surprises or new experiences occur.

Please touch area: Different textures, coldness, hardness (smooth metal, rough bark, sand paper, velvet, corrugated materials), different forms.

Please look area: Mirrors, kaleidoscopes, colored plastic, smoked plexiglass, paintings, videos, wave tubes, fish tanks.

Outdoor areas: Hills, paths, boulders, stumps, shrub mazes, sidewalks, shade umbrellas.

SOME LEARNING ENVIRONMENT RESOURCES

Curriculums

The Creative Curriculum for Early Childhood by Diane Trister Dodge and Laura J. Colker is probably the best resource for helping you move from a teaching environment to a learning environment. The basic book is clearly written, supported by a video, a supervisor's manual, parents' guides, and training around the country by Teaching Strategies (202-362-7543 or <www.TeachingStrategies.com>).

The High/Scope Curriculum detailed in *Educating Young Children* (1995) by Mary Hohmann and Dave Weikart (High/Scope Foundation, 734-485-2000). A *Study Guide for Educating Young Children* (1997) by Mary Hohmann is also available. This work is supported by other books, pamphlets, videos, and numerous training opportunities provided by High/Scope. Highly regarded, the High/Scope learning environment can be adapted to any program.

Books

Edwards, Carolyn, Lella Gandini, and George Forman. *The Hundred Languages of Children*. Norwood, NJ: Ablex, 1993.

Brings together the reflections of the Italian educators who founded and developed the city-run early childhood program of Reggio Emilia, Italy, recognized and acclaimed as one of the best systems in the world.

Greenman, Jim. *Caring Spaces, Learning Places: Children's Environments That Work*. Redmond, WA: Exchange Press, 1988.

Discusses the relationship between children and the environment, offers practical information on developing learning environments, and directs readers to other helpful resources.

Houle, Georgia Bradley. *Learning Centers for Young Children*. Tot-lot Child Care Products, RR Box 1486, Weaver Hill Road, West Greenwich, Rhode Island 02816, 1987.

Detailed illustrations and descriptions of the traditional early childhood learning centers. Includes dimensions, materials, and vignettes about classroom life.

Isbell, Rebecca. *The Complete Learning Center Book*. Beltsville, MD: Gryphon House, 1995.

Description of 32 learning centers.

Loughlin, Elizabeth, and Joseph Suina. *The Learning Environment: An Instructional Strategy*. New York: Teachers College Press, 1982.

Practical information on establishing a learning environment.

WHERE HAS ALL THE SCIENCE GONE?

Children are natural scientists, impelled to dive into the primordial muck with all their powers and make sense of it all. **Make** sense — taste and twist and rub and bang and hurl the elements against each other and themselves.

The problem is that the natural world of people and things is messy — *mucky* even — and quite dangerous, particularly in the clutches of a curious child. The more enthusiasm, the more inelegant the miniature scientist. And the *civilized* world is increasingly fastidious and cautious.

As children have become increasingly valuable objects of consumption — clothes, classes, coiffures — the tolerance for vigorous mucking about is dropping.

An opportunistic insurance industry and a litigious fashion sweeping the culture have banished the notion of accidents from life; there is only negligence and liability.

The child's laboratory is shrinking rapidly in cities and suburbs. Unmanaged experience that children shape and give meaning to through their investigations require some exposure to fields and streams, or vacant lots and rainy streets. The time available for child science and for freedom from the eyes of solicitous and restricting adults shrinks as child care and organized activities fill the child's day.

There are also the laboratories of the kitchen and garage, made obsolete by Betty Crocker and Mr. Goodwrench. Erector and chemistry sets have been replaced by Nintendo and television. The social science laboratory of block games like "Capture the Flag" has been supplanted by littler and littler Little Leagues.

LET THE SUNSHINE IN

If children are to develop a sense of science, if we are to have science in the classrooms, we need to bring life into the classroom and the class out into the world. We must work hard to develop a daily routine that allows children to experience life in gulps and sips as well as measured doses. And life is what? Sunlight and breezes and frost on the window pane. Shadows slowly descending on a corner of the room. Water, seizing the light or revealing mysterious caverns in its shadowy reflection. A parakeet chattering away while martins dine at the feeder outside the window. Sifting and mixing and kneading and baking. Pouring and dripping and spilling and measuring. Feeding and nurturing and breeding and burying guinea pigs, mice, rabbits.

Science takes discipline and order — you don't just groove on nature. But it is a discipline to the task, the investigation, not to the 20-minute schedule allotment or to turn-taking. It is an interest-driven discipline most children possess. Witness a baby investigating the archaeological remains of lunch on the floor — systematically in pursuit of the edible. Or a five year old trying to achieve the right trajectory and distance to hit a floating log with a rock. Or an eight year old trying to build a fire.

A child engages in two worlds — the world that she can measure and calibrate and the world that she can feel with her heart and imagination. When children search and question, they are dogged in pursuit of the answer if they have been taken seriously and listened to in the past. But investigations often follow no straight lines. They are made up of bits and pieces, episodic and varied, which call for a different kind of order, following both heart and mind.

Interesting errors and side effects drive both serious science and child

explorations toward important learning. The critical issue in many early childhood programs: how to allow decidedly non-linear explorations in decidedly adult-oriented linear time and space.

DOES SCIENCE REQUIRE ROLE MODELS? INQUIRING MINDS WANT TO KNOW

In many programs I work with, there are few people on the staff with much interest in the way the world works. In the good schools and programs, there are many people who love being with children and who enjoy the enthusiasm and wonder that children bring to the classroom. They reflect the child's curiosity, but they have little of their own. Why do leaves turn red? Why does popcorn pop? Why is the vacuum not working? Why are people in Afghanistan at war? They live in the world pretty much without question. When they ask questions of the children (and they do so) or respond to the child's questions, it is in a gentle teacher-like fashion, as a good early childhood teacher should respond.

Perhaps that is enough for the most part: teachers who care deeply about the children and listen to them. After all, in many child care programs and schools, one is hard pressed to find many teachers having actual conversations with children, particularly conversations driven by the child's interest.

But what a difference it makes in a program to have an enthusiast or two, someone who is driven to ask "why" and "how," just like a child. In those classrooms, science comes alive, much as music pervades the air in the room of a music lover.

The enthusiast may not be the teacher, or even an adult. In one classroom, the adolescent son of the director with an obsession for bug collecting captivated the class and perhaps added to the future supply of entomologists. In another, it was a

classroom aide who loved plants. It may be the handyman, a parent, even the principal or director — someone who carries with them a charge of intellectual electricity.

I am concerned for all educational programs, but child care in particular, for it has yet to be solidified into a rigid social form. In a rush to credentialize and professionalize and secure our perimeter, I hope we do not eliminate many of the enthusiasts from the scene. In many programs, a rich source of intellectual life comes from people in their early twenties *passing through* child care — working with children for a while on the way to other lives in the worlds of natural science, music, theater, the environment, academia. Most of the men and non-traditional women who ultimately stay in child care fit this description. But if the only positions open for these people are as aides working under teachers with two and four year degrees or less, their numbers will continue to plummet.

COME GATHER ROUND CHILDREN

There is no doubt a role for science curriculum with group activities and experiments in early childhood — just as there is an important role for zoos in preserving and developing appreciation for the wildlife of the planet. But there is a sadness about it all when the artificial replaces the natural. Children are born with the secret of the sensuous life in the rich objective world, and childhood science is inescapably loaded with sensuality. Children come to us ready and eager to know and we put them on hold.

In *Buckminster Fuller to Children of Earth*, Buckminster Fuller writes, "A child is comprehensive. He wants to understand the whole thing . . . UNIVERSE. Children will draw pictures with everything in them . . . houses and trees and people and animals . . . and the sun AND the moon. Grown-ups say, 'That's a nice picture, Honey, but you put the moon and the sun at the same time and that isn't right.' But the child is right! The sun and the moon ARE in the sky at the same time.

Adults are often busy. They don't answer the child's questions. And the child goes to school and the teacher says, 'First you're going to learn A, B, C. . . .' The child still wants to understand UNIVERSE and has BIG questions, and the teacher says,

---

GRASS
by Aileen Fisher

Do you ever think about grass
on the lawns you pass?
The green of it,
the sheen of it,
the after-raining clean of it
when it sparkles like glass?

Do you know what grass is,
those green spears showing
wherever you're going?

Every blade, to be brief,
is a LEAF.
                                    *

I do not know what I may appear to the world; but to myself I seem to have been only like a boy playing on the seashore, and diverting myself in now and then finding a smoother pebble or a prettier shell than ordinary, while the great ocean of truth lay all undiscovered before me.

— Isaac Newton in *Memoirs of the Life, Writings, and Discoveries of Sir Isaac Newton*. New York: Johnston Co., 1965.

'Never mind that . . . you learn the parts first . . . A, B, C. . . .' Then the child goes to college and never does get back to the whole."

FIRST THINGS FIRST

Why focus on science curriculum when the life is being squeezed out of early childhood? When we have established programs with open windows and teeming life inside, and puddle-rich, flowered playgrounds abuzz with construction outside, when programs have people large and small with an enthusiastic appreciation of nature and the way things work, then let us worry about organized curricular science activities for preschool children.

REFERENCE

Fuller, R. Buckminster. *Buckminster Fuller to Children of Earth*. Garden City, NY: Doubleday, 1972.

---

* Every effort has been made to trace owners of copyright material, but in some cases this has not proved possible.

It Ain't Easy Being Green

H ow many playgrounds approach Dattner's ideal? Most early childhood programs don't even try. More typical is a rather small fenced area with a few pieces of playground equipment. But the child's outdoor experience does not have to be bound by the playground. The playground may be planned as part of a larger outdoor context:

- all the accessible outdoor space — the sidewalks, the city parks, the stream nearby.

- all the time the children have access to the outdoors — daily, weekly, seasonally.

- the outdoor experiences that children have outside of the program, in the yard, on the street, in the park.

An Indoor Culture?

We are becoming an indoor culture, more comfortable in malls than cities. Millions of young children are only allowed outdoors with supervision. In many areas, even the backyard or front stoop are viewed as perilous unless closely supervised. Many children come home from school and watch television. On any particular day, they can choose between *Geraldo* talking to "transvestite dads who seduce their daughter's husbands," or "the case of the murdering mom" on *Hard Copy*, or *Barney*.

It is a strange time. We live in an age when our children may know far more about bizarre people we care nothing about or a cartoon world than the workings of their own back-yard — that marvelous ecosystem teeming with life. They may know more about, or rather have more information on, exotic zoo animals and farm animals than the snails, squirrels, birds, worms, and bugs that live outside their windows.

The outdoors for many of us is becoming more and more simply a passage-way, to be hurried through, or often sealed from us by car windows. It is not integral to our experience or a des-tination to enjoy for itself. When it is a destination, it is a task-oriented enjoy-ment such as a ski slope or an outing to a park — a consumable event, not a collection of simple pleasures.

In the world of children's programs, as in schools, the outdoors is often simply

> *A playground should be like a small scale replica of the world, with as many as possible of the sensory experiences to be found in the world included in it. Experiences for every sense are needed, for instance: rough and smooth objects to look at and feel; light and heavy things to pick up; water and wet materials warmed by the sun; soft and hard surfaces; things that make sounds (running water) or that can be struck, plucked, plinked, etc.; smells of all varieties (flowers, bark, mud); shiny, bright objects and dull, dark ones; things that are both huge and tiny; high and low places to look at and from; materials of every type, natural and synthetic, thin, thick, and so on.*
>
> — Richard Dattner, *Design for Play*. Cambridge, MA: MIT Press, 1969.

a place for recess — a temporary respite or diversion for both staff and children and, at best, a place for large muscle exploits. On less inviting days, going out is an inconvenience or pain. It is not uncommon to limit children's time outside to less than an hour per classroom, both as a means of coping with small playgrounds and an assumption that the time indoors is more valuable, more the stuff of school.

What's the result? Two important aspects of life are shrinking in children's lives: nature, in all its transcendent, powerful glory — unpredictable, mysterious, untamed, and infinite — and, nearly as absent, open spaces and physically challenging spaces, places to literally take off, scale, and explore.

WHAT'S THE HARM?

Is there really much cause for concern? After all, much of what goes on outdoors can happen indoors. The danger lies in this — we know a lot about how children physically and psychologically develop; we know less about how they become good people.

How do we become wise?

What is wisdom if not developing a perspective that is broad and deep, placing knowledge in a context that encompasses an understanding of

the universe and our place in it? How can children hope to become wise and develop values within the confines of a narrow, carefully regulated world? Where is their invitation to life's dance? It is the marriage of nature to the soul and the intellect that allows wisdom to grow.

It is not wise to foul your surroundings but that is what our societies are doing. Freeman Dyson is a brilliant physicist and critic who has written widely on a number of scientific topics, including the notion of Gaia — the earth as a living entity. When asked how he could be optimistic that ultimately humankind wouldn't destroy the ecosystem and kill off the vegetation through pollution and global warming, his faith lay in a simple belief: people will always love trees. I am less sure we will develop the wisdom to continue to nurture that love if children are removed from the natural world.

How do we become spiritual?

The essence of spirituality is a sense of miracle, a day-to-day appreciation for the miracle of the world and all its complexity. Without a deep sense of awe at the vastness and majesty of the natural world that humbles us, and a simultaneous ennobling sense that we are intrinsically a part of that world, our spirituality remains shallow.

How do we become sensual?

hot	moist	caresses
oozing	forceful	delicate
hard	soft	tickling
wet	resilient	fragrant
juicy	warm	smooth
silky		

The words above are sensual words — they characterize our sensory experience. They can describe being outdoors, caressed by breezes, tickled by the grass, digging in the wet sand; or they can describe the pleasures of food; or intimate human contact. Our sensuality is a gift, essential to the full enjoyment of life pleasures, but we can lose the secret of the sensuous life in the overwhelming presence of the objective world. The time spent outdoors in a

---

LOBOTOMY PARK

Sign on a school playground:

1. No running
2. No throwing or kicking
3. No climbing up the slide
4. Sit on the swings
5. No digging
6. No climbing on the fence
7. Keep your shoes on
8. Stay off the grass

NO COMMENT

natural setting may well play a fundamental role in the development of our sensuality.

I thought he was just another urban unfortunate — an elderly man grinning broadly and chortling with glee as he almost skipped along the walk, cracking the ice in every puddle along the way. It turned out he had spent his entire life in hot, sunny climates, recently come to the north, and was experiencing snow and ice for the first time. The years peeled away and it was the little boy he once was who couldn't contain his delight and surprise at the CRUNCHING sound of crisp snow and the exquisite feel of ice cracking underfoot: "I never thought it would sound and feel so wonderful," he laughed.

How do we become physical?

We admire the grace of the dancer or athlete — the loose-limbed confidence that allows disciplined muscular precision and explodes into dynamic expression. How else to achieve any semblance of that except repeated exposure to wide open spaces and objects to leap from, and opportunities to use our bodies against hills and winds?

How do we develop a sense of freedom?

When in doubt, twirl.
— Choreographer Ted Shawn

Four year old Marietta was bouncing up and down alone, for no particular reason. The bouncing changed to lying on her back and kicking up her legs, then leaping up, and then back down on her back. Perhaps a Jane Fonda flashback, whatever it was, she was free to do it — as well as accessorize the movement with weird noises. Jerry, George, and Katie were free to hide behind the tree and whisper mysteriously, and race from tree to tree.

Watch children outside when they are free from pinched confines of 35 square feet per child, free to move and make noise and congregate. Watch the vigorous exploration of movement, sound, substances, and social possibilities.

BEYOND THE SQUIRREL CAGE

Playgrounds should have climbers and slides and swings. Children need the physical challenge from a playground — the opportunity to literally "reach new heights." They need the stimulus of risk and choices in climbing, sliding, and swinging. Playgrounds are where reputations are made — whether four or fourteen years old — and they need structures that allow derring-do to build self-esteem. But the outdoors should offer so much more (adapted from *Caring Spaces, Learning Places*):

Places to roll: Children love to roll themselves and objects down slopes. Walking, pulling, hauling up a slope provides challenge. Summer's rolling hill becomes winter's sliding spot, or a water slide with a plastic tarp. Tires, balls, and teachers all roll nicely. Railings can become courses for rolling objects.

Places for jumping: Plato saw the model of true playfulness in the need of young children, animal and human, to leap. Leaping expresses faith in yourself and your environment. The opportunity to jump from different heights and land safely is incomparable, a test of self and gravity.

I AM NOT AN ETHEREAL GUY

"It's easy for you to say. You like being outside! It's your thing. You're one of THOSE!" After a workshop on playgrounds, I was good naturedly dismissed as one of THOSE, an outdoor wonk. It is not the first time I have been dismissed as impractical and unrealistic — thus what I write should be disregarded — but as one of THOSE? Well, that would not be me!

It is time to confess. You will not find me backpacking through the wilds, happily munching trail mix. I never went to summer camp, nor have I kayaked in icy water. I am not in tune with Black Elk's vision. Neither lederhosen nor gortex play an important part of my life. I love flowers but have little patience for gardening. I am not one of THOSE. No, I am a material guy — urban variety.

But not being "one of THOSE" is no excuse. What is teaching all about? We want children to transcend our own limits, to appreciate life in ways we would like to but don't. Teachers need to stretch and be a variation of "one of THOSE" that is at least convincing and inspiring to children — whether "one of THOSE" is someone who likes animals or plants, or good music or literature, or builds with blocks, or enjoys movement and being outdoors. It is hard to do well by children and stay within the confines of our own upbringing.

I watched a group of preschoolers playing in a small fenced play area in a park. Outside the fence was a wooded park with ponds and boulders and high-grassed fields. Standing watch at the entrance, a teacher gently shooed children back to the Spartan play equipment. One boy hung around the gate, resisting entreaties to once again go down the slide. He looked at the teacher with wistful eyes, his body tense with desire to slip around her and take off, and said, "Can't you just get outta the way?"

If we are unable to stretch ourselves, perhaps we can at least set things in motion and "get outta the way."

Places for running: Children run — this way and thatta way, back and forth, round and round.

Places for throwing and kicking: Throwing, heaving, hurling something — to someone, at something, into something — belongs on a playground. Walls and nets, hoops, barrels, and trees can serve as targets; balls, bean bags, frisbees, and, when appropriate, rocks and sticks can serve as missiles. Humankind probably began kicking during the first boring walk, kicking rocks and sticks and small animals.

Places for bouncing and balancing: Children will balance on everything from a crack in the sidewalk to railings on a deck. They love to balance on their feet, stomach, head, and hands. Beams of different size, width, and height; logs, poles, boulders; wobbly balancing surfaces; moveable balance beams; and planks all provide variety.

Places (and vehicles) for riding, traveling, and transporting: Children love pathways and sidewalks that provide a here and there and routes in between — to journey, to race, to haul, to ferry, to caravan. Vehicles that encourage hauling or two child use have special value.

Places to move slowly: In a Japanese garden, one moves slowly along a path — eyes alert to new views, body shifting as the path changes beneath one's feet. On a lazy day, the urge to float and dawdle can become overpowering; on a gray day, the need to hold back can take over. Stone and wood paths or patterned walks that encourage deliberate motions delight children and adults.

Places to watch, to wonder, to retreat: When the challenge of the climber or the commotion on the swings is too much, where is there to go — to be alone or with a trusted friend or fellow temporary outcast? Where is the cork tree, the place to smell the flowers? Quiet spaces scaled to child size — grottos, nests,

perches, miniature picnic tables off a beaten path — all provide wayside rests. Greenery has a calming effect.

Places to eat: What makes life interesting is variation and, when outdoor eating (and cooking) is possible, children are delighted (and so are the local wildlife).

Places to discover: Taking advantage of nature, the busy city life behind the fence, the machinery of bikes or hinges or pulleys, the aerodynamics of kites, great discoveries are possible even in small areas.

Places that feel different: Microclimates — sunny and shady spots, breezy spaces, still spaces.

Places for building: Snow forts and lean-tos, milk crate walls and cardboard castles — the outdoors is a place for children to build shelters and barricades, sculptures and vehicles. With good storage and garbage control, a work yard is possible that encourages construction with or without tools, with driftwood and planks, canvas, boulders, blocks and crates, tires, and rope.

Places for creative expression: The outdoors is a natural site for art. Walls provide easels and perhaps even canvases. Wood, stone, fabric, plastic, and metal are the raw materials for sculptures that play with color, light, and sound. Sidewalk painting, water painting, altering water and sand, rock and wood environmental art that alter miniature landscapes allow children to discover and express their relation to life and beauty.

Places to pretend: Here I am, king of the forest — there is a pirate. Now a race car driver, a superhero, a frontier mother, a tiny rabbit. Where can I roam, walk the plank, save the citizenry, keep my baby safe, or find a good carrot? Children like the realism of a real stripped down car or boat. But structures that only vaguely represent other things or settings benefit from the ambiguity

that allows children's imagination to take over.

Places to dig: George Washington Carver said: "People murder a child when they tell him to keep out of the dirt. In dirt there is life." Digging, burying, making mud, making ditches and rivers, finding life. Earth science!

Watery places: Is there anything more wonderful than water to a child of any age? Water that reflects shadows and faces and flashes rainbows. Water that hides life and bits of past life. Water that moves and makes music with its gurgles and burbles and drips and splats. Water that is still. Water creates ice to crack and mud to squish, tendrils to seep through the grass or sand. Water ferries twigs and leaves and paper boats. Water cools us, runs off our bodies, and livens our skin. Water fills our cup, and jars, and pots. Bird baths, outdoor water tables, elevated streams, splash pools, fountains, sprinklers, and wading pools bring water to a playground.

Places for growing: Growing things allow children to experience the life cycle, to anticipate change in seasons, and to tend and care for life. Gardens, flower patches and boxes, herb gardens, trees, vines and shrubs, weeds (which to a child are simply flowers in the wrong place) provide beauty, life, and loose parts. Leaves and twigs become boats and stew, little people and airplanes.

YEAH, BUT CAN WE CHANGE?

There are real obstacles to fully using the outdoors. But it is also a question of priorities and will. When you build a building, it costs over $100 per square foot to create a great place to be a child. When you build a playground, you can create a wonderful environment for learning and living for $10 to $15 per square foot, a place where children can soar. Beyond the fence, there are resources available in the community. The purpose of life is, after all, to inhale — to live it fully and reach out eagerly and without fear for new experience. Our children deserve our effort.

CAN'T FIND IT, CAN'T GET TO IT, CAN'T USE IT

The doorknob was dusty and the door creaked as it slowly opened. I quickly stepped back, recoiling from the fetid air, narrowly avoiding being crushed by the large box hurtling down towards me. Taking it all in at a glance — the violent disorder, the rubble, the sad soft creatures with missing limbs, the half-empty crates, and here and there through the chaos glimpses of once strong airplanes and garages and other remnants of the Fisher-Price civilization, I now understood the knowing looks and cruel laughter of my new colleagues when, in my innocence, I volunteered to organize the storage room.

Storage is not a glamorous or gripping topic, which is probably why Elizabeth Prescott and Tom David (1976) commented that storage has not been given enough attention as a key factor in providing good child care. The inattention is unfortunate because Prescott's finding that better and more conveniently located storage was often the first step to program improvement is an insight worth putting in neon lights. Effective storage maximizes a program's resources — material resources as well as human resources of time, energy, and peace of mind.

objects protrude; too long, clutter is inevitable as more items are placed on each shelf. Distinctive display advertises the potential of the materials.

• **Good storage is the right size and shape for the space.** Floor units that are too high block necessary sight lines. Units that don't fit a space may leave protruding corners or irritating gaps that collect dust and worse.

• **Good storage is aesthetically pleasing.** A too odd assortment of storage units can be a jarring, disjointed landscape, even when units are visually connected through color.

• **Good storage has a visible order, clear and understandable to its user**, whether ten months or ten years old.

• **Good storage is safe.** This last criteria deserves special mention. Almost every program owns at least one harrowing tale of a cabinet or shelf collapsing or pulling out of a wall, or a floor unit tipping over and narrowly missing a child. Children have been killed by falling storage units, and seriously injured by collisions with sharp corners at a child's eye level.

CLOSED STORAGE

Closed storage is necessary for materials dangerous for children, materials likely to be misused or disappear, rotation of materials, and personal possessions.

• **Good storage is located close to the point of use.** This is the cardinal rule. When things are about, people make more use of them.

• **Good storage comfortably holds and distinctly displays the contents when open.** If it is too deep, materials are hard to remove; not deep enough,

Teachers *and* parents need places to safely stow their coats and purses — often loaded with lethal materials like keys, medicine, pins, and so forth. Teachers need a secure place to accumulate the tools of their trade: scissors, tape, markers, staples, and the stuff they deem essential. Poor storage that allows open borrowing inevitably results in needless irritation and conflict.

Wall Cabinets, Shelving, and Hooks

Wall cabinets are useful because they allow the space underneath to be used for storage or play. It is absolutely essential that they are attached securely to the studs in the wall or the cinderblock. Don't assume the volunteer putting them up for you, or whoever put them up for the last occupant, knew what he was doing. From experience, well-made kitchen cabinets from a home improvement store with good hinges are adequate.

Shelving is cheaper and provides more flexibility than cabinets, and the height restricts child access. Visual clutter can be reduced by using storage boxes or fabric covers. Some shelving systems hold more weight than others, and staff vary in their sensitivity to issues of structural integrity. Flexible shelving using tracks and metal brackets is not designed for heavy loads. Shelving or counter space as an open surface is necessary to prevent cubby tops, diaper tables, and table tops from being used as inappropriate resting places for wayward bottles, unidentified objects, and temporary storage.

Walls are wonderful places to store things, provided the right storage hardware is used. Wheel toys, wading pools, and all sorts of things can be hung on hooks or pegs. Pegboard systems for smaller tools are useful; flexible metal track systems are available for larger items.

Storage Rooms and Sheds

Storage rooms have their place — close to the point of use of the materials. Centrally located supply storerooms and outdoor sheds can be effective if superbly organized and maintained. Taking advantage of the burgeoning science of storage evident in home magazines, storage rooms need flexible shelving, labeled compartments, hooks, and whatever else will organize the contents.

Floor Units

Closed floor units are often necessary to provide more convenient access to a central location. Open storage can be made closed and flexible by combining two units with a hinge and closing it off or by using inexpensive fabric curtains to shield the contents from view.

Creative Closed Storage

It is the programs with the fewest resources or the most restrictive conditions that have the most need for storage. There are alternatives to cabinets which are costly. Pillowcases can be used to store extra dress-up clothes and fabric. Fabric sacks can be hung from the wall or ceiling in an artful, charming fashion. The space under cribs can be used and hidden by fabric panels. Storage boxes can become tables, space under platforms can be designed for cot storage, and the ceiling can be used to store projects and works in progress.

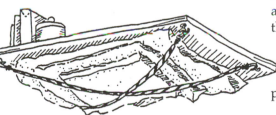

OPEN STORAGE

Good open storage allows children to be independent and responsible. The layout of materials suggests concepts and possible combinations of materials for creative play. Materials can be organized around a property: color, shape, size, transparency; a function: communication, pull toys, tools, building; a relationship: pencil and paper, dolls and clothes, *my* work, an action or effect: sound making, dissolving; or other concepts. Layout of materials can teach left-to-right sequencing, perceptual discrimination, or a sequence of motor skills.

The organizational scheme has to be appropriate for the developmental level of the user — both in terms of the conceptual scheme and the distinctiveness of the display. Distinctiveness can be achieved by limiting the number of items on a shelf, by compartments or clear boundaries using tape or color, or by juxtaposing contrasting items. The younger the child, the simpler the concept and the more distinctiveness necessary in display (e.g., for infants, the concept of *sameness* and one item per compartment).

Personal Storage

Every child needs a place of his own to store the considerable assortment of personal possessions — multiple sets of clothes, diapers, boots, blanket, artwork, and personal treasures. Older children need space for works in progress. Programs use lockers, cubbies, storage tubs, hooks, pockets, and various combinations of all of these. Some of the issues involved:

Protection. How are children's clothes and possessions kept intact and safe from curious cohorts and the child's own actions? Labeling with a name and a picture makes the place their place. Storage for oversized artwork (e.g., computer paper and larger) shows children that their art really is valued.

Infant/toddler diaper bags often contain pins, medicine, and other unsafe materials, so the bag needs to be stored safely or the offending items removed.

Ventilation. An important solution for wet or soiled clothes is provided by pegboard backs or, ideally, an open place to hang wet clothes or set out wet boots.

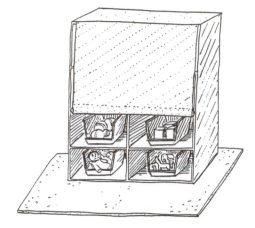

Aesthetics. Nothing adds more to visual clutter than loaded open cubbies. Fabric curtains that children can pull aside are simple and inexpensive.

Activity and location. Cubbies or lockers are, at times, centers of activity — the site of dressing and undressing, sulking, longing, rummaging. Personal space is not simply a functional space, it is an emotional space; generally the only *my* place in the setting. Having a my own place is important in an institutional setting lodged within a culture that from birth invests enormous importance in personal property. Is a cubby a place for a child to sit and be alone, or to put on a boot? A social place to show off personal treasures and exchange tokens of affection? If not, where are these places? The cubby design and location should take into account all the activity that will take place there.

Activity Storage

Flexible storage is a key to a successful learning environment. Too much fixed or uniform storage limits a program. Built-in storage often becomes sacred ground; covering or blocking part of it with a couch or display becomes unthinkable. Some uniformity in height is aesthetically positive; but the ability to vary shelf size and length, compartmentalize, and have or not have a back (thereby allowing one or two sided access) increases the utility of the shelf storage. Shelves are only one way to store materials. Hooks, bags, barrels all have their place.

Portable Storage

Storage that is easily portable allows a program to continually expand and contract spaces as the need occurs. Small shelf units and units on casters provide that capability. The plastic milk crate storage can be relocated and recombined easily.

Portable in another sense is storage such as table tops or nets that can be raised or lowered from the ceiling using pulleys. Also useful are racks and hooks attached to the underside of shelf units and cabinets.

For multipurpose space and hallways, transportable storage is useful. This may be a trolley, a wagon, a suitcase, or a duffel bag, within which is an activity and/or the makings of a space (such as a rug).

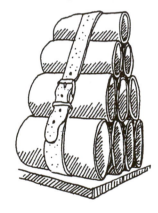

Adapted Storage

The back of a shelving unit that serves to divide two groups can be removed to create a shared zoo with fish tanks, gerbils, and birds, Cubbies laid on their side may make acceptable shelf units, enabling a program the opportunity to purchase more workable cubbies.

Storage Containers and Display

The kind of container used to store materials can work for or against the program's goals and objectives. Considerations:

Visibility. Does a child have to take the container off the shelf to see the contents? Younger children will invariably dump it out and then decide whether to use it. Spend more and purchase clear, soft plastic. The shape, color, or texture of the container can highlight the materials displayed.

Motor skills required. Does a child have the motor skills to remove the container from its place safely and transport the container? The act of transporting buckets with handles, dish tubs, single handle bowls, baskets, trays, and different sizes of containers are all learning activities in themselves.

Social skills required. A container that requires two or more children to transport builds in a cooperative activity.

Classification. Defining the nature of the activity and/or the location of the activity by the color, shape, material (wood, metal, plastic), or kind of container (basket, tub, box) can build in classification and develop an order that children can understand and help to restore.

Aesthetics. Does the container help to set off the materials in an attractive manner? Do the containers contribute to visual clutter?

In *The Learning Environment: An Instructional Strategy*, Loughlin and Suina make a number of important observations about material display — among them:

- Stacking hides materials.

- When items are spread across a shelf, specific items don't show clearly.

- Empty spaces, contrasting color, or framing around materials focuses attention on the material.

- Sets in commercial boxes look alike when left in the box.

- It's easier to remember where materials belong when they don't look alike.

"Write What You Want But We Live in the Real World," My Father Said to Me

It is easy to write about the power and utility of organized storage, the wonderful potential for storage to teach. It is also true that organization can oppress and restrict. There is a place for toy boxes and casual storage where speed and convenience take precedence over teaching concepts. The materials, staff-child ratios, and time schedules may dictate when and where toy boxes are appropriate.

It is also important to recognize that an organization takes an incredible amount of time to establish and maintain, easier for programs with

down time, lots of volunteers or student teachers than for understaffed child care programs always awash with children. Programs do what they can do. The resources freed up to improve storage will pay rich dividends to staff and children.

Resources

Prescott, Elizabeth, and Tom David. "The Effects of the Physical Environment on Day Care." *ERIC Document No. 156-356*, 1976.

Loughlin, Elizabeth, and Joseph Suina. *The Learning Environment: An Instructional Strategy*. New York: Teachers College Press, 1982.

CHAPTER 4

CREATING A WONDERFUL PLACE TO BE A CHILD

CREATING A WONDERFUL PLACE
TO BE A CHILD

by Elizabeth Prescott

A wonderful place to be a child is a place where a child can fall in love with the world. It is a place where children can rely on adults to introduce them to the joys that are to be found in daily, ordinary routines and to the possibilities that exist for dealing with the unexpected. When I think of wonderful moments, it is no problem to recall children creating good, rich play. To remember adults creating wonderful moments out of daily tasks takes more thought:

A teacher is seated casually at a table where she can observe the play. Next to her is a boy leafing through a book. He points to a picture of President Lincoln and the conversation takes off — about presidents, top hats, other places named Lincoln — moving from one topic to another.

It is bathroom time before afternoon naps. The teacher of this youngest group is seated on a long bench, her lap available with room on each side for children to cuddle. Children are in various states of undress, some are playing in the water, others are enjoying their nudity and examining their bodies. A girl pulls a small partition over to a toilet so she can have privacy. It is a relaxing transition from an exciting morning to the solitude of napping.

A plumber is at the center and some of the children have followed his every move. He talks as he works and lets the children hold his tools. When he announces to the director that he is finished, she says he can't go until he has explained to George and Jimmy exactly what he has done. She escorts a surprised plumber into the nap room, where he sits on a cot next to enthralled listeners.

It has been a busy morning making Valentines and the mess to be cleaned up is impressive. At the word, children spring into action like a well-choreographed ballet. Never have I seen a clean-up time performed with such dignity and skill. At the end, the children and their teacher gather to inspect their work and, with pride, pronounce it done. Then everyone heads for a pillow-laden corner to sing, as the good smells announce that lunch is almost ready.

In the child care center in a desolate town in Siberia, a teacher places a small red glass vase with three dandelion balls on a child-sized table. It has been carefully positioned so that a thin ray of sunlight strikes the vase.

The cook calls in sick and the solution is that the prekindergarteners will prepare the lunch for everyone. Never have tuna fish sandwiches been prepared with greater zeal!

I think these memories stood out because they were both rare and showed adults being uniquely themselves. The incidents say something about skills that are important across the life cycle, namely, knowing how to make conversation, tuning into your body to make it comfortable, the dignity of maintenance, the art of transitions, seeing adults work and getting the feel of it from observing and being close, finding beauty, and converting problems into pleasure or at least interesting challenges.

THE SCHOOL AS MODEL

Jim Greenman reminds us that child care for all kinds of families is a relatively new social form and suggests that the school is the model that governs our thinking about it. Actually, child care centers have been around for a long time, though not very visible and, for many years, they served only a handful of the children. They were mostly small and the staff had little or no training except for their experience as mothers. In those days, parents talked about their feelings of guilt, and staff worried that they might take over the mother's role. The advent of Head Start marked a big change. Early education emerged as a profession with curriculum models and standards of certification. Parents began to see child care as a positive experience for their child, not as an unfortunate necessity.

Today centers are becoming much, much larger, and increasingly they offer care from birth through elementary school. Although staff have more formal training, they have less parental experience and turnover is high. These factors all push toward a more stylized and less personal approach to children. Children sometimes seem to rely heavily on each other for support and continuity, while staff try very hard to "do things right" when neither space, scheduling, nor personal experience are helping them to grasp what "right" might be.

THE HOME AS MODEL

I am further troubled by the possible consequences of defining "right" in terms of a school model. After years of observing in centers, our staff began to observe in family day care. On the first day in a family day care setting, I felt strangely disoriented, as if I had moved into another culture. It was hard to decipher the exact beginning and ending of an activity. Children seemed to move back and forth between several activities, making it difficult to name them. Then lunch time came and the caregiver said to the children, "What shall we have for lunch?" For a moment, I froze, because I had never heard this question. The children volunteered suggestions, and what followed was a discussion that went something like this: "Spaghetti? That would take too long to cook. Scrambled eggs? Remember, Timmy is allergic to eggs. Tuna fish sandwiches? Oh dear, I'm out of tuna. Let's put it on the shopping list. Grilled cheese sandwiches? Yes, everyone likes that."

Of course there is conversation about lunch in centers, but it is more about labels and categories. "The peas are green, the carrots are orange, the peas are round, the carrots are cut in squares, but both are vegetables." This is what I would call the logic of schools; children will get much more of this. Figuring out what to have for lunch requires pulling together diverse pieces of information and applying them in a way that will meet human needs. Much of adult life centers around making people comfortable, keeping order, fixing things, and solving a myriad of problems. Children need to see adults doing such things, and they need opportunities to participate and to play out these real-life events. I worry that if young children do not have opportunities to see how adults handle themselves in the world, they will be at greater risk during their adolescent years. Certainly child care centers cannot solve all the problems of child rearing, but I would like to see models that were more like a village than a school.

IF I HAD A HAMMER

A new age of child care center construction is upon us. As we leave the subterranean age of church and school basements, what new age approaches us? And will it prove to be an improvement?

If our standard is the design of places where a child can *spend a childhood*, rich with developmentally appropriate experience, much of the new construction is mediocre or worse. Many new buildings may look good; but under close inspection, they do surprisingly little to support creative programs and hardworking staff. Why is this? It is more than lack of resources because some of the most expensive new buildings, designed as showplaces or for upscale families, have major problems.

A good deal of the problem is due to the fact that child care centers are still a new social form relative to schools and other institutions. Most people have a pretty simple model of what it takes to provide good child care: throw enough good people (read women) and enough materials together with the children in a not too crowded space, and it will work. This seems to be the model many early childhood people have, only their definition of good people involves more than being the right sex, it includes extensive training and support.

Child care centers are systems of space, people, and program assumptions. Often there is a failure to *connect up the dots* — to understand that choices a center makes about program (group size, adult-child ratios, office-to-teaching-staff ratios, type of curriculum) interact and together have implications for program architecture.

Another problem is that after years of resourcefully making do with all sorts of spaces, child care people often take poor space for granted; and their conception of good space is limited. When a new building is to be built, architects take their clues from elementary school construction and from the information provided them by child care experts, who are often projecting from their limited experience with one or two programs.

So off we go, armed with state licensing standards, limited vision, and an often hazy sense of both the scale necessary for early childhood and the real-world behavior of young children and teachers, and buildings get designed. Those buildings become models for others and patterns are set.

Here we will explore the major problem with many of the new *state-of-the-art* buildings — in short, they are too small (pun intended). In the following article we will look at the all too common mistakes made in plumbing, electrical, and interior design that are sure to plague staff.

BABY, IT'S CROWDED IN HERE: NOT ENOUGH SPACE IN THE CLASSROOM

Thirty-five square feet per child of indoor classroom space (not including bathroom, storage, and crib space) is a MINIMUM amount of space, not a desirable amount for a place where children may well spend 10 hours a day — eating, sleeping, and otherwise living. We seem to have forgotten what minimum means — you know, like minimum wage, minimum standard of living. Minimum means barely tolerable, and perhaps not even that, if other elements like staff-child ratios or staff qualifications or supplies are at minimums too. It might be good for us to live on the minimum amount of daily calories needed to sustain life to remind us of the consequences of living by minimums.

Unrecognized Truth 1 —
The younger the child, the more space necessary.

In many new buildings for good programs, classrooms are unbearably small, an effect that often catches designers by surprise. Why? Because group sizes are good. In an infant room with excellent group size and ratios, 1 adult to 3 children and a group size of 9, 35 square feet per child puts those 12 people in a tiny space. Remember, any room with 6 or 12 babies needs some of the same space-consuming furnishings — diaper table, couch, rocking chair. Perhaps we need a couch-to-child ratio.

If it is a good program that encourages parent involvement, attracts visitors, allows prospective parents to visit, and encourages some involvement of grandparents and older siblings, those additional large size bodies will make the space intolerable. A room with 8 babies and 2 staff or 10 toddlers and 2 adults presents almost the same dilemma. Modified open room designs with common space may help compensate

in terms of a sense of spaciousness, but usually have other drawbacks.

Unrecognized Truth 2 —
Total square footage affects the sort of program possible.

There is a long tradition of environmentally based curriculums in good early education. Active learning and learning through play lend themselves to interest areas and learning centers. Sensory motor play calls out for built-in learning. An understanding that child CARE requires a soft, homey environment to live in for 10 hours a day also requires accommodation. Today, the increasingly scarce supply of trained teachers also argues for a rich learning environment approach.

But the number of learning centers possible, the built-in learning, and the home-like care depend on the amount of space available. Again, the new and largely positive concern for small group size may result in small rooms that require substantial accommodation in the learning environment.

Large programs often add multi-purpose space as a space-enhancing element; but, in the real world of inter-classroom negotiations of space and schedules, multipurpose space rarely compensates and may increase *herding* transitions. A very good program can develop shared multi-purpose space centers, portable learning centers, and prop boxes to overcome small classroom size. But doing so assumes a high level of knowledge and expertise and a collaborative working relationship between classrooms, increasingly scarce commodities.

Unrecognized Truth 3 —
Bathrooms are busy social places.

Bathrooms and diaper areas in almost all new buildings are designed for efficient, compact use of space: the minimum number of toilets and sinks and minimum floor

space. *Compact* and *efficient* are not the first words that come to mind in a description of a high quality program trying to make diapering and toileting unhurried, relaxed, and not unpleasant times for children and adults. These are occasions where children struggling for self-control should not have to wait, and adults periodically struggling for a different kind of self-control should not have to work around space limitations at extremely close quarters.

WE GOTTA TALK: NOT ENOUGH SUPPORT SPACE

Good programs have an active collective intelligence. People are observing and thinking and communicating. Team planning is going on, and cross classroom collaboration. Parents or prospective parents are present at nearly all times: involved with hiring, participating in comprehensive intakes, or having conferences or informal chats.

The live connection to the community is evident in the meetings with employers, human service agencies, staff, or community groups. Where is all this to take place?

Good programs are increasingly recognizing the value of support staff. The solitary director with no other office or support staff in medium size and large centers is no longer the rule.

Unrecognized Truth 4 —
MULTIPLE office and meeting space is essential.

Good communication requires space. Respect for people — children and adults — requires confidential communication in conferences, discussions about people, and supervisory interactions. Good meetings are likely to happen in comfortable space that allows the proper room arrangement. The result is that good child care needs the capacity to accommodate a number of two and three person meetings and small group meetings occurring simultaneously.

LOOK WHAT I FOUND. CAN I KEEP IT?: NOT ENOUGH STORAGE IN GENERAL AND IN THE CLASSROOM IN PARTICULAR

Walk into almost all good programs and the need for more storage assaults the eye. The tops of cabinets are cluttered, storage rooms are jammed, and bathrooms and offices double as storerooms. Creative teachers collect, good teachers need storage for projects that carry over beyond a day, and then there are the prop boxes which are necessary to vary the few learning centers that small rooms allow.

Unrecognized Truth 5 —
Calculate the amount of storage you think is necessary and then double it.

In these new buildings, where are we going to put the car seats that parents leave with the program to exchange between mother and father? Where do staff coats, purses, and other belongings go? Where do the personal belongings of visitors go? If we invite parents into the classroom and they feel out of place because there is no place to store their things, or if we find Johnny snacking on Mrs. Brown's medication because she innocently laid her purse down on the toddler room couch — the clear message of the space is "stay away, parents, you don't fit in here."

Where are we to store the six toddler carts, plastic wading pools, wheelbarrows, inner tubes, in-process school-age projects, diapers in quantity, and all the other *stuff* that one can find in the hallways and common spaces of good programs?

There are creative ideas to improve storage, but the amount of space available sets a limit on what you can do. The other reality is that the psychology of moving into a new or renovated space is often to NOT be creative and resourceful. We want to savor the newness, the order — not *junk it up* with all the tried and true accommodations to less desirable space.

WAIT UNTIL NEXT TIME: ADDING SPACE

Essentially we are providing child care in efficiencies, and the only reason that is acceptable is that we are used to it. For a good program, there are few alternatives to adding square footage, despite the cost of construction and renovation. The size of the building can put an iron cap on quality. In programs aspiring to quality and faced with tough choices, it is almost always more cost effective in the long run to try to upgrade quality through larger and better space than through greatly improving ratios or hoping for higher quality staff.

There are no magic numbers to recommend as guides for increasing square footage. A smart program with low staff turnover and a well developed program culture that encourages collaboration may make good use of shared space, thus allowing classrooms to be less self-contained. In a warm climate, a deck or porch may make smaller classrooms tolerable.

A good architect may come up with a creative solution for more office and meeting space, perhaps using corridor or reception space the way hotels do to allow two or three person semi-private conversations. The first step in improving new construction is accepting child care as a complex, multifaceted operation. When that is done, creative solutions will begin to flow.

"AVOID THE KILLER MICE"
OR
"WHO PUT THOSE OUTLETS HERE?"

All the ribbons are cut, the champagne is gone, the dollars are spent, and the new or renovated building is now filled with staff and children. No more basement. No more ill-suited storefront. You look at the new space like an adoring lover and see, if not perfection, at least a damn fine piece of work.

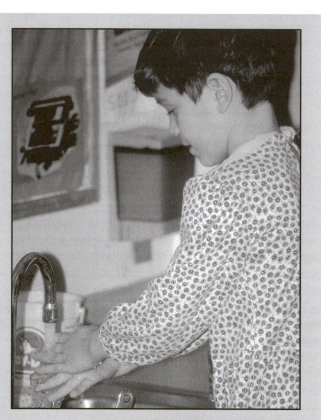

And then it starts; the honeymoon was all too short. Little imperfections begin to grate, like mice nibbling away at your ankles. Staff apologetically (for the most part) point out this flaw and that idea whose time should not have come. At first you want to deny the problems; you don't want to hear about the latches that don't work and the counters that are too high. You begin to cringe when you hear, "I really love the new building, but do you know what drives me crazy . . . ?" How did this happen, all these little mistakes, after so much planning?

A lot happens in a child care center — a lot of work and a lot of living. The work of the child is developmentally appropriate play, learning to live and work in a group social setting. Obviously, the work of the adults is the care and education of the children — well, most of the adults, because others are cooking, administrating, and maintaining the building. *The ultimate test of the worksite is whether it supports the competent performance of the work.* Whether for a chef in a kitchen, a doctor in a hospital, or a teacher or child in a classroom, the environment either works for or against them.

In child care centers, a common failure of design stems from failure to recognize the necessary scale of things. It doesn't take a scientist to discover that young children are very small: they have small hands and feet, and ride low in the saddle. Their size is a factor in everything, from window height to door hardware. Other problems result from failure to take into account the scale implications of a largely female staff.

A second set of problems arise from failure to understand the scope of what goes on in the center beyond teaching — caregiving, administrating, transporting, maintaining, cleaning, and communicating.

And third, not taking into account how children and adults really behave, as opposed to how we plan to have them behave or would like them to behave, results in design mistakes.

"IT DOESN'T BELONG HERE"

Inquisitive children love cracks and crevices, like **electrical outlets** that are within reach. Electrical outlets often are a foot off the ground or near changing and activity counters. It is common for both architects and contractors to assume standard placement. Outlets either should be high and well away from children (which can be annoying to staff), or better, child-proof with built-in covers that have to be twisted to insert plugs. It is useful to have outlets throughout the room, including in the center of the room in larger classrooms.

Thermostats need to measure the temperature close to floor level and at the same time be out of reach or have tamper-proof covers.

Fire alarm pull boxes are often located at an entrance location precisely where a parent is most likely to be holding a bored baby looking for action.

"They got tiny little hands and tiny little feet"

Sink hardware is often beyond the power of children under three years old and may be awkward for older children. Photo-electronic sensors are becoming an affordable option, and levers instead of handles are easier for children to use. When the hardware is placed at the back of the sink instead of to the side, children often have to lean over the sink and into the water to use the faucets. Sinks and drinking fountains are usually too high. Hardware for paper towel or soap dispensers, or drinking fountains, may be beyond the reach or competence of little center dwellers.

Railings on lofts or platforms may be at a safe height when children are standing on the floor, but what about when they are standing on something? Generally another 12 inches is necessary to accommodate anything, including pillows, on lofts.

"It seemed like such a good idea"

- **Skylights** over classroom areas that sooner or later are areas where children nap.

- **Custom cabinets** designed for specific equipment at great expense that don't work as the use of the room changes.

- **Varying floor heights** or fixed platforms that limit the possibilities of

rooms and may wreak havoc with traffic patterns.

- **Large lofts** that are out of scale for the room, or poorly designed for safety or planned use as either motor or quieter space.

- **Directors' offices** that are so visually accessible that supervision or other confidential interactions always take place in a public context.

"Go with the flow"

"Where art thou dumpster?" The farther away from containers laden with dirty diapers or the remains of lunch, the less often the trash will leave the room. Child care generates a lot of messy, smelly garbage, and the flow of garbage is no small program issue. Complicating matters, dumpsters rarely add to the aesthetics of entrances.

"How do I get this stuff in?" asked the surly deliveryman with ten cartons of canned goods to the loading-dockless director.

"How do I get back in?" It is not uncommon to find doors that close and lock automatically used for access to and from the outdoors. Not allowing propping open the door to alleviate the hassle inevitably reduces the time children spend outside. Propping may damage the door and cause security concerns.

"I hope that's your child's hand I feel." In some centers, all the parents come and go at almost the same time. Entryways, corridors, and cubby areas should reflect that.

"I didn't know that they would do that"

Children are designed to test the possibilities of everything in their environment. It is why we have emergency rooms. When we focus on equipment or space for one use, or use by one age group, we may

not anticipate all that children will do with the object or space. Older children may climb and walk along the tops of playground equipment designed for younger children. Locker doors may become clanging musical instruments.

"Oops"

"It looked like enough tile or linoleum on the blueprint." On paper, the lunch tables or high chairs, the space for an easel, the activity sink, or the diaper areas all fit because there was not enough accounting for the programmatic effects of children and adults bumping up against each other. But packing together at lunch is no fun. Try telling a toddler to wait for a toilet, or to wait until we go back inside.

"Imagine that"

There are good ideas that improve worksites once the range of activities that may happen within the worksites are understood:

- Dumbwaiters and laundry chutes that ease the transport of things from floor to floor.

- Ceiling beams that allow use of the ceiling to hang large muscle equipment or infant equipment.

- A wooden plank or panel attached to cinder block walls that enables easier attachment of hooks and other things to the wall.

- Window seats with storage under higher windows and windows that extend nearly to the floor.

- Rain gutters positioned so that children can see and hear the rushing water.

There will always be mistakes. But ones like those mentioned above are avoidable if the program people think through the issues, understand the complexity of their reality, and impose their reality on architects and contractors.

"So You Want to Build a Building?" Dancing With Architects and Other Developmental Experiences — Part 1

Y ou've made the decision to build a building or renovate a space and you have the financing. Great! What happens now? If you are smart, you'll find an architect.

Why Use an Architect?

Even if you know what you want, even if you have a contractor or developer who knows how to build buildings, even if you have a child care consultant who is an *expert*, get an architect.

Why? Because child care centers are not simple facilities, and most existing examples are hardly models — based on too little thought and too little money. *Knowing what you want* is usually knowing how to correct the flaws in the few centers you are familiar with. To make the most of the opportunity, work with the best architect you can find and afford, and together think through the center that will fit your demands for the next 10 or 15 years.

Architects know an enormous amount that you don't and can apply skills and perspective that few builders have. Architects are trained to see the possibilities inherent in space; balance numerous factors of form, function, structural integrity, codes, and regulations; and provide design alternatives you are not aware of.

The Role of the Architect

The function of an architect is to take the goals, design program, and cost specifications of the clients and use their expertise in design and construction to develop facility alternatives and ultimately the most appropriate facility design. In many cases, the architect may function as a project manager as well, working with the contractor to ensure that the building is built to specification, meeting the budget and agreed upon timetable. Or an architectural firm may offer design and building services, serving as general contractor too. Going beyond the interior design to specifying and purchasing interior furnishings and furniture is a common architectural service. Generally, architects will work with landscape architects on projects that involve landscape planning.

Choosing an Architect

Architects range from would be Frank Lloyd Wrights — artists determined to create new visions of place and form — to pedestrian souls whose ambitions begin and end with sensible structures that won't collapse. Architectural firms range from large offices with dozens of architects and support staff to small two or three person operations.

You should solicit a number of proposals and choose based on their proposal, interviews, and references from past clients. You might also want to see their work before selecting who you wish to work with. When considering an architectural firm, make sure you assess the particular architects that you will be working with.

The architect you work with should be:

• **Respectful** — The architect should be someone you enjoy working with, who respects your ideas and prerogatives as the client. Really listening to you and having patience with you as you struggle to understand his perspective while he is struggling to understand yours is absolutely essential. You have to be comfortable pointing out the 100th small change you probably should have caught earlier. (Please note that architecture, like law and medicine, has always been a *white male profession*. One shouldn't assume a respectful *bedside* manner.)

• **Modest** (at least about child care architecture) — The best architects (and directors, consultants) know what they don't know and approach every building with some humility. While every building presents different challenges of balancing cost, square footage, site issues, and learning from past problems, child care centers present more challenges, reconciling competing demands of child and adult scale, care and learning, order and chaos. Simple formulaic answers will lead to mediocre buildings.

• **Competent** — Basic competence is more than knowing design solutions to your building needs. It includes knowing all the building codes and regulations that apply to child care and understanding the diverse alternatives to meeting codes. Knowledge of local processes, such as zoning boards and planning commissions, is important. Competence means that the contractor will have detailed blueprints and specifications that actually work without major on-site

revisions so you end up with a building with level floors and tight roofs and balanced heating and air conditioning. It means managing projects for on-time completion.

• **Experienced** — There is no substitute for general experience. An inexperienced architect will learn from mistakes made on your project. One of the advantages of going with a larger firm is the likelihood of more experience and a team process. But specific child care experience is less important than respect, humility, and general competence. Because so many child care buildings are mediocre, simply having done a child care center is in itself of limited value. It is what the architect learned in the process or how much he is willing to unlearn.

• **Creative** — When confronted with the challenge of limited space and dollars, the creative architect can generate design solutions by looking at the challenge from a number of angles. While most creative solutions *don't work,* the ones that do might give you a much better building. The ideal is a creative architect with a well-honed sense of realism who can knock down his own creative ideas that won't work.

• **Flexible** — Architects (like us) get stuck. They may fall in love with a design or — the opposite — intensely dislike an idea of yours. The creative architect has to be flexible enough to be brought down to earth to design a building you can work with and afford. The less creative architect has to be able to allow your creativity or the creativity of others you may bring in to enhance the process.

• **Cost conscious** — Architects want to do the best building they can. They often chafe under budgetary constraints. You want an architect who can accept budget limits and apply tight dollars with precision to produce the best building — balanc-

ing form and function. Money spent on an ornate building, or expensive moulding or light fixtures, or high price custom cabinets leaves little for the quantity of cabinets you need, or higher quality wall and floor finishes, or photo-electric faucets at changing tables that have higher functional value.

• **Playful** — Child care centers are *places for childhoods* and the major business of childhood is play. An architect who has a sense of play — a spirit of whimsy and the magical properties of childhood and relates to child's play — is more capable of designing a building that works as a child's place.

ARCHITECTURAL FEES

Fees are based on the scope of services that the architect provides. Once the services are established, fees are usually set based on a percentage of construction cost — usually 6% to 10% — depending on the services, or a fixed fee, established early on, though sometimes subject to renegotiation.

A WORD ABOUT CONSULTANTS

There has been a great increase in the number of child care consultants claiming to be able to do nearly anything, including help design centers. Increasingly, proposals from architectural firms in a competitive market will include a child care consultant as a member of their design team. This may not be an advantage. The value of a consultant comes from the *breadth* of her experience with child care program and facility design, the different perspectives she can bring to bear to complement yours, and the creativity her thoughtfulness can add. A good consultant can help prevent a number of mistakes and add to the design process. Look for a consultant with both expertise and humility.

"So You Want to Build a Building?" Dancing With Architects and Other Developmental Experiences — Part 2

T he financing is there, you have an architect in mind, now what? Do you plan to build, incorporate your center into a new building, or renovate in an existing space? The following are what you should probably be thinking about:

Selecting a Building Site

There is no easy formula for site selection. Foremost it is a marketing issue — will it work for your consumers? — and a quality issue — can you run the program you wish to run there? The size, shape, topography, surroundings, and relationship to homes and work sites will shape the building and its use. In the best of circumstances, there is an *essential fittingness* between site, surroundings, building, and occupants or users. But rarely is any site ideal —the best site is typically a site with many positives and the least negative factors.

Factors in selecting a site:

- **Consumers** — Who will be using the center? Parents from one location or a number of locations? Parents who use mass transit, car pool, or walk?

- **Cost** — Acquisition, landscape, utilities, and building cost?

- **Visibility** — Is visibility important for consumer awareness? Is visibility a liability for consumer perceptions of security or desirability?

- **Size** — Is the size sufficient for the building, outdoor play, and parking?

- **Site conditions** — Soil conditions, drainage factors, air, water, or other environmental quality positive or negative factors?

- **Climate** — Environmental protection from climatic factors?

- **Public services access** — Availability of gas, water, sewage, and power?

- **Surrounding area** — Noise, smell, environmental hazards, visual factors?

- **Zoning, local regulations, community acceptance** — Are there town zoning or regulatory issues?

- **Access to worksite** — Convenient and safe vehicle and/or pedestrian traffic?

- **Vehicle and pedestrian access** — Can parents conveniently, quickly, and safely enter and leave the site? Is there easy access for service and emergency vehicles? Is the site on mass transit lines?

- **Security** — Does the site allow for a secure perimeter, controlled visibility, a safe approach for children?

- **Parent perceptions** — Is the site perceived as convenient and positive? Are there ethnic or social class issues? Is the neighborhood changing?

- **Aesthetics** — Will the site provide a positive aesthetic surrounding for the center? Will the center complement the buildings and grounds surrounding the site?

- **Potential for school-age programming** — Potential for school busing?

- **Access to community resources** — Library, parks and pools, museums, stores, community centers?

- **Potential for expansion** — Is there room for expansion?

- **Future** — What will the area be like in five years, ten years? New development, decline, environmental problems?

The relative importance of any of the above factors depends on the particular circumstances. Some factors can doom a project — bad location, high costs never recoverable, poor site conditions. To minimize risk, don't jump into anything. Think carefully about your market niche — who you expect to be your customers — and your finances — what you can afford. Also critical: work the numbers to make sure what you can afford. Subtle factors may be critical:

- A site just a half mile north of a huge office park on a heavily traveled road was a logical site. However, most prospective parents would be coming to work from the south in bumper-to-bumper, two-way traffic. Dropping their child off, turning around, and traveling the half mile back added an annoying half mile to an already irritating commute.

- One site selected by a potential owner seemed ideal. However, the position of the site at a crossroads and the building entrance facing in a particular direction made it highly undesirable for Asian consumers whose culture gives great weight to directionality and relative position. Since potentially 40% of the center's future customers were Asian, using the site was not wise.

RENOVATION VS. NEW CONSTRUCTION

Most of the site selection factors come into play in the decision whether to renovate or build: does the site of building to be renovated work for a child care program?

Child care's historical affinity for adapted spaces leads to the conclusion that renovation is fairly easy and a great way to keep costs down. This is true to a point and may result in wonderful, homelike buildings with character. Yet **quality** child care centers often cannot be easily fit into buildings designed for other use. Windows, child access to bathrooms and water, good circulation patterns, the right size spaces, and logical space relations may be either difficult or costly in renovations.

Renovation may or may not result in cost savings worth the inevitable loss of some functionality as buildings are made to fit the requirements of child care. Renovating space for child care use has some particular issues that will influence the decision:

- Ground floor space — Many states require ground floor occupancy, at least for children under two.

- Sufficient entries and exits outdoors — Meeting codes for fire exits may incur additional costs. Convenient access to the outdoor play area is a program quality issue.

- Visual access to the outdoors.

- Meeting codes for Americans with Disabilities Act may incur additional costs.

- Meeting new fire codes requiring exits, sprinkler systems, and other improvements may incur additional costs.

Adequate distribution of plumbing — Easy access to water and toilets is a fundamental characteristic of quality programs. Sinks and toilets are distributed widely throughout the building, present in or adjacent to every home base.

- Non-institutional lighting and aesthetics.

- Interior circulation patterns that accommodate adults and children.

- In an existing building, the relationship to the other building occupants may become an issue in terms of noise, social density, and perceived distractions, incurring the cost of sound conditioning or redesigning circulation.

SUCCESSFUL RENOVATIONS

A successful renovation usually requires creativity and flexibility both from the space and the program. A program locked into specific age configurations, room (and staff) relationships, and the tendency to *do what we do* may find any renovated space difficult. And even creative programs may not flourish when too much of the program has to be taken as is — walls, doors, floors, plumbing, and lighting — and the program made to fit.

"So You Want to Build a Building?" Dancing With Architects and Other Developmental Experiences — Part 3

The design of a child care center begins with a site, an architect, and a design program. From that basis, the design process has a number of steps, including:

- Conceptual design — developing the concept of the building: structure, location on the site, look of the building, and general organization.

- Schematic design — developing the building specifics, mechanical and structural elements, relationships, floor plans, and major details.

- Schematic pricing — establishing a detailed cost estimate for the schematic design.

- Design development, value engineering and construction documents — developing the specific plans that the contractors will use to construct the building.

Each of these steps involves taking the design program, site, budget, and all the regulations that the building will have to meet and struggling to craft a building that best meets the design program.

Successful Design: A Collaborative Effort

The most successful facilities grow out of a process that recognizes the need for a design team: the architects, the owner or developer, the child care consultant (or the director) representing the owner, and — fairly early on — the contractor. All of the above have specific expertise and work most effectively when they are acknowledged as *players*, with legitimate interests and ownership of the project.

Developing the Design Program

Buildings suggest and support, to one degree or another, a range of activities and relationships. Buildings also evoke feelings. The design program is the statement of all the desired qualities and functions of the child care facility: reflecting the philosophy, goals, and standards of the child care center program. It provides the initial basis of the design requirements that architects translate into conceptual schemes, floor plans, elevations, and specifications:

- Age and number of children.

- Group size and grouping patterns.

- Range of activities.

- Designated spaces.

I. Program Configuration

Program Component	Child Ages	Group Size	# Home-Base (Classrooms)	Staff/Child Ratio	Total Children
Infant	6 weeks to 18 months	8	2	1:4	16
Toddler	15 months to 3 years	10	3	1:5	30
Preschool	2.5 years to 5 years	16	3	1:8	48
				Total Children	94

- Square footage requirements.

- Specific technical and design considerations (including specific furnishings).

- Assumed flexibility.

- Applicable regulations.

- Quality assumptions.

- Aesthetic assumptions.

The design program is an architectural starting point. It should include everything you care about and want included. The program represents all the knowledge generated through experienced research, visiting other programs, and discussions with staff and parents. The more you can articulate, the better.

It should list design criteria or principles that you want the building to be based on (home-like, ample light, and storage) as well as design specifications particular to child care (e.g., two child size toilets, 16" high activity counter). If you want floor drains, flexible lighting, bike paths, include them in the program.

However, there is a difference between a design issue and a design solution; and you may not want to lock yourself into a particular solution (particularly a costly one) or one that no longer makes sense because of technological advances. For example, it is desirable when standing at the changing counter sink to be able to turn the water on and off without using your hands, contaminated from diapering. Wrist blade handles are a reasonable cost alternative. Until recently, foot operated pedal controls were functionally a step up. Those are now a poor choice because of a better alternative — photo-electric sensor controls.

Included in this article is the suggested contents of a design program. Here are some examples of how you might detail various sections of this program.

(Note: Lists of criteria and elements in these examples are not complete, they are illustrations only.)

II. Overall Design Criteria

Four interconnected functional areas:

- Infant component.

- Toddler component.

- Preschool component.

- Support/public spaces.

All components easy access to outdoor play areas.

Sufficient multipurpose play space to allow for indoor large muscle activities for all ages.

Ample visual access into each home base and to the outside.

Ample storage distributed throughout the building.

Layout organized for:

- Support functions at core, surrounding entrance — with one secure public access to the building.

- Limited walking/carrying distance from entrance to home base.

- Central, visible kitchen is desirable.

III. Interior Program Components

A. Infant Component — Children from 6 weeks to 18 months

Home Bases: A total of two home bases each 750 net square feet (nsf) organized into a module of two home bases.

Function: Location for the principle caregiving and learning activities — play/learning, eating, sleeping, diapering/toileting, parent-staff conversations.

Elements:

- A separate, carpeted crib/sleep/quiet area for the module, visually accessible, with access from both home base areas with 8 linear feet of cabinets.

- A program/play/care activity area.

- A service area that includes child cubbies, parent communication area (display and writing surface), conversation area, adult coat closet.

- A food prep mini-kitchen including sink, microwave, and bar size refrigerator, and cabinets in each home base or accessible to each home base without losing visual access to each home base.

- A combination of carpet and tile floor (60% tile).

- Porch or deck areas desirable.

D. Administrative and Support Space

1. Entry / Reception — 200 nsf

Function: A friendly entrance to the program, a security checkpoint, a comfortable setting for visitors to wait, and a communications area for program information, parent materials, children's display.

Elements:

- An energy efficient vestibule.

- Reception desk.

- A controlled exterior door with buzzer.

- Seating for 4 to 6 adults and children (3 unrelated groups).

- Two communication locations — 20 square feet of communication / display area — wall or kiosk.

- *Signature* art piece or fountain desirable.

- Parent access to telephone.

- Visual access from offices.

G. Mechanical Specifications

1. Heating, Ventilation, and Air Conditioning

- Maintain all occupied rooms at no less than 68° F in the winter and 78° F in the summer.

CONTENTS OF THE DESIGN PROGRAM

- Heating devices must protect children from injury and contact with surfaces above 110° F.

- Allowance for open windows in different rooms.

- Mechanical exhausts for kitchen, laundry, bathrooms, and changing areas.

- Adequate heating at floor level.

- Tamper-proof thermostats not accessible to children.

TRADE OFFS

Design would be much simpler if there were no concessions to be made for budget, site considerations, fire and health codes, and the peculiar ideas of other design team members (not, of course, our own ideas). That is not the real world. Good design comes from thoughtful considerations of all factors and awareness of negative side effects of any solution.

WHY DID IT TURN OUT THIS WAY? HOW BUILDINGS GO WRONG

Buildings go wrong in large and small ways. They go wrong when dollars or lead time is limited or when they are not. They go wrong despite good people and experience, whether the plans are ambitious or cautious. Candlestick Park in San Francisco is a horrible place to do what it was designed for, watching baseball at night. The glass in the all-glass John Hancock tower in Boston popped out. Thousands of large and small buildings are, to one degree or another, ugly, non-functional, instantly obsolete, and decidedly not user friendly.

Buildings go wrong because designing and constructing a building is complicated in conception, detailing, and construction; there are many occasions for oversight, compounding small errors and inspired, wrongheaded thinking.

Child care buildings usually face very limited budgets, confusing requirements, and a simplistic view of what is needed. It is amazing how well many centers turn out. Drawing from numerous misadventures, this article looks at what goes wrong.

DESIGNING UP THE HILL AND DOWN THE HILL

It can inspire creativity to begin the process by assuming money is no object or, at least, not THE only concern. But in a number of projects, not having (or

disclosing) a realistic budget led to wasted time, frustration, and less of a building. With the encouragement of the developer or client, the design team went off in a creative and expensive direction without a real sense of limits, leading to buildings that would cost considerably more than would ever be available.

It was not easy going back to boxier, less elaborate buildings, when little of the creativity proves useful. It is better to start with a sense of the limits and encourage creativity in how to best spend the dollars.

WHERE HAVE ALL THE DOLLARS GONE?

There is a chronological aspect to designing a building and allocating dollars. The first decisions generally involve purchasing the site and agreeing on a building concept — including square footage, the building footprint, and the basic elements of the building. Will the walls be bearing walls? What sort of roof? How spread out will the building be?

The cost of the shell will be largely determined by the nature of the walls and roof, the amount of perimeter wall and the volume of the space, the materials used, and how much repetition there is between sections. Architects are often more heavily invested in the form and nature of the building shell than a child care owner can afford to be. Asserting the importance of functionality is critical

MOST COMMON FACILITY OVERSIGHTS OR ERRORS IN GOOD BUILDINGS REQUIRING CHANGE ORDERS, POST-CONSTRUCTION ADAPTATION, OR WHEN UNCORRECTED — PROGRAM STRESS

Footprint
crib rooms too small for number of cribs
too narrow corridors

Electrical
electrical outlets — too few in kitchen, corridor,
    home base, offices; inconvenient for offices; not
    tamper proof
equipment and kitchen equipment
uniform institutional lighting
single-switching on lights in classrooms
overlighting in all locations

Millwork
child activity counters too high
changing counter overhead cabinets too high,
    too close
no 3 inch lip on changing counter
knob hardware on cabinets instead of wire pulls

Plumbing
changing counters faucets NOT photo-electric,
    foot or wrist lever faucets
activity sinks NOT lever or single action
activity sinks centered reducing counter surface
drinking fountains NOT lever operated
goose neck spouts in changing counter or
    bathroom sinks (causing splashing)
goose neck spouts NOT in activity sinks
no plastic bag holders over changing counter sinks
no soap or paper towel dispensers over changing
    counter sinks
dispensers NOT recessed in children's bathroom

kindergarten bathrooms without full doors
child-size toilets (10 inch) in kindergarten room

Telephone
no phones in classrooms
no phone in conference room

Storage
inadequate storage, both closets and shelving close
    to point of use
no large storage space for multipurpose space for
    mats, planks, vehicles
inadequate in-kitchen wire rack storage

Floors, Windows, Walls, Doors
corridors with institutional tile flooring
windows too high for child viewing out
no window treatment in director's office or
    conference room
vision panels in doors too small and/or too high
no protective wall surfaces in multipurpose space
carpet/tile ratio — recommended 40% broadloom
    carpet (infant 60%)
no means for staff to easily keep door to play-
    ground open for re-entry

Outdoors
inadequate shade
too much asphalt
combined walk and bike path
too little challenge for school-age children
inadequate edging to keep in sand/wood chips
no vehicle gate to playground

---

at the initial stages of the project. The more expensive and elaborate the shell, the fewer dollars for functional details like interior cabinetry, quality of furnishings and finishes, conveniently located plumbing, or interior windows and exterior doors to the playground.

PENNY WISE AND POUND FOOLISH

The building is a two decade investment, subject to a lot of hard use. Year after year, both the appearance

and the user-friendliness of the building will impact on the quality and marketing of the program. Allocating as much money up front as possible on square footage, aesthetics, durability, and program support is a wise investment.

Always consider the value of an item (cost and length of potential use) and marketing value (will it make you appear more desirable?). Low-quality finishes, sparse playground, and cramped space are shortsighted.

ASK THE EXPERTS AND LISTEN TO PRACTITIONERS — CAREFULLY

Yes, listen to teachers and directors, but put what they say in perspective. Child care practitioners often know what is wrong or right — and that is what should be given serious attention. However, their suggested solutions to a problem under consideration may not be the best solutions. Why? Because they may be unaware of the down side of the solution or unaware of other possible solutions.

Enrichment rooms, a library, a lunchroom, or a parent lounge are all spaces that might be good things; but they may not be worth the loss in square footage to child activity space. Or they may be limited in understanding developmentally appropriate play.

The teachers that insist on mostly carpet may not want to allow much messy play, play which a more knowledgeable future staff may appreciate. Those that want all tile for sanitation may neglect softness, or they may not recognize the issue of tripping on area rugs.

A recommendation may be based on a limited view. Many of those who believe crib rooms are unnecessary (when allowed) in an infant room have an undeveloped sense of the infant as a competent, active learner.

REDESIGNING YOUR LAST BUILDING

Instead of asking yourself what your program needs, ask what your program could be. What will it be like in 2000; 2005? Will you want more space for school-age children? Should you design and site your building to allow for expansion? Does new technology exist now that you can use in lighting, heating, and plumbing?

WHO TOOK NOTES?

In one renovation, the trusted contractor appeared to be taking in all the precise requests and design details elaborated by the staff and child care consultant. When the building was done, it appeared either he was deaf or forgetful, because few details were correct. Make sure that the architectural program incorporates all that you think is important.

DO WE HAVE TO WADE THROUGH ALL OF THOSE PRINTS AND SPECIFICATIONS?

In most construction, how the building is to be built is detailed in a set of prints and a book of specifications for the contractor. Lodged amidst detail after detail you may not understand — on valves and vapor barriers, masonry construction techniques, air intake, etc. — are all the things you do care about: counter top height, sink hardware, lighting, and so on.

Plow through the prints and the book looking for your details. If you are unsure of what is there, give the contractor or the architect a list of those items you feel may not be included.

IF YOU BUILD IT, THEY WILL COME

They WILL come — to inspect, license, certify. The unwritten rules, the obscure municipal sanitation codes, and the inspector's not-so-charmingly idiosyncratic interpretations can lead to last minute changes, both expensive and awkward — the additional sink or the toilet in the infant area, the loss of child usage space, or the new door. Find out if there are local amendments to building, fire, and sanitation codes.

While child care operators are often faced with the tight rope of wondering whether or not to bring up a question for interpretation because asking forces a response, it makes sense to take advantage of the courtesy reviews of building plans that most regulatory agencies will provide.

DO I HAVE TO BE THERE?

The ultimate check is to be on site often, very often. Often, you will catch a number of errors and oversights. Often, changes may happen at the last minute because of any number of reasons: an unavailable item, a need to adjust when the paper reality turns out to be incorrect, or even the attempt to make a buck by substituting another product.

I FEEL SO PUSHY!

Be pushy — direct and assertive — but listen to the architect and contractor. Don't underestimate what you know and don't underestimate your concerns that the building support the program.

LIVING WITH THE NOT SO PERFECT BUILDING

No building is perfect. Don't let the 1% imperfections bring you down from the pleasure of enjoying the 99% that went right. Ultimately, buildings can be made to work. But one important last word. It always takes awhile to get comfortable with a building, even when it's not a new staff and program. Before you redesign, settle in and live with the building. Maybe those ostensible oversights and design questions are livable, even desirable.

OF TOYS AND STUFF

What is a toy? An object used in play. Great, what is play? What we do for pleasure — *not work*. But play is a *child's work*, right? So toys are the child's tools? In fact, tools with educational import. Serious business, futures are at stake here. And if it is serious, then, of course, play and toys are the subject of serious research: "the metacognitive effects of stacking rings on infants with crossed eyes." Even more important — if it is serious and this is America, there are fortunes to be made; toys are big ticket consumable objects: "Go plastic, young man," Horace Greely said to Benjamin Braddock, "and make it bright red."

Perhaps play and toys are serious, too serious to take seriously. Play is what children do when allowed to — self-initiated, spontaneous, and voluntary *messing around*; and the child is in control. Toys are all those things that kids play with, from blocks and rocks to computers. In fact, the frequency with which children are told "Don't play with that" in the real world illustrates that anything can be a toy — from food to body parts. Children create toys everywhere, in the harshest of worlds, even concentration camps and impoverished desert camps.

TOYS IN THE CHILD CARE CENTER

To say that toys are all those things that kids play with is not to say that all play is equal or that all toys are equal. Good child care centers are play environments where a wide range of play is encouraged. The materials available facilitate that play. But the selection of the materials — the toys — defines more than the play possibilities. The toys also represent feelings, values, and aesthetic choices:

"ROSEBUD" — OBJECTS OF ENDEARMENT

It may have been your teddy, or your Chatty Kathy, or My Little Pony or that Raggedy Andy. Somewhere in your past are toys that evoke memories that bring smiles or tears to your eyes. While child care centers are collective environments where little is allowed to become "Mine!," the evocative power of a toy to become a loved object should be considered, if child care centers are to become *places for childhoods*.

"DROP THAT CARROT" — TOYS AS OBJECTS OF REPRESENTATION

Anything can be a toy for symbolic play: the block as truck or person,

We planned to keep your first toys,

preserve them; one day,

when you are grown, lead you

to a secret closet, watch you

pull wide, amazed,

re-discover your treasures.

But we can't; you're eating them.

— Michael Dennis Browne, *Light Year 87*.
Cleveland, OH: Bit Press, 1988.

the chair as train, the scarf that transforms the child into princess or witch. Children need objects that are not detailed, literal representations. And create they will, whether we like it or not:

Johnny was a determined terminator. First we found him shooting away with his plastic gun, carefully smuggled in from home. "No guns at school," we gently insisted and confiscated the weapon. Then he mowed down a row of his friends with a homemade Lego blaster. The quiet "no hurting people discussion" followed, complete with active listening and affirmation. Later that morning, eyes glinting with revenge, he slowly raised his hand and gunned me down with a carrot.

"FEEL THIS! — TOYS AS SENSUAL OBJECTS

There is a sensual quality to toys for young children — and adults. The softness and responsiveness of a doll or stuffed animal. The smooth warmth of a beautiful wooden toy, rubbed smooth and oiled by human hands. The cool metallic strength of a truck. The smell and feel of the leather mitt or the silky feel of the doll's hair.

"A good toy leaves room for the free exercise of a child's imagination. It can be used in different ways. It is handsome in shape and color and good to touch, beautiful in line, and interesting in texture. It is sturdy and will take heavy use." (Caplan and Caplan, 1974)

"BUY ME" — TOYS AS COMMERCIAL OBJECTS

We live in an age where things only have value if they become objects of consumption. We buy leisure, learning, fitness, and fun. Children and parents are marketed from birth to desire toys, and they do — often only the real thing, the store-bought thing, will do.

To the extent that child care centers replace toys with recycled, found, or real materials, they give off a counter message — "anything can be a toy." Often if scale is not a factor (like with tools), the real *real thing* is best — real pots and pans and dishes, not the toy versions.

"ME TOO" — TOYS AS SOCIAL OBJECTS

Some things lend themselves to social play — blocks, dolls, wagons, manipulatives, costumes, and so on. Others — computers, puzzles, solitary trikes — do not. Children need both.

"HEIGH HO" — TOYS AS TOOLS

"I did it," she said after digging out the hole, unscrewing the screw, or painting the wall. Toys allow children to accomplish, sometimes with a struggle.

Is there a better piece of equipment than a wheelbarrow to challenge a child? It requires both motor and cognitive learning because the ease of maneuverability changes depending on the load and the surface. At one center a four year old, struggling heroically with a wheelbarrow she had loaded with wood, looked up at the teacher and said angrily: "Damn! Teacher, there's a wheel missing." While the teacher was tempted to put away the wheelbarrow as developmentally inappropriate, she realized that the child's struggle to make it work was the real learning.

There is a nature store where one goes to buy, well, nature. For sale are pine cones and acorns, shells and all sorts of pebbles, gnarled branches, and driftwood. There are leaves of eucalyptus and pussy willows and even dirt of different colors and consistencies.

"I WANT THAT NEW ONE" — TOYS AS NOVELTY

Yes, children love novelty. But the idea that children need continual variety reflects an adult sensibility about novelty, and we unfortunately teach that to children. The rapid development of young children has the effect of transforming objects. A few weeks pass in a young child's life, and it is almost a new child who returns to an object to explore different dimensions and uses of an object.

"BRIGHT AND CHEERFUL" — TOYS AS AESTHETIC OBJECTS

Toys in themselves may be objects of beauty or garish additions that detract from the general aesthetic.

Toys play a large role in the overall sensibility of the center. One real dilemma: adults know that *children love primary colors*. They do, and all toymakers have that fact emblazoned on their brains.

There is a wealth of inexpensive, useful, quality plastic toys, all made in vibrant primary colors. Yet an abundance of primary colors creates a kaleidoscopic chaos that diminishes the attraction of all colors. With our greater cognitive and perceptual skills, we may look at a shelf and see a brightly colored truck. The very young child sees another brightly colored plastic object amidst a sea of bright plastic. Unless we wish to raise another psychedelic generation, programs should try to moderate the use of primary colored toys (and furniture, walls, and floors).

THE IMPORTANCE OF UNSTRUCTURED MATERIALS — AKA JUNK

Unstructured materials are *loose parts* to be used by children in ways that are not predetermined by adults. These are *toys* that you won't find in a catalog. You find them in salvage stores, teacher resource centers, children's museums, or suppliers like Creative Educational Surplus (800-886-6428). The objects tend to be simple and perhaps *junk* to the adult eye, until a child recognizes the potential of the item.

What do young children do with these loose parts? They sort, put together, line up, drop, fill, stack, and on and on. They try to combine the materials in ways we would not think of. In fact, the best way for adults to approach *junk* is to determine if the item is safe (and that means safe to explore with the mouth for a child under three), and then give it to the children and see what they will do with it.

Some examples include:

plastic film canisters
canning jar rings
large washers
fabric pieces
wooden knobs or spools
plastic balls
whiffle balls
plastic tubing
clothes pins
plastic hair curlers
funnels
plastic or metal cylinders
small brushes
wooden dowels
wooden rings
pebbles
washers
sticks
bottle caps
paper tubes
medicine vials
shoe laces
key chains
plastic and wood scraps

Combine these materials in a variety of ways and store them in containers that require different motor skills to use. Carrying containers without handles requires different skills than containers with handles, and there are numerous variations of handles — jug handles, wire or rope, fixed, etc.

When using **small unstructured materials**, keep in mind:

- Be extra careful about health and safety issues — sanitation, choking, sharp edges, toxic materials or finishes.

- Rotate materials in different combinations, and facilitate play by putting out different materials every week or so. For example, some jar lids on a plate next to a teddy sitting in a chair suggest biscuits for morning tea.

- Every so often, casually plop down and play with the materials yourself, but don't assume the child will do what you do.

- Use the materials in a bounded area to reduce the pick-up, and incorporate appropriate ones in other learning centers.

Large unstructured materials:

Remember the Little Rascals? Spanky and Alfalfa were always making contraptions out of tires, crates, rope, planks, wheels, and nearly anything else found in vacant lots or trash cans. Large unstructured materials allow children to create, construct, and represent.

planks and beams
rope
large wooden blocks
plastic blocks
tape
wooden and plastic crates
webbing
boxes
parachutes/sheets
pillows/bolsters
sawhorses/triangles
tires
large and small wheels
driftwood
throw rugs
wood rounds
cans — large and small
doors/wooden sheets
wading pools
small boulders

A FINAL NOTE

Parents expect a well-equipped program to be loaded with toys and teaching materials. To provide quality care for young children, we must constantly promote the child as an amazing miniature scientist, artist, social scientist, and architect who can use much of what the world has to offer.

REFERENCE

Caplan, F., and T. Caplan. *The Power of Play*. Garden City, NY: Anchor Press/Doubleday, 1974.

A Guide to Equipping the Developmentally Appropriate Center

In a developmentally appropriate center, the program fits each child, not the other way around. The furnishings, equipment, and expectations of the child are age appropriate and appropriate to **each** individual child. A center is developmentally appropriate if:

• care is individual, personal, and responsive.

• learning is individual and child choice is valued.

• learning experiences are active, concrete, and relevant to the child.

• all developmental areas are addressed in the learning environment.

• a wide variety of experience is available to accommodate wide ranges in interests and development.

• adults respectfully facilitate, guide, encourage, and nurture each child's self-esteem, competence, and self-reliance.

• the child's great need for movement, expression, noisemaking, and exuberance is planned for.

A quality center is experientially rich and alive with child-directed activity; the adult focus is more on learning and facilitation than on teaching and direction. Adults listen and carry on individual conversations with children on real issues of concern to the children. Care is responsive, personal, and respectful. Full-day care takes place in a comfortable setting with ample time and space for privacy and quiet times.

A typical developmentally **inappropriate** early childhood setting is likely to require children to be too passive and group oriented, allow for little individuality, and focus more on instruction and child listening than learning and child doing.

In developmentally inappropriate settings, toddlers are often in programs designed as if they were young three year olds, preschoolers as if they were second graders, and school-age children as if they were old four year olds. A long, structured, group-oriented day (or very unstructured day) puts the burden of adjustment on the child.

Principles for Equipping the Center

The right equipment and furnishings support a developmentally appropriate setting for care and learning. The goal is to maximize both child and adult competence. With furnishings and equipment that support appropriate, independent child use and easy adult use, children will have more experiences that accomplish developmental goals, and caregivers will have more time to care for children and to support their learning.

A well-equipped developmentally appropriate center provides the following:

Soft, comfortable furniture:
Couches, easy chairs, futons, pillows.

Child access open storage: Shelves, bins, cubbies, carts, bags.

Variety of play materials: Sufficient variety to rotate play materials.

Sufficient quantity of play materials: More of the same item, such as blocks, are usually preferable to a smaller number of similar items. These items require large quantities per child for their potential value to be realized.

Duplicates: Duplicates of popular items are important to facilitate smooth social relationships, particularly for toddlers and young preschoolers.

Learning materials offering a balance of:

• *open/closed:* Open materials have no **correct** outcome — blocks, clay, painting; closed materials involve a right answer or a clear ending — puzzles, Montessori materials, or worksheets.

• *plastic/wood/metal:* An imbalance of brightly colored plastic is a common problem that creates an over-stimulating aesthetic.

• *commercial toys/stuff: Stuff* is everything not designed to be toys that children play with — pots, pans, cardboard, twigs, tools, and other **junk**.

• *novelty and challenge/familiarity:* Opportunities for practice and mastery, as well as novelty and challenge.

• *active/quiet play materials:* Trucks and balls and boisterous dramatic play as well as books, stuffed animals, dolls, and manipulatives.

• *individual/social play materials:* Some equipment requires children to use it as a group; other equipment allows for solitary use.

• *simple/complex materials:* A simple item has one obvious use — a rattle, a car. A complex item has subparts or multiple uses that allow children to improvise — play bus with people.

CRITERIA FOR EQUIPMENT SELECTION

Durability: How long will it hold up? Center use is probably 10 times as hard as home use.

Safety: Sharp edges or corners? Parts to swallow? Toxic surface? Pull or tip over? How will it wear or break?

Health: Does it allow for easy cleaning and disinfecting?

Size/scale: Is it the right size and scale for projected **and** unanticipated use by children or adults?

Quality of play experience: Can it be used by different children (age, size) for different activities? How long will it hold a child's interest? How long will it challenge a child? What developmental needs or educational skill does the use of the equipment engender?

Quality of caring experience: Is it consistent with the child/parent experience? Does it facilitate the caregiver's task? Does it add to the child/parent's sense of security?

Accessibility/independent use: Does the equipment require adult assistance in display, preparation, or use?

Aesthetics: Is the design attractive? Does the color, size, and shape add or detract from the overall aesthetics (e.g., will there be too much primary colored, plastic equipment)?

Appeals to a variety of sensory modalities: A mobile with sound appeals to sight and hearing, a beautiful wooden shape.

Authenticity: Real items used for real activities — garden tools, workbenches, kitchen and cleaning utensils.

Cost/value: The value of an item depends on the significance and length of its use relative to the price.

	Infant *6 weeks to 1 year*	Toddler *1 year to 2½ years*	Preschool *2½ years to 5 years*	School Age *5 years to 9 years*
Classroom Furnishings	Couch/futon Changing counter Adult rocker Cribs/cradles Infant bounce chair Cubbies/bins High chair/chair with tray Child access shelves Nest/wading pool	*In addition:* Book display Chairs/seating cubes Lunch tables Child rockers Block cart Small water table Cots/mats Pillows	*In addition:* Activity counters Small play tables Work bench Room dividers Small rugs Sand/water table	*In addition:* Easy chairs Bunk beds Tents Hammock
Large Motor	Mats/pillows Beach balls Push/pull toys Small wagon Foam rolls Tunnel 4-6 Passenger carts Strollers Sling/backpack	*In addition:* Stairs/slide Rocking boat Barrel Wheelbarrows No-pedal trikes Variety of balls Simple climber	*In addition:* Balance beam Pedal wheel toys Larger wagons Shovels/rakes Hula hoops Planks/triangles	*In addition:* Sports balls Roller/ice skates Basketball hoop Jump ropes Skateboards Scooters
Dramatic Play	Baby dolls Stuffed animals Rubber animals Rubber people Puppets Hats Plexiglass mirrors	*In addition:* Large doll furniture Dress-up clothes and hats Child-size furniture Plastic cooking sets Blankets Tents Boxes Cars/trucks Pots/pans	*In addition:* Doll houses Plastic food Clothespins Play money Cash register Kitchen utensils Prop boxes Purses/luggage Play telephone	*In addition:* Small dolls Castle sets Mobile Balance scale Microphone Stage Fabric Planks/boxes
Blocks/ Construction	Fiberboard blocks Foam blocks Bucket and blocks	*In addition:* More blocks Large trucks Large train Snap blocks Waffle blocks	*In addition:* Unit blocks Hollow/perma blocks Planks Derrick/pulleys Wheelbarrow Woodworking tools/hats/belts Dominoes/lots of blocks	*In addition:* More hollow blocks More planks Plastic crates More tools Tri-wall cardboard Traffic signs/train set Plastic/wood wheels, nuts, bolts
Creative Art	Finger paint Simple prints Wall hangings Sculpture Mobiles Messy mats	*In addition:* Block crayons Large brushes Chalk/markers Chalkboard Play dough Ink stamps Paste	*In addition:* Easel Small brushes Water colors Modeling clay and wax Collage material Glue Scissors	*In addition:* Tri-wall cardboard Styrofoam pieces Clay Sewing machine Badge maker Camera Camcorder
Sensory/Sand/ Water/Science	Dish/garden tubs Tub toys Sponges Plants Aquariums/birdfeeders Animals Wind chimes	*In addition:* Buckets/jars Funnels/sifters Measuring cups/pitchers Magnifiers Large markets Flashlights	*In addition:* Electric frying pan Incubator Ant farm Balance scales Thermometer Magnets/prisms	*In addition:* Microscopes Rock tumblers Tape measures Oven Motors
Books/ Language/ Music	Cloth books Hard board books Posters Photos Records/tapes Music boxes Musical mobiles	*In addition:* Picture books Read-to books Play telephones Simple instruments Listening center	*In addition:* More books Magnetic letters/Lotto Typewriter Telephones Thick pencils Musical keyboard Instrument set Scarves/ribbons	*In addition:* Computer and software Easy read books Chapter books Time/Life type books Maps Dictionary/encyclopedias Historical books Notebooks
Perceptual/ Motor/Games/ Manipulatives/ Math	Mobiles Cradle gyms Busy boxes Rattles Prisms	*In addition:* Pop beads Stack/nesting toys Large pegboards Lock boards Pounding bench Poker chips Sorting boxes	*In addition:* Small pegboards Puzzles Thread boards Table blocks/parquet blocks Tyco/Lego/Lazy blocks Abacus Lacing boards Nuts and bolts	*In addition:* Board games Skill games Cards/checkers Dominoes Looms Cuisenaire rods Calculators Models

GUIDE TO EQUIPPING YOUR CENTER

THINKING ABOUT THE AESTHETICS OF CHILDREN'S ENVIRONMENTS

A ll spaces have size and scale, aesthetic qualities, entries and pathways, and a degree of spatial variety. These characteristics together give a space its *feel* and its sense of workability.

AESTHETICS

Imagine a room where there are bright splashes of color, often attached to moving bodies, and warm muted hues on carpet and walls. Sunshine catches the light of a prism in one corner, and there is a small patch of sunlight so bright you have to squint. There are soft indirect lights, shadows, and cool dark corners.

There are hanging baskets of trailing green plants, flowers, pussy willows and cattails, angel hair and dried grasses. The beauty of life is captured by Monet and Wyeth and assorted four year olds.

There are the smells of fresh dirt, lilacs and eucalyptus, garlic, and baking bread.

One hears laughter and singing, animated conversation, soft classical music, and the back beat of reggae from somewhere in the corridor. There is a ticking of clocks, chirping of birds, and the squeaking and rustling of a guinea pig.

There is a breeze from an open window as one walks around feeling heavy dark wood and silky fabric; hard cold metal and warm fur; complex textures and watery, slippery, gooey things.

Everything somehow seems to fit together in a comprehensible way. The elements are not random. These are the aesthetic elements of life, of what makes the world a rich experience. They stimulate and nurture our many moods. Through them we glimpse the soul of nature and of humanity. They are the elements we hope to have in and around the places where we live, settings where children and adults spend days together.

The aesthetics in a children's setting are, as is everything else, a tradeoff of cost, convenience, and health concerns. Plants and animals require tending. Fluorescent lighting is cost effective; uniform lighting results in maximum flexibility. Washable surfaces are healthier and more functional; water, earth, and clay are messy, and so on. Too often the tradeoffs don't take into account equally important concerns — appreciation for the rich sensual nature of children and the importance of beauty in our lives.

If a children's program is a *work* or *school* site geared to accomplishing narrow objectives in a constricted time frame, then aesthetic appeal may be secondary. All we ask of lecture halls is reasonably comfortable seating, good lighting, and a clear view of the teacher and the black-board or screen. In a room with no highlights, the teacher is the high-light. For a child or adult in a setting for a few hours a day, beauty and character are nice, but not essential; we have that in our other settings. But as Golan et al. (Prescott and David, 1976) found, we often lose the "essential totality" and continu-ity in a child's life. Children who live in crowded, dingy apartments are likely to go to crowded, dingy schools; walk on congested, dingy streets; and use crowded, dingy transportation.

For babies, the importance of the perceptual environment, particularly the visual environment, cannot be underestimated. The more an infant sees and recognizes, the more an infant wants to see. Vision is the means the baby uses to make the world familiar. It is not simply a matter of quantity. Visual environ-ments that are dull and sterile, or random and chaotic, or that contain busy murals that appeal to adults, or complex (to a baby) images that appeal to older children are negative learning settings.

Consider the world of care and liv-ing: restaurants, motels, apartments, playgrounds, and nursing homes. These settings often lack character and a sense of beauty. Child care programs, with a diversity borne of homes, churches, and storefronts, tend to have character. But as the child care industry has grown and

ITALIAN SCHOOL

The preschool programs in the schools in the Commune of Reggio Emilia in Northern Italy embody an appreciation of beauty and a sense of the whole-ness of life: "The rooms are simply beautiful. There is attention to detail everywhere: in the color of their walls, the shape of the furniture, the arrangement of the simplest objects on shelves and tables. Light from the windows and doors shines through transparent collages and weavings made by the children. Healthy green plants are everywhere. Behind the shelves displaying shells are mirrors which reflect patterns which children and teachers have created. But the environment is not just beautiful — it is highly personal. For example, in one of the halls, a series of small boxes made of white cardboard create a grid on the wall. On each box the name of a child or teacher is printed with rubber stamp letters. These boxes are used for leaving little surprises or messages from one another.

Walking a little further, you see a display of pine cones placed in order by size, and next to them a series of round, polished pebbles arranged in rows by shades or color from white to dark gray. The natural beauty of these found objects, along with their form and size, is highlighted by the careful attention with which they have been arranged on a lighted shelf just at children's eye level.

Children are encouraged to bring in tokens of their home experience con-nected with daily or special events. They bring home shells from the seashore in the summer or traditional decorations when they return from winter vacations. Teachers collect these items and child displays where each child's contribution is respected and at the same time becomes part of a larger picture. For example, the children's decorations were each put in a transparent bag; the bags were all put together into a huge transparent hanging which caught light from a nearby window. Children could simply watch the play of light on the hanging, they could play counting games with the objects, they could gather round and compare what each of them had contributed.

The space in the schools of Reggio Emilia is personal in still another way: it is full of the children's own work. Visual expression is so important in the curriculum that an art director . . . works with teachers to help them display children's work. The results literally surround the people in this school. . . . It turns up even in unexpected places like the stairways and bathrooms."

From: "Not Just Anywhere: Making Child Care Centers into 'Particular' Places" by Lella Gandini, Beginnings magazine, Summer 1984.

standards rightfully increased, char-acter has sometimes given way to the pleasant and impersonal uniform aesthetic, indistinguishable from that of fast food places or branch banks. It is often an adult aesthetic designed to offer parents the images they associate with younger children and their needs: bright colors and Sesame Street characters, and furnishings clean as new that appear riveted in place.

It does not have to be that way. Programs for children should take their ideas and inspiration from those places where we experience the world of people and things most fully.

ASPECTS OF AESTHETIC APPEAL

Lighting: Few of us choose to live in windowless basements or light our homes uniformly with banks of fluorescent lighting. Uniform fluorescent lighting washes out colors and flattens perceptions; there is no focus and all subtlety is lost. Lighting can give space warmth and character and highlight specific areas and features. Light and shadow alter perceptions of things — their volume, shape, color, and texture. A mixture of lighting of different wattages and types as in homes creates a variety of living and learning spaces.

Color: Like light, color creates moods and highlights features. Human beings react physiologically to color. Cool colors like blues can exert a calming effect; warm reds and yellows stimulate us. Preliminary research in a new field of color therapy indicates that a bubble-gum color called passive pink may have an almost immediate effect on aggressive behavior (Hiss, 1987).

FLETCHER AVENUE
by Myra Cohn Livingston

In my
grandmother's house
sun comes through leaded panes
on the front stair landing, creeping
softly

over
the red carpet,
flashing yellow circles
and white dots, with ribbons of blue
dancing

on the
bannisters and
balconies, coming to
rest on warm wood walls in the dark
hallways.

Color can tie spaces together or create boundaries. Bright accent walls or patterns (visual texture) draw children to spaces. Whites (and mirrors) make a space feel larger, while dramatic colors and patterns have the opposite effect.

Art and Display: Many programs use pictures that seem to appeal to children to signal that it is a child's place, like figures from children's books and cartoons and cute childish images. It is a signal both adults and children recognize. But cute and commercial does not have to be the dominant image. Images that appear to children and represent higher artistic standards than mass cartoons can be selected. There are photographs and illustrations from children's books and numerous images from the art world that might compete with Mickey Mouse.

However, because the children's own artwork should be displayed in abundance, added pictures and murals in a group space often create visual clutter. Bright, cheery graphics present the same problem. Some programs seem kaleidoscopic; one is assaulted by colors and shapes — brightly clad children moving around bright primary colored plastic furniture and toys, encircled by bright graphics, murals, and children's art. Pictures, bright colors, and contrasting shapes are targets for attention. Too many targets create a sensory overload and exact their toll in fatigue or dulled senses, no matter how acclimated everyone becomes. Limiting the amount of display and locating display areas carefully improves the program aesthetics.

Texture: Texture is appreciated almost entirely by touch. Even when visually presented, it is the memory of tactile experiences that we appreciate. The skin is the largest organ of the body

---

MEDITERRANEAN BEACH, DAY AFTER STORM
FROM "LOVE: TWO VIGNETTES"
by Robert Penn Warren

How instant joy, how clang
And whang the sun, how
Whoop the sea, and oh,
Sun, sing, as whiter than
Rage of snow, let sea the spume
Fling.

Let sea the spume, white, fling,
White on blue wild
With wind, let sun
Sing, while the world
Scuds, clouds boom and belly,
Creak like sails, whiter than,
Brighter than,
Spume in sun-song, oho!
The wind is bright.

Wind the heart winds
In constant coil, turning
In the — forever — light.

Give me your hand.

---

and provides our most personal sensations. For most people, life's most intimate moments are associated with touching and being touched and with the changing texture of skin. For children, this is unquestionably true. If young children were designers, the textural quality of the space would be one of the first orders of business.

Nature: There is a tremendous aesthetic and learning value in living things. Plants and flowers add aesthetic appeal to the setting. Because they are alive, they also add complexity and novelty. Aquariums offer patterns of form, color, and motion, while birds offer color, motion, and sound.

Sounds: Our sense of space is derived from the sounds we hear and the silences. Sounds evoke strong physiological and psychological reactions. Sounds can soothe or jar, help one to focus, or serve as a bridge from one activity to another. Music can be a stimulant more potent than caffeine. Because adults and children differ in their tolerance for noise and in their drive to make noise, the acoustical properties of settings are extremely important. Making noise is a powerful experience for a child, not being able to is a heavy restriction.

A great need to prevent noise is hard on teachers and children and will color all interactions. Keeping noise down becomes a test of a child's self-control and the teacher's competence in her own eyes and the eyes of other staff. The crowding voices of children close in on adults, and the felt need to control noise can alter both program structure and content.

Children and poets, Robert Penn Warren and others, bring inner sounds with them to spaces, sounds that often must get out. Yet the absence of silence can be equally oppressive to children, silence to hear their inner sounds. Noise is a major cause of stress for both adults and children.

Ideally, spaces in children's settings would allow for silence, the steady hum of play, and the explosive noises that punctuate exuberant living. Sounds from the outer world would neither be absent nor intrusive.

Smell: Researchers take seriously the view that we respond to smell much as we respond to color. Some smells, cooked onions for one, cause us to salivate and feel hungry. Others, like pine, seem to have a calming effect. Certainly, the psychological effect of a smell such as baking cookies is obvious.

REFERENCES

Hiss, T. "Experiencing Places." *New Yorker Magazine*, June 22, 1987, pp. 45-68; June 29, 1987, pp. 73-86.

Prescott, E., and T. David. "The Effects of the Physical Environment on Day Care," *ERIC Document No. 156-356*, 1976.

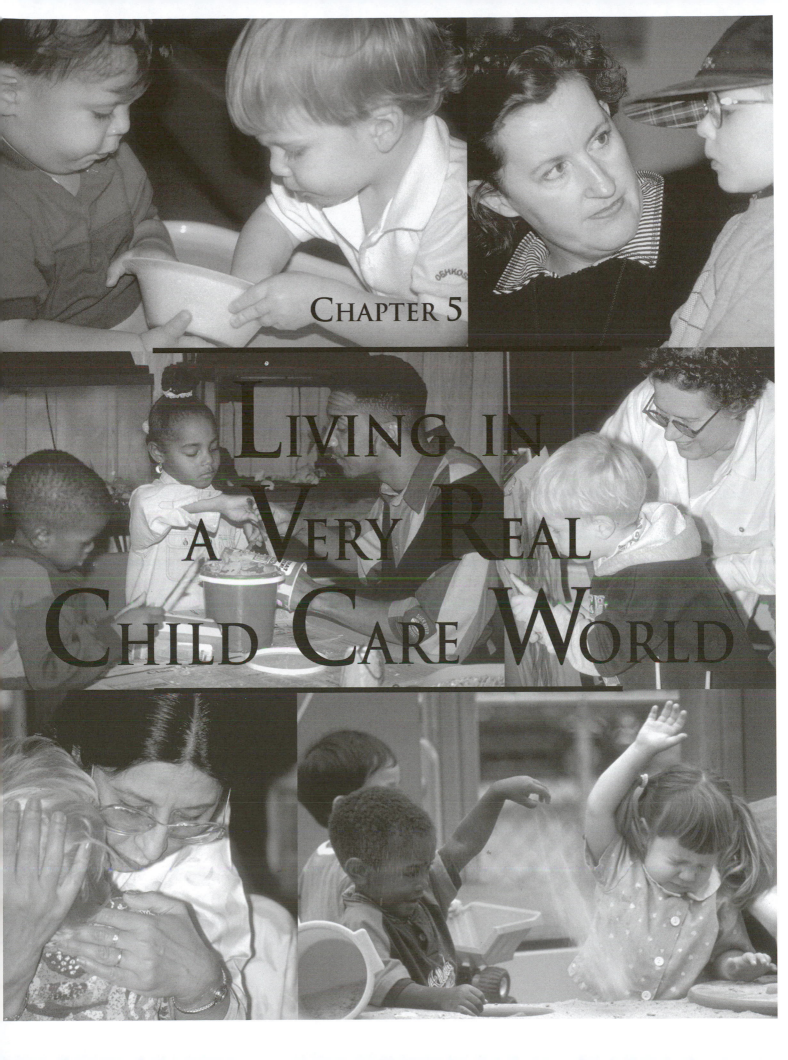

CHAPTER 5

LIVING IN A VERY REAL CHILD CARE WORLD

LIVING IN THE REAL WORLD

by Janet Gonzalez-Mena

It is easier to be a theorist than live in the real world of child care. It takes a lot less energy to deal just with ideas than to deal with children, staff, parents, regulations, ratios, funding, and all those messes!

I remember when I first realized the appeal of the theoretical world. I had spent a Saturday morning at school cleaning cupboards. When I got home to the mess that my four children had created while I was gone, I went to work to clean that up. As I opened a cupboard to put the toys away, junk spilled out on my feet. It was then that I realized I could spend the rest of my life cleaning cupboards, and I would never keep ahead of the game.

It's so different to read books and then sit at the computer and click out words that stand for ideas. Not that the theoretical world is never messy. But running into a confusion of ideas to sort out somehow seems a lot neater and cleaner than dealing with the real world of unplugging toilets, picking up messes, untangling scrapping kids, and picking play dough out of the rug.

Some people balance home and school well. I didn't. I never did get those cupboards cleaned at home, unfortunately, even though I left my on-the-floor job and retreated to administration and finally to the land of teacher education. In my spare time, I live in the world of theory. It's fun there — figuring out what is and what should be — a real intellectual exercise.

MAKING CHILD CARE BETTER

Of course, it isn't all intellectual; feelings come in, too. I have lots of passion about making child care better. So that passion always bring me back to real teachers in real programs. Every time I step into a center, I breathe a sigh of relief that I no longer have to clean out school cupboards.

Teachers remind me of the limitations of theory. Though theory and practice should go hand in hand, they seldom do. Reality keeps getting in the way of theory. There's much that can be done to make teachers' jobs better, easier, more financially rewarding, and more effective. I have these tendencies to become a crusader. The problem is, I can't just make things better for teachers. If I take a narrow focus, I forget about families. Making things better is about quality, and improving quality means making things better for *everybody*.

There are three sets of players in the child care scene. Child care is about teachers *and* parents (families); it's also about *children*. Those three groups each have slightly different viewpoints and sometimes they conflict with each other. THAT'S the real world. Teachers have to figure out what to do about those conflicts. They have to serve the family, look out for the best interests of the individual child, the group of children, AND take care of themselves — all at the same time. No easy job!

"BAD" CHILD DEVELOPMENT

I've had plenty of experiences with teachers who thought of something a parent did as "bad" child development without understanding anything about that parent's culture or individual motive. Toilet training done any way but the way that the *experts* advocate is an example. I also was once very critical of parents who started toilet training before the second birthday. I've read enough Freud to know what early toilet training does to the psyches of innocent children who were born to pee and poop their pants for the first two years.

I'm singing a different song since I began to look into cultural differences in child rearing. It is indeed possible to eliminate diapers in the first year. Some cultures never use diapers at all, but start at birth tuning in to elimination patterns. By training themselves and conditioning their babies, some parents can actually forego using diapers. Even dominant-culture Americans can do it. A letter to the editor in *The Compleat Mother* out of Minot, North Dakota (Spring 1997), describes how one mother managed to train her newborn. Of course, this wasn't an ordinary working mother in Big City, USA, but rather a person who lives in "an intentional community" in the deep country of Virginia.

After having only read anthropological studies about toilet training young babies, I was thrilled to read a first-hand account. And you know what? I believe it! Forget the label "bad child development" — let's open our minds and embrace diversity! We may not be able to do in the center just what every parent does at home, but we can at least try to understand and be respectful of differences.

The Down Side of Diversity: Inevitable Conflict

One thing I've had to do in order to embrace diversity is to embrace the conflict that comes along with differences. If we're truly celebrating diversity, we will often be walking a fine line between being culturally responsive and standing firm on what we believe is best for children. And we'll make mistakes.

We have to decide that we'll do the best we can and forgive ourselves for not being perfect. There is no easy method to decide ahead of time which thing we do will have a drastic effect on a particular child or family. We just have to be sensitive, responsive, and still be who we are.

I used to worry a lot about the mistakes I might make that would affect young lives for ever. I know better now. It's not likely to be a single action on the part of an adult that ruins lives. It's a whole set of circumstances and repeating patterns, coupled with the individual's makeup that make the difference between healthy outcomes and less healthy ones. It's hard to tell during the child care day which of the millions of things we can do will truly matter in the long run. We do the best we can. And when things go wrong, we have to try not to blame ourselves or others.

Staff Turnover Rate

None of us single-handedly can change the fact of high staff turnover, yet we have to work at it. Without consistency in staff, how can children ever build a feeling of security? This is part of the real world of child care that we cannot continue to sit back and accept. It's not good for children to have a constant parade of teachers coming and going in their programs.

The staff turnover rate affects quality and how teachers feel about the program! I wonder how many teachers feel so good about the program where they work that they would be or are happy to have their own children there. Some are, I know. But every time I hear a teacher or caregiver say, "I wouldn't want my child in this program," I look around at the children who are there and feel sad.

We're a field with many profoundly difficult issues. But we're a field with a lot of dedicated caring people who are working to make things better. People who can manage to see the positive side of the negatives seem to regularly find new energy to figure out what to do to make child care better. Jim is one of those people. I like to think that I am, too.

SEEING CHILDREN:
A QUESTION OF PERSPECTIVE

My daughter, Emma, lives life as an opera. Since birth, she has attacked life with no-holds-barred pleasure, incapable of understatement. She overwhelms spaces with her large and dynamic physical presence and her enthusiastic loudness, seizing the life around her — perpetually moving, gobbling up experience as well as food and drink. The tribal delights of childhood fuel her day.

Love relationships go through phases of congruence. When Emma was nine, I looked at this nine year old Bette Midler daughter of mine and craved the polite-mannered, anorexic delicacy of some of her friends. Our life together seemed like a series of short, dispiriting skirmishes as we navigated hurried days and small spaces. Emma was definitely situationally disadvantaged, sharing small living space with a father who worked and traveled too much. I wanted a quieter, and perhaps more socially acceptable, way of being. The relationship slowly worsened as I lost sight of all those qualities I loved in her. We were out of synch; it was not a happy time for either of us.

I happened to be listening to an artist, Red Grooms, talking about his childhood. He creates delightful, energetic paintings and walk-in tableaus (you become part of a cartoon-like scene) and is a large bear of a man. He described

himself as a child much like Emma, and he used the term ebullient, bubbling over with energy, enthusiasm.

As that year's up and down life with Emma went on, I clung to that term. When I looked at her and saw a huge, clumsy, loud, grabbing child and began to cringe, I thought "my wonderful *ebullient* daughter — such a strong life force." And I soon began to really **see** her again, as a complete person. I relaxed and became more accepting; and, as I relaxed, she relaxed (although with Emma, relaxing still involved a good deal of high drama and chaos).

Coming upon a **positive label** for Emma saved my relationship with her that year. It changed my perspective, which badly needed changing.

Positive labeling is a useful device when we are locked into negative interactions with others. It is an attempt to try to change our perspective by helping us see beyond the behavior that is disturbing to us or driving us crazy to the positive human qualities that underlie that behavior. Emma's Rabelaisian charm was always apparent to my friends and family, even when it was wearing thin on those of us who had to live with her.

Having to search for positive labels forces us to really see the children we work with. In Marlon's case, his energy, social curiosity, and charm were enormous assets, except when driven by his insecurity and occasional boredom:

"Marlon, that's the last straw," I yelled. Actually, more than breaking the camel's back, Marlon had bludgeoned the camel senseless with a ton of straw by creating an aquarium tidal wave as he *accidentally* dropped the guinea pig in the aquarium. Not a good day for Marlon, not a good day for me, and not a good day for Adolpho, the diving guinea pig.

"I don't know, Marlon," I said later, trying to allow the humor of the situation to overcome my urge to heave him through the door, "you just have a certain *Je ne sais quoi*." "I got what?" he asked, alert to the fact he might not have to take his record-breaking fourteenth time out of the day. "*Je ne sais quoi* — it's an expression from France and means *I don't know what*, a certain hard to describe quality."

From that time on, Marlon held on to his label with pride. "What's that I got? Jenny what?" He had *Je ne sais quoi* and none of the other kids did. Not Chad who was always good, and Paul who had a father, and Willy who always had little cars to play with. He didn't have much, but he had *Je ne sais quoi*.

His label was important to me as well as I struggled with the havoc this beautiful, undisciplined, wild child could bring forth in my classroom.

As a teacher, there were many other children:

May Her — passive, withdrawn, and silent at four. Sadness clung to her like a shadow, and soon she was defined almost entirely by her sorrow and suffering. I tried to think of her less as a victim and more as *careful* — choosing carefully the level of interaction she would risk.

There was seven year old Joey, who seemed to delight in tormenting other children. Joey's problem was that he was a jerk (at child care). When he got together with Shane, it was *jerks on parade* and senseless carnage would soon follow. He became the *social scientist* as we worked on developing his embryonic pro-social skills.

Angela was almost four, but always quick to dissolve into a whining, clinging, contrary toddler. She was unpopular with children and adults. *Sensitive* was the only term that seemed to be positive enough to describe her.

And now my seven year old step-daughter and I have left a four year plateau of smooth sailing and seem to be sliding toward more conflict. Annie is a bright, cautious child. She is also funny with a sly, off-the-wall sense of humor.

Unlike Emma, who plunges into any situation without a lot of thought, Annie holds back until she is assured of safety. She watches the news, carefully and seriously, and then catalogues the risks — earthquakes, war, asbestos, abduction, bankruptcy, accidents, cholesterol; and each day

the world becomes a more dangerous place. She observes social situations closely. She is not unhappy or insecure (or serious for that matter — she has a delightful sense of humor), nor is she a coward or cry baby, just fundamentally cautious, often infuriatingly cautious.

Here is a child who would prefer to do her own criminal records check on her school bus driver, conduct a soil test of a picnic area, and wait to cross a busy street until there is no car in a five mile radius. Annie can be difficult to be with when she is holding back, especially for a type-A personality like me. It is easy to view her as a *baby*, a *wimp*, a *scaredy-cat* as the approach-avoidance pull of a new experience often results in indecision and sometimes panic.

What word can I hold on to as I struggle with helping this child into an active exploration of childhood possibilities? George Bush has given *prudent* an even more prissy connotation than the word normally carries. *Thoughtful* is accurate but not quite specific enough. *Cautious* is not positive enough. *Mindful* seems to most clearly describe the underpinnings of her caution.

It is not easy to step back and think about what we are doing, particularly aswirl in the churning waters of classroom or family life. Positive labeling is perhaps necessary for me more than others because I am a labeler, and perhaps because I am given to high expectations. Alas, what labels do others apply to me?

A Question of Perspective: Situationally Disadvantaged

Coping with day-to-day life is often a matter of developing a sense of perspective. Working with children and families is stressful, *being* a child and a member of a family is stressful. It is easy to get swept away and lose our balance as we struggle with the slings and arrows of outrageous fortune, especially the outrageous fortune seemingly brought on by the people around us.

In "Seeing Children: A Question of Perspective" (page 117), the concept of *positive labeling* was discussed as a coping strategy for use with children we were struggling with. This article addresses another concept that might alter our perspective and help us see others in a more positive light, helping us to think through difficult situations.

SITUATIONALLY DISADVANTAGED

I sat around the breakfast table of this sturdy farm family where I would spend the next few days. We talked of fences to be mended, calves to birth, carburetors to rebuild. I, the urban consultant, post-modern man, was polite and charming and absolutely useless. What I knew and knew how to do was of little value here. My daily rhythms had no correspondence with this sunup to sundown physical life. My cheery cynical wit brought no smiles. I generally felt incompetent, bored amidst the hard work others were doing, and increasingly reclusive. Inwardly I was getting a little surly, my smile growing a little frozen. This was not a situation I was quick to treasure. Over time, I became more comfortable as I adapted to the situation. But the me they saw was not the me I felt the best about.

Many children in child care are *situationally disadvantaged* in analogous situations. Just like me on the farm, the situation they find themselves in puts a heavy burden on them to use all their personal resources to adapt. They are *situationally challenged* — their energy, patience, flexibility, and reservoirs of good will are put to the test. Certainly new situations that require stretching may be necessary, and actually *good for us*, in that they broaden our experience. Growing is learning how to handle an increasingly widening world. But the immediate result is that we are not at our best.

MAMA, DON'T LET YOUR BABIES GROW UP TO BE TODDLERS

Thirteen toddlers sit at tables smearing paste on paper bunnies; cotton puff tails are ready to be attached. Two children are happily sucking on the paste brush, another is beginning to resemble Colonel

Sanders as cotton clings to her chin. The harried teachers are not amused.

Nineteen month old Jordan arrives home from child care at 5:30. He's whiny, negative, and tired. He fusses, eats, fusses, and crashes by 7:00. His disappointed parents hope they might have the delightful toddler they know and love back with them on the weekend.

Toddlers are clearly the most situationally challenged in child care. Unfortunately able to periodically pass as younger, ersatz preschoolers, they are often treated as such. Made to fit into structured schedules and activities and expected to conform to group life, they use up much of their daily quota of energy. Often, as in Jordan's case, they have little in their reservoir of good will left for the people whom they must spend the rest of their lives with — their parents. It is developmentally appropriate for toddlers to be anarchists with a blind herd instinct, alternately contrary and eager to please. They are also relentlessly mobile, quick to climb, dump, and explore the world in an often clumsy fashion. In most child care programs, these behaviors are *situationally inappropriate.*

How Much of This Do I Have to Take, Oh Lord?

Eight year old Jacob is bored, tired of the program he has spent most of his life in, tired of the block corner, tired of clean-up time, tired of jigsaw puzzles, tired of games. If he were home, he could work on his models, meet with his secret club, or make some money raking his neighbor's lawn.

School-age children are the other group in child care subject to benign neglect. The opposite of toddlers, they are often treated as if they are old preschoolers, with little allowance for their interests in a complex social life of teams, clubs, and cliques

— or projects that span days and weeks. Escaping from the classroom or bus, and thrust into a limited or structured situation, some school-age children will present less than their best side.

Hey, What About Me?

It's 1:40 pm and, as usual, Allison can't sleep. What to do — considering she can't get up until 2:30; and in the last hour she has already explored her cot, her clothes, and each nook and cranny of her four year old body? What about trying to sneak over and wake up James?

Group settings inevitably force individuals to accommodate to the group. The less flexibility in space, time, and expectations, the more accommodation required. It may be necessary, but nevertheless unreasonable. If the situation cannot be changed, at the least we should recognize the child's difficulties in coping as legitimate.

Doing the Best You Can

Adults are situationally disadvantaged in child care as well: toddler teachers trying to provide a developmentally appropriate program at 1 to 7 ratios, or the teachers coping with non-nappers with neither the space nor staff for awake children. It is also hard to maintain a thoughtful perspective on daily life without time off the floor and time to talk to co-workers.

Parents (the other adults in child care) who take their responsibility for their child's care seriously and assertively seek personalized care from a program unable to provide it are equally disadvantaged. In that situation, they are often viewed not as conscientious but as demanding.

While outside of our relationship with parents, we might imagine the

ideal parent as one fiercely protective and conscientious about his or her child. The ideal parent in our minds is too often one who is willing to back down quickly when we counter with our assertion of our needs.

Judge Not, Lest Ye . . .

Situationally disadvantaged is a particularly useful term for teachers and other professionals because it is a constant reminder of the influence of the situation on behavior. To look at an adult or child as situationally disadvantaged *does not* remove responsibility for one's actions or excuse behavior; but it puts it in perspective as we struggle with the consequences. At the least, it may help us be less judgmental about the behavior that confronts us. Hopefully, it also focuses attention on what we may be able to change in order to remove the often developmentally inappropriate pressure on the child.

It is interesting to note that in child care and education we usually implicitly recognize situational effects even while we are locating causality elsewhere. For instance, when a child is biting, our discussion often puts the weight of the problem on the child or that too frequently used, convenient, root of all evil — *problems at home.* Yet when we actually try to attack the problem, we don't change the child as much as tinker with the situation, addressing the experience of the child in the environment, relaxing the schedule, improving a crowded situation, or reducing stimulation.

The more perspective we have, the less likely we are to lapse into the debilitating and self-defeating self-righteousness that too often leads to power struggles with the children and parents we are committed to serving.

PILLARS OF SECURITY — PART 1

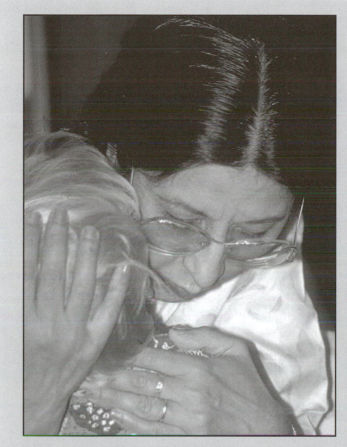

Is there anything more basic than feeling secure: feeling that I am all right, right here, right now? If we can't safely relax, feel *at home* where we are, how can we work? How can we learn?

We feel secure in places where we know the life that happens there. The world is safe, predictable, manageable; we know we can fit into that world, as ourselves. We will be accepted by the people we encounter. When we travel, we can relax when we know what is in store for us or when we have confidence that our life experience gives us the skills to cope with whatever will come our way, or when we are with trusted others.

Young children are perpetual tourists without much life experience, truly strangers in a strange land. They are developing their minds and bodies at such a rate that they are literally new people with each sunrise. Their backlog of life experience is so slight that each day, each new place, each *old* place brings surprises. Their courage rises and falls like the tides.

If child care centers are *places to live*, given all the business of living that takes place in the course of ten hour days, and if they are *places for childhoods*, given that many children will spend much of their childhoods in child care settings,

then the issue of feeling secure takes on the same level of importance that it does in homes. Children need to feel at home. When we are anchored at home, we are at a place where we know we are safe, accepted, and allowed to be ourselves. We can open ourselves up to the sting and caress of new experience.

FOUR PILLARS OF SECURITY

It is no small task for child care centers to be secure places for children, places where they feel at home. Four key program elements underlie the security a child experiences in child care.

■ *People*

For most of us, the most insecure feeling of all is feeling alone — no hand to hold, no one to look up to, no arms to hold us when we stumble. The second most insecure feeling is to feel surrounded by strangers who are clearly important to our experience but unpredictable.

Imagine changing parents every year, or every few months — or brothers and sisters or friends. Turnover of staff and children wreaks havoc on feeling secure. Familiar, trusted faces can make most places manageable. Without them, we are on guard, ready to retreat.

Yet turnover of staff and children is to one degree or another a reality that all programs face. The more

Home is where when you go there,

they have to take you in.

— Robert Frost

turnover, the more importance the other pillars of security assume. We have entered the Blanche Dubois era of child care: our children increasingly depend on the kindness of strangers. For the children, these people are large and powerful, arbiters of their fortune, regulators of their possibilities.

■ Place

In *our* living places, we can relax. We take comfort in the familiar order, the sounds and sights and smells. We know our way around and how things work. There are few surprises. Our treasured things are there to reassure us, as are our memories.

A new place makes demands on our awareness. After a time, our steps are sure and we more fully explore the new territory.

In *our* places, we have the freedom to find or create sanctuaries and places to pause. Where do we adults go when the world falls apart? Some of us head for the bedroom, others for the bottle, still others for the refrigerator door. Perhaps an amniotic soak in the bathtub provides respite from an indifferent world. We find security in soft, private places when we are feeling unimportant, tired, unhappy, or out of control.

Whose places are child care centers? Children need a soft, responsive, physical environment. The moments alone *spaced out* on a swing, rocking in a chair or a rocking horse, or kneading dough allow children to recharge. Comfortable places provide the security for fledgling disciplined scholars to tackle the demands of

sustained concentration. They mask and mute the necessary efficiency and order of institutional life. A physical environment that yields (yielding to the pace, interests, and sensibilities of the group) compensates somewhat for the imposing demands group living requires of individuals.

■ Routine

We all need routine to give shape to the chaos of life: patterns of actions and expectations, welded to the clock or the rhythms of inner needs or the outer world. Routine in group living prevents anarchy and conflict; it is what *we* do, over and over until it becomes part of *us*.

Routine reassures each of us and stabilizes groups — the regular meal, the prompt dry diaper, the inevitability of sleep. In early childhood settings, basic time blocks and the day's rhythm are defined by the tasks of living: eating, diapering and toileting, sleeping, and housekeeping; staffing schedules and breaks; and the physical space, particularly the amount of scheduled shared space. Routine marries the tasks and times.

The structuring of time has an enormous impact on how we feel — Lucille Ball trying to keep up with an assembly line that speeds up on the one hand and Vladimir and Estragon waiting for Godot with time an open and terrifying expanse on the other testify to this. Institutions of social control use the structure of time to discipline, torture, or drive people mad by assuming absolute power over the rhythms of living and applying varying amounts of ran-

domness amidst a rigid order. Yet a too casual approach to the clock or control of our own time and establishing our own patterns can be at once exhilarating and scary.

■ Ritual

Our individual lives are ordered and made meaningful with daily rites: the first cup of coffee, goodbye kisses, how we enter sleep, the routes taken to work or school. Social and group life has its own rites: from the Walton's "goodnights" and holiday ceremonies to pregame warmups and pledges of allegiance. Ritual joins routine and the physical order as the secure skeleton that holds individuals and groups together in those times of stress, against the uncertainties of staff and children who come and go — and change from mood to mood — day to day.

Adults have rites to help live their lives, of beginnings — weddings, baptisms, housewarmings, dedications; of renewal — birthdays, anniversaries, holidays; of endings — funerals, graduations; and of passage — firsts (kiss, job, car, sex, child), coping with aging, responsibility, and loss. These rites are marked by symbolic acts that have great meaning and emotional power —exchanges of words and rings or paper, breaking glasses, dances, chants and songs, and, very often, the taking in to one's body of food or drink.

Ritual serves the same purpose in children's programs. Group daily rites — i.e., sharing the same song and the same story day after day — reassure against the unknown void. Children under age three will listen to *Good Night Moon* by Margaret Wise Brown with delight every rest time. There are acknowledged rites of passage — children give up diapers, bottles, and naps, or leave for school. Individual rituals between children and caregivers can become pinions of security — a special touch, a shared joke, any regular shared exchange. Groups might experiment — rites of destruction perhaps.

Pillars of Security: Making Child Care Centers Secure Places — part 2

If people, place, routine, and ritual provide the basis of security for each child, how do centers use this understanding to make child care centers more secure places?

■ People

It's easier to pronounce from on high "reduce staff turnover" than to achieve it. But, sadly, some turnover is a given and programs can offset its worst effects.

When a caregiver leaves, children face the loss of a familiar, perhaps loved, person. Early childhood professionals have long understood this is a time of trial for children and teachers.

But a replacement is found and now, at least as long as he remains, classroom life returns to normal. Only it's a new normality — new person with new language (verbal and non-verbal), new looks and interests and warning signs, new favorites.

And what does this stranger do? He begins to alter the world as they know it. He begins to make the classroom his — a new room arrangement and perhaps new spaces, slightly altered routines and new rules. The schedule may change — story before nap, snack a little later, playground a little earlier. Very shifty sands under very unsteady little feet.

It doesn't have to be that way, if there is an expectation that teachers assess the environmental impact of their plans for change on the children's sense of security and adjust the extent and pace of change accordingly. A program rich with rituals and low staff turnover may sustain quite a bit of change in the physical environment when a new teacher arrives, provided the rituals remain. A high staff (or child) turnover program may need all the rituals and environmental predictability it can muster and may need to delay change for quite a while. The following also may help programs:

- **Three-staff groups.** They may allow for more human stability, both in the sense of less chance all familiar faces will disappear and of maintaining continuity of collective intelligence and practices. The resulting larger group size can be offset by environmental and program changes.

- **Extended-age groupings.** This reduces the transitions to different teachers.

- **A feeling of *centerness*.** Fostering a sense of connectedness between all staff and children can overlay and strengthen individual relationships.

- **Primary caregiver systems.** Systems that allow a child (and parents) a special adult but avoid too much ownership of child — the hen and chick model — that collapses with turnover.

■ *Place*

In the absence of beloved people, places and objects take on even greater significance.

- **Places of delight and wonder.** We become attached to spaces that charm, delight, or move us. What brings this on? — a certain slant of light, an intriguing staircase, an alcove, or the feel of smooth wood or unexpected beauty or forms. Children have, or can acquire, more taste than we expect. The ubiquitous murals of Disney or Sesame Street have limited staying power for many children.

- **Places to pause.** As Fred Osmon observed, these places often have a found quality and may not be obvious to adults. They convey a *sense* of privacy rather than total physical isolation.

Places to pause are not all the same. There is a distinction between enclosed spaces that allow a teacher to see in, enclosed spaces that allow children to see out, and spaces that may not be enclosed but have a

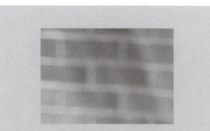

How does it feel?

How does it feel?

To be on your own

no direction home

a complete unknown

like a rolling stone.

— Bob Dylan
(Like A Rolling Stone)

defined sense of place and that allow lingering. Children need places to watch from, to hold back, to hide and seek things, and places to pause and reflect.

- **Child-created places.** Given the freedom and the necessity, *children invent the spaces they need*. They squeeze behind furniture, climb on whatever is available, seclude themselves under blankets, build forts or houses.

- **Personal treasures.** Loved things help, at least a little, to still troubled waters.

■ *Routine and Ritual*

Centers have to balance the stability that routine provides with the flexibility necessary to fit individual needs, both dimensions essential to security. "You see a lot by observing," noted Yogi Berra, pointing to the route to ensuring sensible routines and achieving that balance. Rituals tied to caring routines allow the routines themselves to bend — mealtimes for instance.

- **Individual rituals:** a kiss, hug, touch, joke, task, question, or exchange ("How's my pal today?").

- **Group rituals:** stories, songs, calendar, questions, chores, teacher's actions or responses (feigned surprise or anger, etc.).

Children, like adults, don't wear insecurity on their sleeves. Nearly invisible, it has to be uncovered in their hesitations and fears. Undetected, it collects and resides forever to some degree in the nerves and heart as anxiety and mistrust. Child care centers owe it to children to leave no stone unturned in making the center a secure place.

DIVERSITY AND CONFLICT: THE WHOLE WORLD WILL NEVER SING IN PERFECT HARMONY

C an there be diversity without conflict? I doubt it. Woodstock nation never came to pass. Little creatures of the forest haven't come together. We don't have many models of diversity functioning without conflict.

We don't like diversity in this country, but we like to believe that we do. We pretend a lot. We pretend that we don't have social classes. We pretend that racism is something of the past. We don't really want group homes for people with mental disabilities in our neighborhoods — or even group homes for adults with physical handicaps. Most religions are broken up into a lot of splinter groups. Even roommates don't get along well if they are too different.

Diversity, like many things that are good for us, usually isn't comfortable. The problem is not just in a failure to communicate or in ignorance, the common and convenient characterizations of the problem.

CHILD DEVELOPMENT STORIES

I was watching a little boy in a program in Chinatown who was about to conduct an experiment in the water table — "Can gerbils swim?": a follow up to his dramatic investigation — "Can gerbils fly?" A very patient teacher, at the end of her rope (not unlike the unfortunate gerbil), said, "If you do that, we are going to have to tell your grandfather." When I asked several early child educators what they thought of the story, there was agreement that this was bad child development. But why is it bad child development in a culture where disgracing your family actually means something, where grandfathers are important, where children have genuine respect for their grandfathers? Why is that bad child development to bring in the family context?

Another story. . . . There was a wonderful man working with babies in an infant program. While very gentle and quiet, one of the things he did a good deal of was active physical interaction with the babies, which they loved. He was cautioned that this was bad child development. Well, is it? Is the male caregiving style, which often is much more physically stimulating and less soothing than most female caregiving styles, bad child development? Or is it just different? Is the fussy caregiving of a 68 year old woman (or man) of various ethnicity bad child development?

Another story. . . . Visiting a child care program in the Arctic, I watched a five year old Eskimo boy working with an 80 year old man. They messed about with a motor for 45 minutes. The silence was deafening, hardly a word was exchanged. But the unspoken communication between the old man and the boy was incredible. Forty-five minutes with no words spoken, was that bad child development?

There has been an influx of Hmong people from Laos and Cambodia to Minnesota. A child care center with many Hmong children was trying to improve the infant and toddler program by hiring more Hmong staff. The center believed, as I do, in a language-rich environment and much personal one-to-one interaction between caregiver and baby. With Hmong staff, they got very little language and very little interaction with toddlers. Bad child development?

What would be normal in Hmong society? Mothers strap their babies to them, and this happened at the center. They have constant bodily interaction, but not the interaction we know. Toddlers are often the responsibility of older children, not just the mother. In the Hmong world, once a child stops nursing — when the mother turns her attention to the new baby — the older baby begins to be cared for by the four year old or the seven year old or the other older children.

It was hard for the Hmong caregivers to suddenly relate to children in a new way — our way — a way where children are divided into tight age groups and children have no responsibility for caring for siblings (often, ever!). A Hmong child care center would be organized very differently.

DIVERSITY ON THE JOB

What is good work behavior? Nearly all directors would argue that being on time is essential to good work behavior. If you are not on time, you are a real pain to many. It's hard to conceive of people who are not on time as responsible or good workers.

I worked with a very talented teacher, a young Indian man who had one problem — he was rarely on time. There are all sorts of jokes about minorities and their sense of time — black people time, Indian time. There is always some truth behind the usually derogatory joke. Cultures have different sets of time and the importance of "on time" varies. You only "miss the boat" if the boat leaves on a tight schedule. An alternative — the time the boat leaves is when everyone is there. In this case, the teacher also had public transportation to deal with, during Minnesota winters. No matter, his lateness was usually viewed as a character flaw. Staff who are often late fall prey to our cultural stereotypes — they are lazy, disorganized, they can't get it together.

But we (speaking for American middle-class white people, I guess) are very strange about time. If I — the director — was late, people assumed it was because I was so busy. We are willing to grant dispensation for some people because we assume it is due to factors beyond their control, socially redeeming factors at that. Not incidentally, many of these people are higher status or social class, and in more powerful positions. Interestingly, it is usually acceptable for these individuals to keep those lesser souls waiting, perhaps even for the supervisory conference to lecture on the importance of on-time behavior.

Another situation will come up in how the work is divided. Many of our models of good infant care include adults who are on the floor with kids. There are cultural and age differences here, and a lot of people aren't going to feel comfortable rolling on the floor with babies. If our model of good infant care is that everyone has to be on the floor with babies, we are not going to be able to tolerate as much diversity.

DIVERSITY WITHOUT CONFLICT?

No room for diversity. Where in the midst of diversity is there less conflict? One place is where there is no tolerance for any diversity in thought or behavior, where diversity really doesn't matter. You're not going to get much conflict from diversity on an assembly line. If there are clear behavioral prescriptions, diversity isn't an issue. Many child care centers manage this way. Everything is prescribed, routines are clear, and it works smoothly. Make it routine, and issues, however important, are less likely to come up.

Room for diversity. Allowing room for diversity is another and more preferable way to reduce conflict. If there is room for territories, and clear boundaries, then individuals can do their job their way. Public schools are often an example of this. The right of the teacher to close her door and do her own thing makes public schools, given the right administration, places where very talented, diverse individuals flourish side by side. The doors are closed. No one is going to see it. Yet room only makes a difference if there is enough autonomy so I can be myself in my space.

Diversity also requires times and places to retreat. A black teacher I worked with periodically would say, "I've just got to find a place where I can get away from white people." I understood entirely because usually as one of the one or two males around I needed the same thing — I needed to get away from women. For women who work in all male environments, the feeling is the same. We need to get away; we need to be with people that we feel we can be ourselves with.

Sufficient numbers. Another thing that supports diversity is sufficient numbers. I was director of a center for a long time that always had a lot of men, and I'm convinced that one of the reasons is that we crossed the critical threshold of numbers. There were three men, so it was much more comfortable for men to work there. Once you have more than one or two of any given minority — age, gender, race — the organization is under more pressure to accommodate. Numbers count.

Beyond Coping: Valuing Diversity

There are places, but not many, where diversity really works and greatly enriches the organization. Based on appreciation and understanding grounded in respect, these child care centers have a basic belief that good care and education comes in different forms — that what is good care is allowed to be arguable. There is a high tolerance for difference. In most organizations, the earnest proclamation of valuing differences is instantly contradicted by talking to those who are different.

For a person or a program, the key to understanding and respecting differences is having a good sense of who you are and knowing the boundaries of what you are. Not too many child care programs are that self-aware, and there is a reason for this. In child care, you have no time to talk, so you really don't talk about things that may lead to controversy. You don't thrash out what exactly you are, what you believe.

What are the boundaries of how much language you need to have in your program? If you really believe that classrooms have to be incredibly verbal, it's going to limit the kind of cultures you have in that classroom. If you believe that all children process information the same way or use the same social behavior, it's the same thing. Knowing who you are, being comfortable with that, and knowing the boundaries of your ideology and the program will reduce conflict.

What becomes a staff issue when you have diversity? The same things that become an issue when you don't have diversity. Who is in charge here? How can this person tell me what to do? What am I supposed to do, as opposed to this other person? A program that is going to have a diverse staff or treat parents with respect has to articulate what they expect from staff and parents. If they don't, there will be conflict with racial, ethnic, or gender overtones.

Good programs have to problem solve. They have or make the time and energy to do it. They discuss social issues, and they discuss the issues that come from diversity. I worked in a center that believed kids should get dirty and be little scientists — it had a wonderful adventure playground. Parents, particularly black parents, would say: "We don't want our kids going outside. We spend an hour and a half on their hair. Two minutes later they are covered with sand. We can't get that stuff out and we spend our whole evening cleaning it up. So we don't want our kids going outside."

For awhile, our earnest and empathic response was: "Gee, that is too bad. But this really is good for the children." Of course our knowing response implied, "You poor, ignorant person, valuing appearance over good child development." Conflict continued and we learned. Now the response to these sorts of issues is: "Okay, let's figure this out. Obviously it's important to you how your child looks. And you know it's very good for these children to have these sorts of experiences. Let's come up with a solution." The assumption is two legitimate points of view — let's work it out together. In this instance, the answer was shower caps for the kids.

The sad reality is that all many programs have time for is often the doing — not thinking, problem solving, growing. If things are going *well*, it means smoothly, comfortably — which means that the gerbil doesn't die dramatically after all and people do not fight. But it doesn't mean that children are not getting less than they deserve, that some are not lost in the cracks, that cultures are not being devalued and diminished, and that we are not losing all the wonderful ways that people are different.

Diversity is the spice of life. It also makes us sneeze a lot. If we believe in it, we have to take the time to think it through for our programs.

LIVING WITH DIVERSITY:
A MEMO TO
ALL PARENTS AND STAFF

Differences are not deficiencies. It is inevitable that some of us — parents and staff — have trouble accepting this. And truthfully, probably all of us at times struggle with complete acceptance. The children, however, rarely have trouble because they have no expectation that we are all the same. But some adults are uncomfortable with male caregiving, or with care that reflects differences in culture or class, or language differences. Often we then characterize the issue as simply *their* competence, not any limitation in our incomplete understanding of differences or our own struggle for tolerance. Competence is defined by *our* terms and reflects the style and practices we are familiar with and prefer.

Diversity is important to our program. We believe strongly in having a multiage, multicultural, female, and male staff from a variety of ethnic backgrounds with a range of experience and training. We also enjoy serving families from all economic, ethnic, and cultural groups.

Understanding diversity means recognizing and accepting that people are not the same and that quality care comes in different forms. Individuals' caregiving styles are different, male and female styles are different, cultural groups have different styles.

A child care center is different from in-home care by a nanny, relative, or family child care provider. You have to put your trust in the whole center, not just the person who happens to be your child's caregiver. Caregivers come and go: on vacation, on leave, on to other things.

Trusting the center means trusting the center leadership to hire the best people available and to be competent and conscientious supervisors. While staff come to us with a variety of training and experience, *everyone employed at our center meets the center's high standards.* When we have substitutes or new staff with less training and experience, they work under close supervision.

This letter was sent to parents and staff annually at a center where diversity was ever present and can be adapted for use in other programs.

All staff have different strengths and weaknesses, some that parents are aware of, some that they are not. Staff have different personalities. Because we are all different, not all staff will be equally loved by all parents (and vice versa). *But **all** children will receive excellent care and education; the entire center is responsible for seeing to that.*

The diversity of our staff is an inherent aspect of our quality. It extends the world available to the children and adds both breadth and depth to the perspective of the staff. That diversity also brings occasional confusion and awkwardness, and friction is not unexpected — learning and growth rarely flourish in teflon smooth environments.

When a parent or a staff member has a concern about a staff member, we take it very seriously. We carefully check out the concern through observation, discussion with co-workers, and other parents. When the concern is whether a particular teacher characteristic compromises program quality (such as limited English fluency, which is not harmful; or questionable expectations of a child, which may be a cause for concerns), we also research the issue with other child development authorities.

Sometimes the concern is with a behavior easily correctable through simple awareness, training, or, occasionally, a timely restful vacation. In other cases, the real concern is with the style, language skills, or person-ality of the caregiver, although not always couched to us in that way. It is no accident that more concerns surface around staff from other cultures or ethnic groups or male staff. In other words, the concern is most often about caregiving different than the white, middle-class, female norm.

In the best of programs, *adults have to grow* as the children grow: we come to terms with some of our own stereotypes and narrow thinking. We probably all have these, whether we are willing to admit it or not.

Our center is what it is: a multi-cultural program committed to excellence, with staff and families from all sorts of backgrounds. That is precisely what we want to be.

CHILD CARE AND EARLY EDUCATION: NO "JUST" ABOUT IT

"We are not just day care," sniffed the director to the prospective parent. *"Can you not see by our sign that we are **a child development program, a preschool**?"*

*"We are, of course, **not child care**,"* huffed the Head Start administrator. *"We have a higher calling. We are Head Start. We teach the children."*

*"We are an all -day Montessori program, **not child care**,"* firmly explained the Montessori teacher.

In the February 1989 issue of *Child Care Information Exchange*, I wrote a column on the unfortunate distinction between child care and early education ("Is Everybody Singing Our Song? Child Care and Early Education"). It was written in those heady days when early education and child care was finally on the national agenda and there was talk of actually increasing funding.

Times change and the 90s have largely been a time of limited funding. This is changing with welfare reform. But whether a period of feast or famine, a strong message on the ill-used distinction between child care and early education is still appropriate.

The "just day care" label is still alive as an epithet to be applied to other programs. The two important studies that brought into the open the poor quality of many existing child care centers and homes is already fueling the increased use of "child care" as a negative label (see "Cost, Quality, and Child Outcomes in Child Care Centers: Key Findings and Recommendations (*Young Children*, May 1995) and "The Study of Family Child Care and Relative Care — Key Findings and Policy Recommendations" (*Young Children*, November 1994).

ALL CHILD CARE IS EDUCATION

Is there such a thing as *"just day care"* or *"just child care"*? Perhaps in result, but rarely in design — what center, home, or preschool (or elementary school) sets out to be purely custodial care? Isn't a better term for "just day care" or "custodial care" simply "lousy education"? All child care is educational; children learn something in every setting whether we acknowledge it or not, learning that has implications for future learning. Is it all good education? No, some is actually quite awful.

Child care settings are early education settings often *not adequately funded* to provide quality education — or care. One can look at the marginal quality of much of current child care and make a distinction between child care and *more* educational programs, but that doesn't alter the fundamentally educational nature of child care. Poor under-funded learning environments provide poor educational preparation and, most often, poor care as well.

The program name or sponsor is no sure indicator of educational value. Good and bad care and education take place in "child development centers," "day care homes," "academies," "Head Start," "nursery schools," "learning centers," and "Montessori programs." (NAEYC accreditation has considerable value as a national standard because it makes no distinction between child care programs and "educational" programs. It is in the interest of all child care providers to support the concept and work towards accreditation.)

Educational Quality Depends on Funding and Training

What is the difference between a quality early education setting and a mediocre one? Not the length of the day, the sponsor, or the name. Most often, it is the funding.

Quality education and care is not likely with the deadly combination of $6 an hour teachers, high turnover, minimum staff-child ratios, minimum space and equipment, and minimum training of staff. This is true whether under the auspices of a school system, a corporation, a social service agency, or a private provider — non profit or for profit. Provide the funding for trained and committed professionals, support staff and services, and decent equipment, materials, and facilities, and quality early education can and does happen in a range of settings.

Child care providers are essentially asked to build the moral equivalent of shanty towns. Visit the thrown together housing by the desperately poor on the outskirts of many third world cities (and in some U.S. cities) and you're struck by the wonderful ingenuity and sheer effort that is possible when men or women strive to meet basic needs. You are left with

---

> ## MAMA LOVE
>
> Cornelia Anne Washington Breedlove was known by all as Mama Love. Her husband, Marcus Aurealius Breedlove, was also known throughout the neighborhood as Mr. Mama Love. They took care of kids. They assumed that they were just day care — actually even worse, *baby-sitting*.
>
> "I just loved those children," she said, "and tried to raise them right." Walk into her home and the children would be sorting clothes by item, color, and size; or making bread or muffins; or helping with the "little ones," all the time chatting with her about family and life — "telling my stories or listening to theirs," she said.
>
> Children might be out in the garden with Mr. Mama Love, planting tulips, carefully arranged by time of budding, color, and height; or in his garage "helping" him fix the car by handing him tools. When I tried to help and hand Mr. Mama Love a wrench, five year old Darius couldn't contain his condescending smirk while letting me know I was reaching for the wrong wrench — he needed a metric wrench.
>
> If this was *just day care*, I would have loved it for my kid. Yes, as the study makes sadly evident, there is a lot of miserable family child care. But when it is good, it can reach heights of individualized care and education many centers cannot reach.

---

great admiration for the builders. They have created a place to live. But not a very good place. Shanties, after all, leak or blow away, and their inhabitants alternately broil and freeze.

And that is what we often are asked to do in child care, construct shanties — out of the inexpensive staff we can find and keep, the found and low-cost purchased spaces and materials that we can afford, and all the energy, love, and commitment we can muster. Even the better programs with newer facades, with private or public support, and glossy brochures are never far from the minimums.

It isn't all funding, however. What is quite astounding is not the number of poor quality programs but that there are so many that are not mediocre. It is a tribute to how terrifically resourceful and committed child care providers are in crafting programs.

Child Care and Society

There are three vehicles for early education and child care in this society:

- children cared for in their own homes through parents and home-based programs;

- part-day programs such as Head Start, nursery schools, and early childhood programs in the schools and other agencies; and

- full- and extended-day programs serving parents who are working or in training.

Advocacy efforts and any public or private support for early education should begin with a commitment to acknowledging the fundamental educational nature of child care programs. As a basic premise, children should receive early education through the vehicle appropriate for their families.

The Price of Division

The artificial devaluation of child care hurts children and families — both because it keeps child care down and because it results in a fractious "system." Millions of at-risk children attend all day child care. Attempting to serve them through separate early intervention programs or preschool education programs outside of child care has two consequences.

One is that the thousands of children in child care because of parent need simply will not have real opportunities to take advantage of the intervention programs.

The other alternative is that children attend two early childhood programs: one for a few hours a day, well funded and equipped, called "early intervention" or "preschool education," the other struggling with all the minimums and called "child care." ("Wrap around care" is a term already in use to describe programs that wrap around Head Start, nursery school, or kindergarten.) The programs funded for "early intervention" or "early education" are inevitably better staffed; they pay better salaries than child care programs, thus drawing talented staff from child care.

The result of an artificial two track — child care over here, education over there — system is the needless child

---

"DAY CARE"

I think it's somewhat unfortunate that the term *day care* has become politically incorrect ("I don't take care of days," the advocate huffed.) In designing programs and viewing the child's experience, the most significant distinction is between all-day and part-day care. While it is, of course, a challenge to provide good early childhood education, it has always seemed to me that the great challenge is to provide good *care* over a long day to a child in a group setting — care that is actually personal, individual, and responsive, in a setting that feels like a good place to be a kid. Day care was a useful shorthand for "all day care" and good day care, inherently to be good, had to include good early childhood education.

---

and family stress of complex schedules, transitions, and transportation; ultimately, the child will spend the bulk of the day in a child care environment barely able to recruit any staff at all. What kind of a day will a young child have — filled with transitions and busing and many different adults from two programs, one of which has high turnover? What kind of parent involvement and parent empowerment takes place if two programs ask for their trust and precious time?

Marissa is a beautiful, shy, three year old with slight physical and language delays. She attends a good child care program and is eligible for two intervention programs — a Head Start type intervention preschool in the morning and a program for children with special needs in the afternoon. Her mother gets Marissa up at 5:30 AM and uses public transportation to get her to the child care center.

Marissa arrives at the center at 7:00 and gets on a van to the educational program at 9:00. Greeted at the preschool by two ex-child care teachers now making $2 an hour more and working with a 1:7 staff child ratio, Marissa spends the morning in developmentally appropriate play, precisely what she would be doing in her child care center with less trained staff making $2 an hour less.

She arrives back at the center, presumably enriched, demonstrably exhausted. After staff help her gulp down food with no time for self-help or conversation, Marissa is bussed to a developmental activity program for some one-to-one with a special education teacher working on motor skills in self-help care and language.

Arriving back at the center, half asleep and disoriented for the rest of the day, she is for the most part allowed to finish the day at her own pace, unlike the more inflexible schedule at her previous child care center. Her mother arrives at 5:00 PM, after ten and a half hours of work and public transportation, to hear about the parent/child program activity night at the center, which begins at 7:00. The teachers really hope she can make it. ("She needs it," one told me).

Marissa relates to seven different adults a day as teachers or therapists. Her harassed low-income mother has trouble finding the time to talk to the staff at the child care program without missing busses, let alone to staff at the other programs who she hardly knows. Some staff at all three programs see her failure to seek them out or come to conferences as a lack of motivation, which contributes to Marissa's problems.

The very sparse and erratic communication between the three programs is not perceived to be a problem of professional motivation or a contributing factor to Marissa's problems. They do not see that when Marissa's mom chooses to go home and give Marissa dinner, put her to bed, and not return to the parent meeting, it is a rational conscientious parental choice.

Each program does its piece of Marissa's life relatively well, confident of helping Marissa. The state is proud of its comprehensive services. No one is responsible for asking whether Marissa is having a good day if all the pieces are put together, nor, in fact, is it clear that Marissa's development is helped or hindered by the abundance.

There are many Marissas, not all are low income or with special needs. Some ride in nice cars and shuttle between enrichment programs instead of remedial programs.

A FINAL NOTE

Every time early child care educators or advocates play the "just child care" card to promote their own territory, they do harm and diminish the possibility for improving children's lives. Funding and support for early education, intervention, or enrichment for young children should build on the existing network of programs — helping programs to afford trained and talented staff, improve their ratios, and upgrade their facilities.

Amidst the Daily Sound and the Fury — What Is Important?

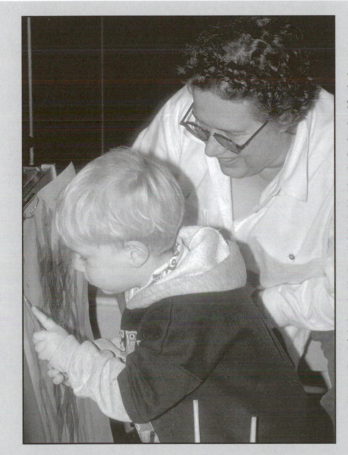

During the national obsession with the O. J. Simpson trial and the daily assault on our consciousness, I was struck by the observation made by one of the ubiquitous legal commentators. He was asked about the importance of the trial to American jurisprudence. Certainly an event that monopolized nearly everyone's attention for over a year (even those of us who claim to only watch public television) would have some great import for the future.

The commentator (nameless because I don't remember who he was) noted that "There are many things that are significant today but not really important, certainly in the long term. There are also many things that are important, but not significant; they don't receive the attention that they deserve."

The Simpson trial was obviously significant enough to cast its appalling shadow over the country for more than a year. But it probably was not particularly important for the legal system, or much else. On the other hand, there were probably a number of little known decisions that will have major effects on jurisprudence for years to come.

It might be useful if we apply a similar analysis to child care. It is hard in child care not to be resolutely focused on the present and confuse what is significant, but not particularly important, and what is important, but often not significant, in day-to-day child care life. What follows is wholly subjective (of course what writer isn't?) and reflects my concerns of the day — hopefully significant and important.

It Seemed Important at the Time

Jesse took her first steps today! And she's only 11 months old!

Did you hear Michael? He sang the whole alphabet.

Milestones are wonderfully significant to parents and caregivers — eagerly anticipated, anxiously analyzed when thought overdue, and joyfully heralded the moment they occur. But milestones usually aren't important in any developmental sense. Unless very early, or very delayed, they are simply a measure of how individuals develop normally at a different rate.

On the other hand, how parents and caregivers feel about the milestone can give them an importance that they do not deserve, particularly if the milestone is perceived to be late. The concern can result in parents and teachers constructing a lasting image of the child. In other words, the milestone is significant to all, but what is important are the actions of the center to place the milestone in perspective.

Did you hear Tyler's new word? Let me just tell you it involved a sex act that four year olds aren't supposed to discuss.

Bad words, sexual curiosity, and other social transgressions are often the cause célèbre of the moment in a preschool classroom; particularly when interest sweeps over an entire multiage preschool room. Swept along by a worldly five year old, a clueless three year old once asked a visiting dignitary, "Do you have a vagina, too?" The speechless visitor and the mortified director survived the very significant — but thankfully unimportant — moment.

Albert just bit Emily — again. I'm glad it wasn't me who had to talk to her parents.

Were you a biter as a toddler or a frequent snack for a two year old acquaintance? Does it matter now? Biting is horrific but rarely of lasting importance or an indication of something very important, again except where the adults give it unwarranted meaning.

How many plastic bags in her cubby today?

My daughter Emma was uneventfully toilet trained for six months. Then, when she was almost three, she became a rectal terrorist for no apparent reason, but the subject of endless speculation. These indiscretions occurred only at the child care center. As director of that same center and a well-known child development speaker on the one hand, and bewildered parent on the other — not immune to reflected shame — it was very significant to me and the staff who felt (or rather smelled) the consequences. Advice (and paternal instinct) was abundant and absolutely contradictory — take a relaxed stance and not make a big deal out of it, or pull out the B. F.

Skinner and apply behaviorist reinforcement. And then, she stopped.

Is toilet training of daily significance? Certainly. Of any importance in the larger scheme of things? No, unless it sets a pattern for the child's relationship with adults.

RESPONSIVE INTERACTION

My boyfriend, actually my ex-boyfriend (but he doesn't know that), gave me lots of attention, but it was usually when he was ready or able to give it. When I made the move, it usually went nowhere. That mattered to me.

Responsiveness is rarely significant except to the recipient — it's hard to keep track of who initiates it. However, it is important to young children, as well as lovers; and human parents are preprogrammed to respond. Watch a typical mother or father in the room with their infant. How many times does the parent not respond to the sounds or actions of the baby? Either with a word, a look, or a gesture, parents tend to be genetically driven to respond. In group care, even very good care, rarely do interactions reach the level of frequency or responsiveness witnessed at home. If you observe closely, often a good percentage of the interactions are initiated and ended by the caregiver. Yes, there is a wide variation between parents, and between programs; but the basic distinction holds.

It is quite natural for anyone on the floor with a group of children in the day-to-day world of child care to lose some perspective and sensitivity. It is an occupational, not individual, phenomena. A teacher almost inevitably gets somewhat desensitized to the reality of nuances of individual experience.

New research on infant cognitive development makes it critically clear that child care's best efforts need to improve. Neurological research using newly possible techniques shows that the experience of the

young child *shapes the physical structure of the brain.* The permanent "hard-wiring" of the brain grows out of the child's first experience interacting in the environment. The quality and the quantity of the child's interactions creates electrical activity that results in brain development.

It is important that we improve our responsiveness to individual children, the frequency of responsive interactions, and the quality of those interactions. Responsive care helps children to learn they can have an effect on other people, that overtures on their part will usually lead to predictable responses; and it encourages them to initiate more interactions.

FAMILY ISSUES

Children are not the only ones in the initial stages of lifelong ongoing development. Most families entering child care are also fairly new, working through the dramatic changes that occur when a couple becomes a threesome or with the advent of siblings. Just as with child development, often the important issues are complex and the issues that generate attention may overshadow more critical concerns.

At a meeting with child care staff, I asked them to list bad things that could happen to a child. Assuming I was talking about their island of the child's world, they listed:

- poor teacher/child relationship
- aggression
- lousy curriculum
- poor socialization/discipline
- too little/too much stimulation
- health/safety issues
- lousy play environment

The list reflects what is significant to them. When I told them not to think as center staff but to list bad things that could happen to the child that would affect his/her future, I got an entirely different list:

- poor parent/child relationship

- divorce

- unhappy family

- homelessness

- violence

- bad neighborhood/community

- poor sibling relationship

- poverty

- family struggles (disorganization, illness, death)

- bad schools

- illness

It was clear to everyone that to a great degree the future well-being of the child was bound up with the future of the family. Thinking along these lines led the staff to rethink what was important.

SEPARATION AND ATTACHMENT

Every day it's a struggle — Alicia clings to her mother, makes a scene about being left, and 20 minutes later is fine. Her mom doesn't help the situation, and sometimes even seems to need it to happen.

Daily separation stress is very significant; it can make or break the child's — or more likely the parent's — day. But daily separation is only important in the long run so far as the cumulated effects and the totality of the experience — the effect it has on the parent/child relationship or the parent's relationship to the program. From a caregiver's perspective, the less parent or child drama and angst the better. But painless separation is certainly not a sign of great attach-

ment. The significance of a child and parent conditioned to dispassionate separation may receive little notice but may have great importance, negative, for the parent/child relationship.

What should really matter to the program? That the parent attains the peace of mind necessary to work, that the child moves on, and that any efforts to change the situation focus on what is important to that individual parent/child/program relationship.

PARENT EMPOWERMENT

Sometimes I feel like they think I'm not a good parent: I work too hard, I'm not organized enough, my kid acts up and doesn't want to leave. The parent conference was mostly about how we could work together. I could work with them to help David adjust. It wasn't their fault, but I felt worse.

The program's relationship with parents is filled with significant interactions, but of what importance? Successful parents share some common qualities:

- **Attachment**: a profound sense of connectedness to my child.

- **A feeling of competence as a parent**: I can be a capable parent and manage the daily array of new and bewildering challenges that the developing child presents.

- **A sense of control**: I can manage the multitude of details and influences on my child's life and provide a decent life for my family.

- **A sense of hope**: life will have something good to offer for my child and family.

How does this translate to the parent relationship with the center? Important interactions or events are those that strengthen or undermine the parent sense of attachment, competence, control, or hope.

THE DAILY QUALITY OF LIFE

Years ago, as a two year old teacher, I had a wonderful child (and, no, they are not all wonderful) — Angelique from the island of Martinque. Angelique had an extraordinary grandmother whose role in the neighborhood was midwife, storyteller/historian, healer, and, many said, witch.

On Angelique's second birthday, the grandmother staged an elaborate party at the center, a mini-carnival riot of food, music, and life — including a live chicken. I'll never forget her incantation (performed on every one of Angelique's birthdays): "My Angelique, being two years old is a very special gift. You will only be two years old once in your life and we will have to make the year very special, très magnifique" — looking at me intently, clearly including me in that we.

Of course, none of the above discussion should imply that daily life is not in and of itself important. If we apply the analysis of significant versus important to quality of life issues, then our perspective changes. Biting is important because it can make everyone miserable, and call into question the parent's (and teacher's) sense of competence and control. An overly institutional concern with schedule, order, the absence of mess, and decorum will wash out the brilliant colors and rich textures of everyday life. Events that ruin days or weeks are important, as are those that give meaning or joy to the ordinary grind.

JUGGLING AND THE LIVES OF CHILDREN

Classifying events as significant or important is only a device for trying to develop a perspective on what truly matters. Child care practitioners are jugglers with lots of balls in the air. Some inevitably wobble or fall. As we juggle, it is important to remember which bounce and which are made of glass.

CHAPTER 6

ORGANIZATIONAL REALITY

WHAT THEY NEVER TAUGHT YOU IN
CHILD CARE ADMINISTRATION 101

by Roger Neugebauer

Without a doubt, the biggest reaction ever provoked by an article in *Child Care Information Exchange* occurred when we published Jim Greenman's article, "Jean's Pretty Good, Kind of Affordable, Child Development Center." The editor of a competing (no longer existing) magazine was so enraged by this article, or so enamored with his reaction to it, that he devoted an entire issue to attacking it.

Jim's article, as you can see for yourselves in this section (and then publish your own rebuttal), is a clever exposition of why it is so hard to provide quality, pay teachers well, and keep fees affordable all at the same time. The enraged editor portrayed Jim as a whining, witless, purveyor of doom and gloom (a portrayal that many of us secretly enjoyed, of course).

He contended that by simply adding some part-time children into the mix, and changing them at a higher hourly rate, any center with a director with half a brain could make a handsome profit. He presented pages of budgets and flow charts that looked ever so conclusive and all ended up with big positive numbers at the bottom.

While our enraged editor acted as if he had just discovered the secret of turning play dough into gold, the fact is that in the real world, offering a bunch of high-priced part-time slots will not meet the needs of most working parents or solve the budgetary woes of most centers. In the real world, the economics of child care are harsh. As was demonstrated in the 1994 *Cost, Quality and Child Outcomes in Child Care* study, in every community fee levels are influenced most by the cheapest, lowest quality centers in the market. Few centers succeed in charging fees significantly above the market rate which would enable them to pay teachers well and improve quality.

This is one of those *dirty little secrets of child care* that they don't like to teach you in Child Care Administration 101, otherwise known as organizational realities. In fact, there are a lot of organizational realities that they don't tell you about until after you've signed on for your first center director job. For example, try these on for size:

DUMPING ON THE DIRECTOR

Remember back in your past life when you were simply an employee? Remember how much fun it used to be to poke fun at your boss with your fellow employees around the water cooler? Your boss certainly made some dumb moves and never really appreciated your talents. Now imagine your current staff gathered around the water cooler making those same jokes about you — because that is exactly what is happening.

When you achieved the position of center director, you undoubtedly believed that you would be a kinder, gentler, more intelligent boss than those you had suffered under. You would inspire staff with your swift and sure decision making. You would treat them all with such respect and fairness that you would earn their unswerving loyalty.

In reality, your vision of your leadership was impossible. No matter how wise you are, no matter how hard you work, no matter how fair you try to be, you will never please all your staff all the time. You will make some decisions that will please some staff and displease others — if you try to reach a compromise decision that will please everyone, more likely you will disappoint everyone. You will make some decisions that staff see as stupid because they don't have all the facts. And, inevitably, you will make some decisions that are just plain stupid.

If your leadership style is friendly and folksy, some staff will see this as manipulative. If your style is cool and professional, some will see this as aloof and uncaring. If you bend over backwards to support a struggling staff member, some will view this as nurturing, others will see it as favoritism.

Your goal as a director should not be to get everybody to work hard because they love you. Your goal should be to build an organization that accomplishes great things for children and families. By crafting an organization that makes a difference, you will inspire top performance in your staff, whether they like you or not.

The Parent from Hell

When you work 40 hard hours a week at minuscule wages caring for a child who is dropped off and picked up by Calvin Klein parents in a Mercedes, it is incredibly easy to find fault with their parenting. As a result, staff room conversations often turn into gripe sessions about the parents.

As the director, it is critical that you put a stop to such parent bashing. If anti-parent attitudes are given free rein to proliferate, they will unconsciously but inevitably damage parent-teacher interactions and finally compromise quality of care. Therefore, a director must be relentless in helping teachers understand and respect the parent perspective.

On the other hand, not all parents are angels. Every center it seems has at least one parent who pushes all the wrong buttons. This may be a parent who constantly complains about the care his child is receiving (as if there is a conspiracy to pick on his child); spreads rumors among the parents about imagined problems at the center; frequently arrives late to pick up her child without warning; or constantly is demanding special considerations for his child.

None of the techniques you've learned about dealing with difficult people seem to work with the parent from hell; in fact, they only serve to encourage irritating behavior. The politically correct answer, propounded by armchair experts such as myself, is that the customer is always right. However, in real life, the politically incorrect, but organizationally ever-so-correct, action may be to show the exit to the incorrigible customer.

Feeling Competitive

People who are drawn to the early childhood field, even those who select the for profit arena, are motivated more by a desire to make a contribution to society than by hunger for monetary rewards. It often comes as a shock to these good-hearted souls when they find their organization engaged in competition. After all, competition is that nasty behavior that goes on among high tech ventures, fast food chains, beer companies, department stores, and car makers.

But even though we are all engaged in doing good, this does not exempt us from the forces of competition. One might expect a fair amount of competition to be going on between for profit centers seeking to attract the same fee-paying parents. However, in today's mixed child care market, non profit centers are increasingly dependent upon fee-paying parents for their survival and are forced to compete for their business. Probably the fiercest competition of all is being waged in communities where public schools, Head Start agencies, and private non profit centers are directing their services to the same finite populations of three and four year olds. Likewise, competition between private centers (both for and non profit) offering after-school services and after-school programs operated by the public schools is intense in many states.

It takes a while for a new director to appreciate that she is in what has become a highly competitive business in all sectors. Being able to move beyond ambivalent feelings about competition and to play the game in an honorable manner that does not sacrifice services for children and families is an important growth step for directors.

LIVING ON THE EDGE

When a child care center is working well, it is a thing of beauty. Children are engaged, teachers are inspired, parents are happy, and the director can sit back and bask in all this wonderfulness. However, in the back of every director's mind, even in the best of times, is the niggling recognition that just slightly behind all the magic are a gazillion disasters poised to strike.

Hitchcock's classic movie *High Anxiety* could just as well have been written about the life of a center director. Directors truly know what it is like living on the edge, because at any time there are so many things that can go wrong — a lead teacher could call in sick, the van could break down in the middle of its morning run, a teacher you fired could stir up a revolt among parents in her room, the licensing worker could drop in and perform an unannounced inspection when two of your four toilets are out of action, your insurance could be cancelled on short notice, an angry parent could falsely accuse a teacher of abusing his child, your best teacher could take a job with your competitor across the street, your landlord could raise the rent, and on and on.

An effective director will implement management practices that can minimize many of the risks of running a center. However, no one can foresee and forestall every conceivable disaster. In the long run, surviving as a director requires a high tolerance for anxiety and a high threshold for pain.

SO MUCH WOE

I am starting to sound like a woeful, witless, purveyor of doom and gloom myself. So I had best close with an encouraging word.

The sad truth is that there are a lot of organizational realities to confront as a center director that are not openly addressed in textbooks or at presentations at NAEYC conferences. While these challenges may be nasty, they are not insurmountable. Most directors survive them and go on to successful if not illustrious careers. What we don't want to happen is for new, highly motivated, talented directors to be surprised and prematurely burned out by these not-so-nice challenges. We need to encourage the open discussion of all problems so directors will understand them and be prepared to deal with them. And, finally, we need people like the writers in this volume to openly address the tough issues.

Do You Have a Credibility Gap?

You are going through the last agonizing steps of the process of firing Sally, the head teacher in the three year old room. Since Sally is one of the most popular members of the staff, you would like to go to the staff and defend yourself by saying, "This is why Sally was told to change or leave, for the good of the center. . . ." However, you know that professionally you cannot do this. Sally, on the other hand, is free to present her side of the case and in doing so is portraying you as quite the ogre.

This is an acid test of your credibility. If your credibility is high, staff members, parents, and board members will trust that you have valid reasons for firing Sally, even though these reasons are not readily apparent to them. If your credibly is low, staff members may line up behind Sally and revolt.

Who Needs Credibility?

A leader of any organization must have credibility in order to be effective. Credibility is really a short term for credible authority. Authority is the power to make decisions and gain compliance. A leader, at times, may achieve compliance through

means of coercion simply because of rank. Staff members will do what she commands out of fear of being disciplined or fired. But coercion is an ineffective means of achieving anything but grudging cooperation, and it doesn't work for long. In order for staff members to perform with dedication and enthusiasm, they

must respect the leader's expertise and judgment, and believe in her vision for the organization. A leader with credibility based on respect can inspire staff members to make the extra effort and to hang in there during times of crises.

While credibility is an important asset for a director in her day-to-day dealings with staff members, it becomes critical in high stress situations. The firing of Sally described above is an example of a situation where a director must have credibility to fall back on. Other examples abound:

• **The center in crisis.**

Last winter, the roof of the center I direct suddenly collapsed. If our center was to survive, we had to find a new site and resume operating as a quality program almost immediately. If this took more than two weeks, parents would have made other child care arrangements, and our enrollment would never recover.

With so much to accomplish in so little time, I found myself acting like a commander, running things like military maneuvers. There was barely time for explanation, let alone a democratic decision-making process. Staff members had to perform whether or not they liked what I said or how I said it. All too often I would find myself saying, "I know you came in last night to arrange your new space, but today you'll have to rearrange it because the fire marshal told me we have to do it this way." If ever there was a time when people were going to shoot me, it was then. Staff members had to believe that I knew what I was doing and trust that I had the best interests of the center at heart.

• **The new director.**

A director I know was required to demonstrate credibility the minute she became a director. She took over a center from a director who was well loved by staff members because she spent a great deal of time chatting and listening to staff concerns. One of the reasons she was able to do this was that she stuffed in her desk drawers all the bills and reports that were due and did nothing about them.

When the new director took over, she had to spend a great deal of time for the first three weeks untangling the books and files, and had dramatically less time for interacting with the staff than her dearly departed predecessor. She was in the uncomfortable position of not being able to explain why this was so without attacking the beloved ex-director. She had to develop enough instant credibility to carry her through these difficult three weeks.

• **The often-absent director.**

Many times a director may find it necessary to spend a great deal of time away from the center on a special project: hustling a grant, negotiating contracts with local employers, lobbying for a new child care bill, or fighting a proposed reduction of the center's state contract. The net effect of this effort may be to bring in thousands of dollars for the center, or to stave off financial ruin.

While staff members may appreciate this in a general sense, what may have a more immediate and negative impact on them is the fact that the director is not around to take care of problems at the center: fixing a broken piece of equipment, talking to a parent about being late, etc. If she does not have a reserve of credibility to draw on, these minor irritations may eventually generate a major crisis.

• **The growing center.**

A period of rapid expansion may strain relationships between a director and her staff. When a center is small, the director may be able to spend a lot of time working in the classroom and interacting with the staff. As the center expands, the director may be required to spend more and more time on administrative tasks, and less and less time with the staff. Time with the staff is not only reduced but also spread over a large number of people.

This may depress staff members — some because they become aware that their distance from the throne has increased and others because they don't get personal time with a person they like. They may come to see this change not as an institutional process but as a personal rejection. It may feel like the director is intentionally withholding time from them. In this situation, unless the organizational role changes are made explicit, the director will lose credibility because she will be judged based on her performance in the now obsolete role.

OBSTACLES TO BUILDING CREDIBILITY

One mistake directors often make is to assume that because we are wonderful people, because we work very hard, and because we are doing a great job, this will automatically translate into credibility. We assume that our expertise, dedication, and professionalism always show. Then when a crisis is encountered, when we try to fire Sally, we may suddenly discover, much to our horror, that we have deluded ourselves. We haven't built a sound base of credibility.

There are many reasons why performance doesn't always translate directly into credibility. Foremost among these is the fact that everyone connected with a center sees only a small piece of what we do. Teachers see us for part of the day, primarily in our supervisory role; our accountant sees us in terms of our budgeting skills; parents see us in terms of our relationship with them, etc. No one person sees the complete picture; and, unfortunately, everyone tends to evaluate us in terms of the piece they see. Thus, a director may be performing exceptionally well, accomplishing 90 tasks out of 100 when completing 50 tasks would be good. But if the fraction of uncompleted tasks is what the teacher or bookkeeper sees, she might well assume the director is doing an inadequate job.

A similar obstacle is that of turnover. In a center where turnover is high, a director's past accomplishments may quickly be forgotten. The director may have struggled effectively to renovate the center in response to teacher complaints or to work health benefits for teachers into the budget; but two years later these victories are ancient history. In a center with high turnover, the question may be, "What have you done for us lately?"

Many of us are also handicapped by inordinate modesty. We feel some need to hide our light under a basket. We may be dedicated professionals with a solid record of accomplishments and well-established credentials, but we do not let staff members know this. In an effort to create an egalitarian atmosphere, we may act as if knowledge and expertise is more widely dispersed among the staff than it really is. In trying to be just one of the gang, we may make it difficult for staff members to accept our authority without resentment.

Another serious obstacle to establishing credibility is lack of time. In many centers, there simply isn't time for staff to talk to each other, to build relationships, to work through problems, and to reach consensus decisions. There often isn't time for staff members to really get to know the director and to develop respect for her.

HOW TO BUILD CREDIBILITY

Since there are such serious obstacles in the way of establishing credible authority, a director may need to take deliberate steps to generate some credibility. In general, credibility is established in three ways. To begin with, you gain *role credibility* simply by occupying the position of director. You may throw this credibility away if you prove to be an ineffective director; but nonetheless you start out with some credibility in the bank.

You may earn *expertise credibility*. By displaying knowledge in the tasks you perform and succeeding, whether it is in the area of management, child development, or marketing, you gain credibility in the eyes of those who observe you in action.

Finally, you can earn *process credibility*. Your credibility is enhanced when you demonstrate that you are effective as a leader — that you can supervise and motivate staff, that you can set priorities, that you can pursue a vision for the program. The following are some specific approaches you may find helpful in implementing these means of establishing credibility:

• Increasing your presence.

Just being around more visibly enhances your credibility enormously. You need not spend long periods of time in the classrooms, but just dropping by from time to time or eating lunch with the kids increases your visibility and your credibility. The more staff see you on the floor, the more you notice and acknowledge staff efforts and achievements (the new room arrangement, the struggle with the difficult child, the creative activity), the more they will believe you are in touch with what is going on. (And they will be right!)

• Being a reliable resource.

Staff members need to know that when they have exhausted all their ideas for dealing with a problem or an opportunity you are always there as a dependable resource. You do not want to become everyone's crutch, so you don't want to provide solutions to problems you know staff can solve on their own. But you do want staff members to know that when all else fails you are there as a resource of last resort. This does not mean, of course, that you need to be the world's foremost authority on everything. But if you can't come up with the answer, you should be able to reliably point people in the right direction for finding the answer.

• Being an effective trainer.

Directors are often lax in an area where they really can let their expertise shine — in training their own staff members. While they may really fire up and prepare well for doing a workshop at a conference or for training another center's staff, they may underprepare for training their own staff. In fact, the reverse should probably be the case. The director should really be prepared to do her best training for her own staff.

• Actively cultivating allies.

It can be very helpful to have loyal allies on the staff. This is particularly true in a center with a large staff. Allies can do two things for you. First, they can present your story to the staff. Particularly with financial matters, I find it difficult to keep everyone fully informed of all the tradeoffs that are taking place. When I am going through the budget to explain why we are trading off some overenrollment to generate more revenues and not raise ratios or reduce benefits, I often see people's eyes glass over. However, if I can fully explain the situation to a few key teachers, they can be very effective in translating the message to the other teachers when the issue comes up. Likewise, if I am away from the center lobbying for long periods, allies on the staff can explain why I am absent.

• Empathizing with the staff.

A director can generate credibility by showing an awareness of what the teacher's role is all about. You want to be able to truthfully say, "I know how you feel; I understand your perspective on this issue." If you have been a teacher yourself, you should periodically remind people that you have had this experience. If you have not, you should demonstrate your sincere interest in learning their perspective. Listen to staff, ask teachers how they view certain issues and situations, find out what is important to them. Try to fill in as a substitute from time to time to keep your views grounded in reality.

• Being decisive.

Nothing can erode your authority more quickly than being indecisive. If you take forever to make routine decisions, if you are inconsistent on decisions you make on similar issues, if you fail to follow through on decisions you've made, if you flip flop about a decision, or if you announce tough decisions with all sorts of reservations and justifications, staff members will (correctly) begin to doubt your ability and judgment. It is important, of course, that you solicit staff input before making decisions, that you take all the time you need when making big decisions, and that you are willing to admit you are wrong and reverse poor decisions. But, to maintain credibility, it is also important that you make decisions on a timely basis and that you announce them clearly, without ambiguity or apology.

We live in an age where appearance is often taken for substance, where all problems are seen as communication or public relations problems. "If only they knew what I knew" is the leader's lament (heard most frequently in Washington to justify dubious battles). The most important source of our credibility is our performance, and that is the first thing to analyze when problems arise.

"Jean's Pretty Good, Kind of Affordable, Child Development Center" Versus the Child Care Trilemma

It was an average day for Jean, an average director of a pretty average child care center which she founded 15 years ago in a pretty average neighborhood. First thing in the morning, a parent was in her office in tears because of her struggles to pay her outstanding bill. Three hours later, one of her assistant teachers told her she was probably going to leave to work as an elementary school aide because she couldn't live on what she was making.

At a staff meeting later, the primary staff complaint was the difficulty of operating at minimum ratios, with an aging facility and not enough materials. Later in the day, she thought back to the leadership conference she went to that made her feel that her ten hour days were too short. She needed to do more marketing, budgeting, coaching her staff, advocacy, developing her board, and more community outreach.

Jean decided it was time. She either had to figure out a way to resolve the problems of her center or go crazy. She noted that she may have already gone crazy if she thought she could improve things. However, feeling plucky, and a little slaphappy after the long day, she plunged ahead.

She didn't know it, but Jean was going to tackle what Gwen Morgan coined the child care "trilemma": the fact that quality, staff compensation, and affordability for parents are all serious problems, and working on one of these problems makes it harder to tackle the other two.

If you try to increase compensation, you have less funds for improving quality by improving ratios, and vice versa. Or, if you work to make your center more affordable, you have less revenue to spend on staff or other quality factors.

Note: The trilemma recognizes that improving compensation also certainly has an effect on quality. However, few would argue that improving wages and benefits does much to reduce the need to improve ratios, administration and support, and facilities and equipment.

The following is the cautionary tale of Jean's late night calculations to shed a little light on a dark and dreary problem:

Budget: "Honest Jean's Pretty Good, Kind of Affordable Child Development Center"

INCOME   (1990 Dollars)

- Total fees $350,000
- USDA   20,000
- Fundraising   5,000

Total income $375,000

EXPENSES

- Teaching staff $213,000
- Administrative staff   63,000
- All other expenses   99,000

Total expenses $375,000

Where the budget numbers came from:

PROGRAM INCOME

Fees

- 16 infants x $120 week
  x 50 weeks x 90% $ 86,400
- 28 toddlers x $96 week
  x 50 weeks x 90%   120,000
- 40 preschoolers x $77
  week x 50 weeks x 90%   144,000

PROGRAM EXPENSES

To honestly cover ratios over the 11 hour day, the equivalent of the following number of full time staff are required:

- 16 infants   =   5 staff
- 28 toddlers   =   5 staff
- 40 preschoolers   =   5 staff

Teaching Staff Compensation:

- 3 teachers ($8.00 hour
  average + 15% tax and
  benefits) $ 57,000
- 3 assistant teachers
  ($6.30 hour average +
  15% tax and benefits)   45,000
- 9 CCAs ($5.00 hour
  average + 15% tax and
  benefits)   108,000
- Substitutes   3,000

Administrative Staff Compensation:

- Director ($12.00 hour +
  15% tax and benefits) $29,000
- Administrative assistant
  ($7.00 hour + 15% tax
  and benefits)   17,000
- Cook ($7.00 hour +
  15% tax and benefits)   17,000

Jean Decides to Improve Quality (*But Not Necessarily Compensation*) and Become "Jean's Mighty Fine Child Development Center"

Jean figured her staff and parents would like better staff/child ratios, more administrative support for staff and parents, and work on the facility. She calculated the cost:

- To reduce ratios by
  1 in each group,
  reduce 12 children   lose $48,000
- To change
  administrative
  assistant to assistant
  director ($2.00 raise)
  and add 1/2 time
  secretary ($6.00
  hour)   add $11,000
- To improve facility
  and equipment   add $10,000

*Total budget cost to
improve quality* $69,000
                        (an 18% increase)

The bottom line. To accomplish this change, the average per child fee would need to be increased by $21 per week — a 40% increase.

Jean Looks to Improve Compensation (*But Not Other Elements of Quality*) and Become "Jean's Pretty Good Child Development Center — A Great Place to Work"

Staff are restless — burning out, leaving, grumbling. New people are hard to get. She decides to consider improving salaries dramatically:

- To increase salaries
  by average of $1.50
  hour   add $56,000
- To increase benefits
  by 5%   add $17,000

*Total cost to improve
compensation* $73,000
                        (a 19% increase)

The bottom line. This change would boost the average per child fee by $17 week — a 21% increase. (**Note:** This is lower than the increase above because we are back to 84 children in this scenario.)

Jean Decides to Become More Affordable to 50% of the Parents and Become "Jean's Pretty Good Community Child Care — A Great Value"

A little less plucky than when she started, Jean continues on with her trusty calculator (next year, she vows, a computer). More of her parents from her lower middle-class neighborhood are talking about having to look elsewhere for less expensive care, perhaps less formal home care.

She has no waiting list. Some of her parents having second children are planning not to go back to work because they can't afford child care. Remembering the request of some parents, she looks into a sliding fee:

- To offer 10% of the
  families a 50%
  discount (off
  current rate)   lose $18,500
- To offer 20% of the
  families a 35%
  discount   lose $32,300
- To offer 20% of the
  families a 20%
  discount   lose $16,000

*Total cost due to
lowered fees* $66,800
                        (an 18% decrease)

The bottom line. The average rate increase for remaining 50% of parents to pay for sliding scale would be $28 week — a 38% increase. Flush with new understanding and fatigue, Jean decides to calculate improving quality, compensation, and affordability all at once, before total collapse:

"Jean's Mighty Fine Child Development Center — A Good Place to Work and a Great Value, Too"

- Quality improvements $69,000
- Compensation improvements   73,000
- Sliding scale   66,800

Total cost to improve quality, compensation, and affordability   *$208,800*
(a 55% increase)

As Jean woozily slid off her chair and struggled for equilibrium, she also struggled for perspective. There were hundreds of centers like hers in her state, and thousands throughout the country.

- What could be done?

- Where should she start?

- Where was that bottle of wine?

Alternate Ending Number 1

Jean woke up the next morning clear headed and resolute. She would seek help. She contacted Child Care Scientific Management Consultants, a new firm with a ten year history of small business consulting. They recommended the following thinking process:

1. Analyze the way to maximize full enrollment and thus generate the most revenue.

2. Improve working conditions and salaries relative to your competition for staff.

3. Offer scholarships necessary for full enrollment but not more.

Jean took their advice on the following:

- She put money into marketing, new materials, and administrative time, hoping to increase enrollment by 4%.

- She developed a series of bonuses that made staff feel better yet cost much less than across-the-board salary increases.

- She increased starting salaries to make her center's the highest advertised starting wage among her competition.

- She used the increased administrative time to improve working conditions like teacher planning time, breaks, clearer policies, and more staff recognition.

- She raised her rates after a concerted internal marketing effort to parents that she was going to spend money to offer some new

enrichment activities and materials and become "Jean's Good, Kind of Affordable, Child Development Center."

- She budgeted to offer scholarships.

Jean knew these short-term measures wouldn't solve her problems finding staff or maintaining full enrollment. She felt a little guilty because she had always regarded bonuses and enrichment activities as mostly cosmetic changes. But it seemed to her that these changes would improve her chances of getting by and maybe society would begin to pay more attention and new dollars would materialize.

Alternate Ending Number 2

Jean woke up in a cold sweat. What a dream! Last year, struggling with the trilemma, she ran into Gwen Morgan. A tireless fighter, Gwen told Jean that the alternatives were limited. She could keep on trying to balance the inevitable scarce resources and organize to advocate for public and private dollars that will very slowly, if ever, materialize; or she could open up a card and gift shop.

"Oh, well," Jean thought, "Time to get up and open up the shop." Later in the afternoon, she had time for tennis.

So Long, It's Been Good ~~Not So Good~~ to Know You

Communicating with Parents When Staff Leave

I didn't know what to think when Maya left. I found a note in my cubby on Monday that Maya was no longer employed at the center. She was Kevin's primary caregiver and had been there for two or three years. It was so sudden and we really liked her. I was confused, anxious for Kevin, mad, and concerned about Maya.

Teachers leave and parents are unhappy. Departures often create an emotional climate that affects everyone. Maya's departure upset Kevin's parents, presumably Kevin and other children, and a few other parents. However, it also caused her co-workers, supervisors, and some parents to breathe a sigh of relief.

In any program, staff will leave — voluntarily and not so voluntarily. As a relatively low-income employer, child care turnover is, and will continue to be, endemic. Staff turnover is a bad thing for programs — in general. But parents (and we) may forget it is also natural, even in good programs, and an individual staff departure may be a good thing — a move toward program improvement. Because turnover and involuntary departures are both inevitable and have important consequences, good centers should not only make the effort to reduce turnover and its impact on children, but also sort out the issues and have a communications strategy prepared to reduce the impact on parents.

Not All Turnover Is Equal

Savvy parents interested in a center often come prepared to ask questions about turnover. They may also have been advised to ask who will be their child's caregiver and are ready to size up and bond with the teachers they see in action. Typically, we offer some reasonable turnover number (say, under 15%) which we think is about right and extol the virtues of Sally the fabulous infant teacher they observe.

The rate of turnover is one of those statistics of dubious value. It makes a huge difference for program quality whether two assistant teacher positions turn over three times in a year or six teachers leave in a year — numerically it translates into the same rate. It also makes a difference which individuals leave.

In reality, informed consumer parents should be most concerned about the center's organizational quality — compensation, working conditions, hiring process, supervision, culture, leadership, the tenure of the staff (how many people stay), and the quality of the staff.

From the Beginning — No Surprises

Much of the tension between parents and the program comes from expectations not being met and from surprises that cause parents anxiety and a loss of confidence in the program's ability to provide for their child. Parents should know the center's expectations of staff before staff departures occur — the general why, how, and when of staff departures and your policies and practices that support staff growth and performance quality.

WHY "GOOD" TEACHERS ARE TERMINATED OR COUNSELED OUT

Not all hires are good hires, particularly when a center has high expectations and a limited talent pool to draw from. When staff are "helped" out the door, sometimes the reasons are obvious to all: visibly poor performance, misconduct, or poor attendance on the job. But, usually, performance issues are not as evident to parents or other staff. While directors are not in a position to discuss the dubious merits of individuals, they can discuss with parents the kind of people who sometimes don't work out. Sometimes good people need to go because:

They don't meet the program's expectations of quality. Natasha was warm and talented but was unable to move beyond a theme-based, teacher-directed curriculum. Her success teaching this way at other programs left her resistant to unlearning her old ways and moving toward the emergent curriculum with the center.

They don't fit the program. Donna was a terrific teacher, if she was teaching in a Montessori program. Danielle would have fit in just fine at the ultra laid back Sprouts and Bliss Child's Place. Neither, however, fit at the Oakdale Child Development Center. A tight labor market and wishful thinking (both the individual's and the supervisor's) led to six uncomfortable months before each teacher left.

They are impossible to work with. It is fortunate that many teachers are able to adapt their personality to

develop a good team. Unfortunately, Steven wasn't one of those. To call Steven rigid and anal retentive was an understatement. He had his own schedule, his own scissors, his own children, his own way of doing things. It got to the point that the other teachers had to bend over backwards so far to work with him that they had to limbo into the room. He was also sweet but needy, so needy that he drained the other teachers of empathy.

They are detrimental to the program culture. The truth was that Barbara thought parents were there solely to support her: genuflect on her masters degree and listen to her advice, praise her sensitive teaching (and she was sensitive), and close the door on their way out. While she might have been tolerated in some situations, her credentials and teaching expertise gave her influence which reinforced the worst instinct of other teachers in a program that was striving to become more family friendly.

They are detrimental to the program's daily climate. Some days Jo would blow in lamenting her hangover, move on to a treatise on her jerk of a boyfriend, deliver her PMS status report, and maintain a running commentary on life as she knew it. Or, like a cold fog, her increasingly frequent sulky, sour moods would chill the entire toddler program.

THE STRATEGIC VIRTUE OF HONESTY

Why do people leave your program, and what should you communicate to parents? Generally there's a lot less harm in being open about your reality than in concealment, denial, or fantasy — which is not to say that you shouldn't put your own spin on it:

- If staff leave because your salaries and benefits are barely competitive, acknowledge the difficulty of balancing staff compensation with

your efforts to keep the rates down.

- If staff leave because of poor performance, emphasize your standards of quality and that not all teachers measure up. You will need to explain why the individual was hired (limited talent pool?) and the supportive supervision process that attempted to maximize the individual performance to no avail.

- If staff leave because of incompatibility with your program, be clear about the virtues of your approach.

On the other hand, if staff leave because they can't work with you, your quality standards are too low, or it's simply a lousy place to work, you might want to take heed and consider changing the center, yourself, or your career. Honesty works when you have justifiable confidence in your own performance and the process of hiring and supervision, backed up by good communication skills.

GOOD BYE, JESSICA

Jessica had been struggling for the past six months with the center's expectations of professionalism toward parents and staff. A good teacher and popular with children and parents, she was also rigid and often judgmental concerning co-workers and parents (unbeknownst to parents). At her final meeting with the lead teacher and director, she resigned one step ahead of termination. Because her continued presence would be even more detrimental to the center than before, she was told that she could leave immediately and be paid for the rest of the week.

The director had a strategy ready for easing the impact. The lead teacher called the parents of Jessica's primary care children, and all parents in the room received the following note when they arrived the next morning:

A Letter to Parents on Staff Departures

When you have to face the departure of popular staff, a letter like the following will reduce concerns.

Recently a few teachers have left the program. I know parents are concerned about turnover both because of the impact on their children and the well-being of the staff person they have developed a relationship with. I thought I would share some of my perspective with you.

We are proud of the stability of our center. Out of 37 regular employees (not counting summer camp), ten have left in the past three years. Out of those, two relocated to another area, two decided to stay home with their children, two went to a public school, and two left the field. No one left to work at another child care center. Eight out of the nine core leadership and teaching staff have been at the center for more than three years and 82% of the staff have been here more than two years.

Most of the time at our center departures are unambiguously voluntary. Teachers leave the center for all sorts of reasons, but most often relocation, personal life choices, and occasionally career change. Sometimes a departure is not so voluntary: the teacher's supervisors are unhappy with the performance of the teacher or the teacher is unhappy with the job of his or her supervisors. Because of the care we take in hiring and our supervision that supports growth, involuntary departures are uncommon.

Sometimes a teacher who is counseled out or terminated is popular with parents, or other staff, and does some or even many aspects of his or her job very well. But there are numerous aspects of the job that parents do not see, including:

- ability to plan and organize curriculum and environment
- responsibilities as a team member
- professionalism in interactions with co-workers
- relationships with supervisors
- commitment to their professional growth and development
- commitment to the center's quality goals

When a staff person leaves, we have to maintain confidentiality as to the specifics of the departure out of respect for the employee, even if the employee is freely giving his or her view of the situation. Unless the employee gives us permission to speak, all we will say is that the employee has resigned or been terminated and the departure was not the result of any inappropriate behavior towards children. Of course, if the reasons for leaving did involve inappropriate behavior toward children, we will always notify the parents and discuss the situation with all families involved.

When a teacher is terminated, counseled out, or leaves the center voluntarily but unhappily, we usually prefer to have the person leave immediately. We understand that this can be difficult for children and parents, but the alternative is often worse — plummeting morale.

As you know, we are proud of high standards for care and education. Many of our staff have little experience with a center that demands the level of quality that we do and our approach that expects individualized care and a customer service approach to parents. Some of our staff are fairly young and have little job experience at all. There is usually a lot of growth expected of staff in their first year of employment.

But there is also a lot of support, particularly from lead teachers, co-workers, and me — training, supervision, and resources. We have a supervisory process committed to development. We want people to succeed and stay. As long as an employee is committed to growth and we believe growth is possible, we are willing to help them succeed, and struggle with doubt, fatigue, and burnout.

We require documentation of clear expectations for each staff person, and opportunities to succeed and meet these goals in a timely manner. No one is terminated or placed on probation without considerable thought.

Any parent with a question or concern on personnel or program decisions is always welcome to call me or drop in to discuss the situation.

Dianna Doe, Director

Dear Parents,

Jessica has resigned from the ABC Early Learning Center. Yesterday was her last day. We wish her well in her future pursuits. We realize abrupt transitions are difficult for all, and we will do all we can to minimize the effect on the children. Alice Johnson, who many of you know, will be substituting for Jessica. We are already in the process of recruiting a permanent replacement. I will be working with Maria (the head teacher) to help facilitate the smooth transition.

We always discuss a teacher's leaving with the children and help them understand that the teacher will miss them. Please feel free to discuss any concerns or questions with either Maria or me.

Sincerely,
Susan Doe, Director

What parents were told in person: Jessica's resignation was voluntary, but there were ongoing serious performance issues that did not have to do with her interactions with children. It was not a happy termination of the relationship, which is why Jessica's separation was immediate. The director explained that she needed to maintain confidentiality and that was all she could say. She also mentioned the policy, noted in the parent handbook, of having an unhappy employee leave immediately.

In talking with parents, Jessica's director understood that the parents had a right to be upset, sad, or anxious. Their concern entitled them to emotional questioning. She listened to their concerns and was empathetic. Her lack of defensiveness comes from her knowledge that the center had appropriate high expectations, a good supervisory process, and that the process was utilized well. She was able to articulate that Jessica's departure was sad but necessary to maintain the program's high standards and the morale of other staff.

A no-surprises approach might lead to the following section in a parent handbook or a parent handout:

- Turnover is a child care reality that affects all: children, parents, and staff. Continuity is important for children and team relationships, so the center does all it can to minimize turnover.

- Given the nature of the talent pool in child care — young women between the ages of 18 and 30 — there is a natural baseline of turnover due to life changes. Children and parents will also experience a turnover when their teachers move to other rooms.

- Describe your hiring process and how it leads to a good hire; and, if your talent pool is limited, discuss how you maximize it.

- Mention your commitment to support and supervision that leads to growth and good performance.

- Discuss why you are a good place to work and why staff stay, why people who leave do leave, and how you try to reduce the effect of departures.

A FINAL NOTE

All we can do is what we can do. But our success will also depend on our ability to communicate our perspective and the logic and limitations inherent in our practice. Directors are responsible for managing complex organizations, usually with limited resources. Staffing the center for excellence is a challenge. The more parents understand the nature of the challenge, the more likely they will be supportive partners and satisfied customers.

OF CULTURE AND A SENSE OF PLACE

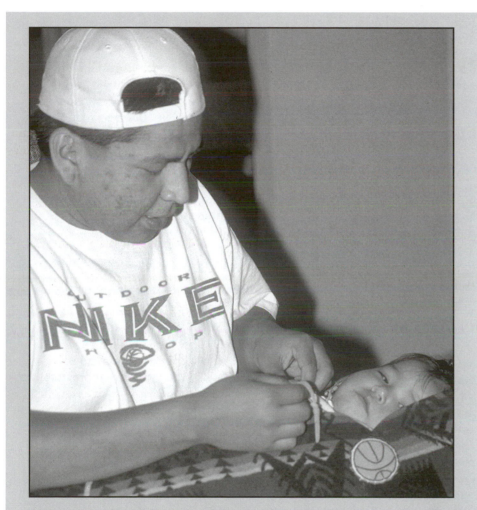

"That's just the way we do things here," said the director. Good child care centers, like any good organization, have cultures that shape how members think, feel, and behave. Just like the culture we are born into, we enter a world of shared beliefs and values, behavioral norms, and attitudes. In programs with strong cultures, one can go to two programs and see very similar people, yet one program feels relaxed and fun-loving, accepting and creative; the other, efficient and business-like, formal and industrious.

In some centers, everyone and everything is managed to the edge of regimentation; in others, spontaneity and discovery rule, flirting with chaos. One program may have a drive for excellence; another is just getting by.

Programs vary greatly in the way people treat each other — whether relations are respectful and caring or not, formal or informal, collegial or distant.

Some centers have no real program culture. Individual teachers set the tone in their rooms. One room feels very different from another and changes as the people change. Or the overall tone is set by the director; and if the director changes, so does the tone.

At Babyland Child Care, Mary and Alicia have a fairly low tolerance for noise and bursts of movement, and their toddler room reflects that. They also pretty much do what they have been doing for the past five years. They are friendly with other staff and parents but seek little input into their practices. Anne's and Mark's toddler room couldn't be more different; toddlers are all over — climbing, jumping, hauling — and the teachers are always seeking out new ideas and critical reactions.

At Child's Garden, the center has worked hard over 20 years to establish a consistent culture. Reading through the parent handbook, looking at signs on the wall, observing in each classroom, sitting in on meetings, and reading newsletters, it is clear that everyone who works there buys into the same basic ideas — messy, active play is essential; teachers throughout the center work together, use each other's good ideas, and look for ways to inject fun and humor into the day; and (unfortunately) all believe that the parent role is to support the program, not offer advice or guidance. The hiring and socialization reinforces the program culture.

Culture is a powerful medium, one of the basic organizational dimensions that create and maintain quality, along with designing the environment; creating organizational structures, systems, and routines; and maximizing human resources. Culture creation is a major part of developing a new center, and acculturation of new staff (and parents and children) is a key task in maintaining quality.

PLACE AND CULTURE

We make the places and the places make us. Places are designed to accomplish functions — what goes into the business of living, working, and playing. We also try to give sensible form to the feelings, mood, and rhythms of life imagined within the setting.

Elizabeth Prescott for years has helped early childhood professionals understand that space provides more than a container or stage — rather it "regulates our experience," influencing how we think, feel, and behave. Space suggests possibilities, enables or restrains, encourages or demoralizes. For instance, a good center design invites active learning — indoors and out — and encourages and supports caregivers to develop a rich and creative learning environment. It does so by providing adequate square footage, storage, both carpeted and washable surfaces, and a varied outdoor setting.

Space also "speaks" to our emotions. Poet Ezra Pound once commented that poetry is language charged with meaning. **Places are spaces charged with meaning.** We build images of places — "meaningful" spaces — out of fragments of experiences — experiences significant to us for reasons of our own. Our memories, sensual experiences of place, imaginings, hopes, and dreams transform places and things. Our houses become **our**

homes with our living, our wear and tear. Features of the house — the sunlight streaming through windows, the emerging shadows, the hideaways that shelter us, the walk-in closet space we lusted after, and all the other features of space we like — inspire our gratitude and affection.

Child care centers speak to children and parents. Some centers, dominated by bright lights, colors, and tile, shout out "bright, gleaming, clean!" Because we are different, some will see a healthy place, others will see it as unappealingly sterile. Another, with classrooms and ABCs and number lines dominating the decor, will proclaim "serious school" to some, developmentally inappropriate to others.

OBJECTS AND PLACES

Objects also lay claim to our feelings because of both associations and the inherent qualities of objects. Wood, leather, natural stone and brick, and some textured fabrics beckon to be touched. They warm us. Metal, formica, vinyl, and polyurethane surfaces, and plastics, generally do not.

To an adult, the smell of a cedar chest; the sight of a toy — perhaps a teddy bear, Raggedy Ann (or Barbie), sled, or wagon — or the form of a chair or table can bring forth a jumble of feelings, some never reaching the conscious level. For young children, each day and place is likely to be a huge leap with fewer associations to anchor their sensibilities. Yet, however limited their experience, they have lived in a world of sensation; and familiarity can bring security (or, of course, the opposite). Echoes of the homes that children come from in both form and objects will reassure children — similar textures, couches, pillows, and familiar toys.

Ronald Flemming and Renata von Tscharner, in their book *Placemakers* (1981), describe **placemakers** as objects or forms that "help to define,

reveal, enrich, reinforce, expand, or otherwise make accessible place meaning" — the fountain in a plaza, a sculpture or iron bench in a garden, the art or photographs in a lobby. Placemakers can transform a place otherwise drab or anonymous and release a particular kind of energy in people, "an energy that is invested in feelings of care and propriety for a place." A placemaker can add "a layer of decorative richness which embellishes and sometimes commemorates." Some provide just a "whimsical bump in the mind," like the giant milk bottle outside the Boston Children's Museum.

Placemakers aren't equal. They can elevate or diminish, be gaggingly cute or trite, or so arcane to be meaningless. In one center, a huge (stuffed) shaggy dog at the reception desk creates an enduring welcoming experience; in another, a fountain; in a classroom, simply a special table or pedestal with changing objects of interest — fresh flowers, crafts, or kaleidoscopes.

Landmarks also help to define a space and orient us. They provide security as we make our way, "Come on, Adam, here's the blue door." A roof or pillar; a tree; a distinctive window; and art — such as a statue, mobile, or painting — all serve as landmarks. In a classroom, maintaining landmarks — such as a couch or learning center — while rearranging a room environment helps children adjust to change.

WHAT KIND OF PLACE?

All centers and classrooms have to decide what kind of place they wish to be and who belongs in the place. My list would begin with:

✔ **A Place for Parents**

If parents are truly desired in the center, the environment has to welcome them in. We feel welcome in places that signal "come in" with "friendly" entrances, signs of welcome, photographs of us and our children, and immediate greetings in well designed reception space and classroom entries. We are welcomed into classrooms by open doors or windows into the space. We feel that **we belong** in places where we understand how the spaces are laid out and how they work — either through signs or friendly assistance, the space accommodates us — and we understand our role at the place, feel competent while there, and feel accepted by others. Some important features of a welcoming place:

- parking

- a phone for parent use

- closet space for parents

- sufficient classroom square footage for parents to feel they are not unwelcome as visitors because of crowding

- adult furniture in the room

- a comprehensible classroom with visible signs and instructions for parent participation

✔ **Place with a Sense of Community and Collegiality**

Community is the sense of *we work together* and *the whole is greater than*

the sum of its parts. The physical space has a major effect on the development of relationships, particularly in larger centers. Self-contained closed door classrooms and out-of-the-way offices spread out over a large area don't easily accommodate a sense of community.

On the other hand, a confusing open layout with limited walls quickly leads to too much togetherness; and teachers begin building walls. Community is supported in larger facilities with central crossroads, multiple **gathering places**, and central office and support space that everyone passes by. Gathering places often include the kitchen, a table in a larger office, a copier, picnic tables, a bench under a shady tree.

Teamwork requires space for meetings and shared materials and equipment, but also individual *owned* space and equipment. When

A construction is a new organization of the world and life.

— Mircea Eliade

all is communal and everybody shares, it can easily slide into nobody *owns* anything. Privacy and places to retreat to are always necessary. Some elements that support a sense of community:

- a coordinated aesthetic, with room for variations

- ample shared storage for shared toys, books, and materials

Creating a sense of place that creates and supports the center culture grows out of a shared vision of what child care and childhood is all about. Every center will vary. My list of that kind of place would certainly include "a place for fun," "a place for families," "a place for wonder," "a place that accepts many cultures," and so on until I have defined the place for a childhood for the children in my care.

It Seemed to Make Sense at the Time: Stupid Child Care Tricks

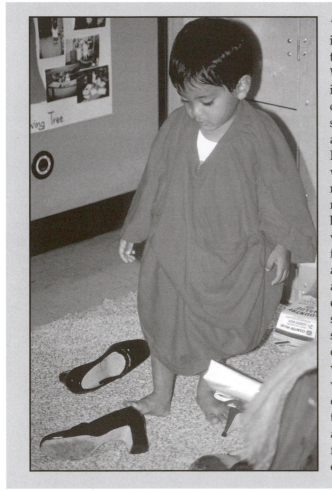

"That's the dumbest idea, what idiot thought of that?" Well, sometimes that idiot would be me, or perhaps you, or some other reasonable human being. Much of the time, we do dumb things, not because we are mindless, but because of tunnel vision. Our mind is focusing on one action, goal, or idea and ignoring other consequences or side effects, like slamming into the car ahead of us while admiring the view. Child care centers might want to look at their actions from a different perspective; examples follow:

HOW TO CREATE A "NO" ENVIRONMENT: PARENT POLICIES AND COMMUNICATION

Some recently observed signs while visiting centers:

You must call before having lunch with your child.

Children with unpaid tuition will not be admitted.

No toys or food from home.

No personal phone calls.

No breakfast for children who arrive after 9:00.

No car seat storage in the lobby.

Often the parent policies are written in the same language: "No . . . ," "Parents must . . . ," etc. Yes, we do need restrictions and we do need to give hard messages. But rephrasing — using "please" and "we appreciate" and more discrete communication of penalties and consequences — at least makes it look like there is some respect for parents.

The Unbearable Wrongness of Being Late

God knows we all hate late parents (except when those late parents happen to be us). In fact, late parents are so frustrating that I would not be surprised to hear about a center charging a $50 late fee or kicking the family out. A not uncommon approach: "Parents will be fined $1 per minute for the first five minutes and $2 per minute thereafter. Parents must pay the caregiver directly."

Here are some absolutely predictable effects of this policy:

• Increased parent / staff tension in front of the child.

• Arguments over what time it is because each minute counts.

• Inconsistent application of the policy based on the mood and assertiveness of the individual staff member and the parent.

By instituting a five minute grace period to reduce wrangling over minutes, scheduling staff to work the predictable late times, and billing parents, tension is reduced. You also might want to look at your hours, or offer extended hours for a separate fee.

DUMB MARKETING — OR — WHY DON'T THEY LIKE US?

The hardest job in marketing is attracting attention, getting the customer interested. So when someone calls your center, you have already crossed that hurdle, and you have a hot prospect — winnowed down from all the potential parent customers who have never heard of you or considered you for their child. What is this potential customer likely to hear when they call your center?

"Hello, ABC Child Care" (neutral, flat monotone).

   or

"ABC Child Care, can you hold?" (frantic, harried voice).

   or

"ABC Child Care, Missy speaking" (bored, mindless, very young voice).

   or

"ABC Child Care" (background noise includes wailing child or raucous laughter).

   or

Ring, ring, ring, ring, and no answer at all.

It is often difficult in the busy world of child care to cover the phones, but let's consider priorities. How much was that call potentially worth to you? Suppose it was a parent with an infant? It may be worth $6,000

this year, $25,000 over the next five years — or even more. How do most people come to know about your center? What if that same parent worked in an office with other young parents and perhaps brought in three or four new families over time or, even if they didn't choose you for their child, mentioned you as a favorable option and generated some interest? That one call alone could be worth $125,000 to the center.

What do parents want to hear from a place where they will entrust their precious, vulnerable child and which will charge them lots of money? — a voice that conjures up images of warmth, trust, and, above all else, thoughtful care. Isn't it worth it to make an effort to make sure a prospective parent gains a favorable or at least neutral impression from that call? If not a warm, welcoming live voice, that same voice on a machine followed up by a call is better than any of the above.

Other First Impression Gaffs

- The lobby or hallway that looks like lifestyles of the poor and homeless — doubling as a storage space and frenetic communication kiosk.

- Dying plants, empty aquariums, lifeless looking staff.

- Unsmiling or involved staff.

- Unexplained eye sores or questionable sights or sounds (e.g., a temporary mess, a distraught child).

"IT LOOKED GOOD ON PAPER" — FACILITY DESIGN

The Big Room

There is a popular large center design that creates multipurpose space by placing the eight or ten classrooms around a central multi-purpose room creating common space — on paper, a great idea, capturing wasted corridor space. In

reality, unless carefully done, it is an out-of-scale space that creates a no-man's land problem for parents during arrival and departure, and an under used space by staff. Usually it is only used by one room at a time and not at all during drop-off and pick-up times. No one feels secure letting children loose, losing the prime purpose of the space.

Little Rooms

We know that small group size is an unquestionable good, right? We also know that 35 square feet per child (50 square feet for infants) is acceptable. So let's create a six infant, 300 square foot room, and add cribs, a couch, staff, parents, a changing counter and see what happens. Take the same scenario with ten toddlers and 400 square feet or 16 preschoolers and 600 square feet. What do we get? — child care in a closet for a ten hour day, AKA hell.

Yes, small groups are good, but then you need more space per child. A room for six infants requires nearly all the same furniture as a room for eight or nine infants. That is even more true of spaces for older children.

A small group packed together allows no room for semi-seclusion, active learning, or a number of learning centers. Children spend the day joined at the hip.

Group size, staff/child ratios, and room size are interactive elements of quality and cannot be applied mindlessly. A small group packed together allows no room for semi-seclusion, active learning, or a number of learning centers.

ADMINISTRATIVE FOLLIES

"Pinch Every Penny"

Enrollment is down, we have to pinch every penny. So no raises, cut back on substitutes, cut out the paste, watch those paper towels like a hawk, freeze all the equipment spending, and "Sorry, staff will no longer receive lunch free."

When the budget is tight and salaries are frozen is not the time to nickel and dime in every area. How can you maintain any semblance of morale and expect staff to perform well? If quality drops, how will you attract more enrollment?

Apply the budget chopping ax carefully, with thought to staff morale and those tools they need to do the job. It may be some of the last and smallest cuts are the unkindest of all.

"I'll Take Care of That"

Like most directors, I enjoyed purchasing. I also firmly believed that I was the most experienced and wisest purchaser (after all, I wrote a book and have a masters degree).

It took me awhile to accept delegating because I knew I would disagree with some purchases. I overlooked the fact that you could fill a room with my own mistakes, and why shouldn't other staff get to enjoy spending scarce resources?

A Final Note

There should be little shame attached to "dumb moves." If we stay in the business long enough, most of us will make our share of them. However, many can be avoided if we look before we lurch and ask ourselves what the more subtle consequences or side effects are of our well-intentioned efforts.

Chapter 7

Places for Childhoods Include Parents, Too

The Heart of the Matter:

Parent Partnerships

by Anne Stonehouse

If I had to give this a title, I would call it "The Heart of the Matter." Jim Greenman gets past the superficial, the trappings around issues related to parent-staff partnerships in children's services, and gets to the heart of the matter. The second reason is that parent-staff partnerships are a much neglected and critically important dimension of quality in child care.

Traditionally early childhood teachers in all types of settings, nursery schools, kindergartens, early years of school, as well as home and center-based care, have prided themselves on building strong links with families. When it comes to child care, however, it may be said that we have perhaps borrowed too heavily from models of parent involvement and participation in other early childhood settings without recognizing some fundamental differences. We need a model for parent-staff partnerships for contemporary child care settings that borrows from acknowledged elements of good practice and also acknowledges the unique characteristics of child care. Both parents and teachers have a great emotional investment in the child. The stakes are high when it comes to parent-staff partnership. It would be easier to get it right if it weren't so important!

Why are partnerships so important in child care? There are a number of reasons:

1. Mutual sharing of information between parents and others involved in the rearing of their child ensures continuity for the child, and makes the task easier for all adults, as they are able to operate with a *full picture* of the child.

2. Parents have a right to have a say.

3. When parents have a feeling of *connectedness* to and investment in the service, there are tangible benefits for the staff in the form of contributions of time, energy, and resources.

The above are not the most important reasons, the heart of the matter, however. The most important reason for partnerships is that if we want to make a meaningful, positive, and potentially lasting difference in a child's life, the best way — in fact, probably the only way — is to influence the child's parents. The best thing that staff can do for a child is to increase parents' understanding of, liking for, and attachment to their child. This is more easily said than done for a variety of reasons. Firstly, child care services are not funded for parent support but rather to provide care for children while their parents work, that is, a kind of maintenance role. There is some confusion in the community as well as in the profession about the role of child care, with some beliefs that it is to replace or substitute for home experience, and therefore that staff are in some way substituting for parents. In contrast, kindergarten and preschool programs are seen to provide carefully planned and evaluated experiences for children, to *supplement* the experiences provided by home and parents.

This notion that child care is simply substituting for parents interferes in a major way with partnerships. Firstly, it denies the professional nature of working with other people's children, and lends support to the mistaken notion that what a child care worker does is no more than what a parent does and therefore does not require much training or skill. Secondly, the notion that someone can take the place of parents — and that children who spend substantial amounts of time in care will become more closely attached and more greatly influenced by child care staff than by their parents — is not only nonsense but also interferes in a major way with healthy partnerships.

A further impediment to partnerships is the notion held by some child care staff that they know what is best for children. In combination with judgmental attitudes towards parents who (appear to) choose to work when they don't have to, this can lead to a mission to *rescue* children from uncaring parents, to *child saving*. This escalates tensions, which are further fueled by imagined or real lack of valuing and appreciation by parents of the care provided by staff.

What is the nature of good partnership in child care? Firstly, it is a *relationship*, and it is not the same as participation and involvement. Having parents contribute to the life of the service, whether through fund raising, serving on the management committee, helping out at working bees, contributing junk materials, or providing assistance with the actual program for children, is valuable and may contribute to the establishment and maintenance of a partnership. However, *participation and involvement by parents in and of themselves do not constitute partnership.* These are ways to connect with the service, and they are an important means to an end; but there is no necessity and therefore should be no pressure placed on parents to undertake these activities.

The critical element of partnership is the quality of the daily interactions between staff and parents at arrival and departure times. "Partnerships on the run" is the name of the game in child care. And these times when partnership can be forged are not ideal. Parents and staff are busy, rushed, and, at the end of the day, tired. Over time, if there is good will and commitment to partnership, however, it will happen.

What follows is a brief look at some of the key elements of partnership in child care. Interestingly, these elements apply also to business or personal partnerships.

Mutual Respect

Respect is easy to list and hard to put into practice. It requires that staff genuinely believe that the vast majority of parents are doing the best job they can, with the resources they have. Staff as a group and as individuals have to resist imposing on others their beliefs and values about what they would do or have done as parents, and ultimately to understand that it is not for them to make judgments about what is best for others. This includes respecting parents' decisions to use child care in the first place.

A second manifestation of respect arises from accepting that parents have a perspective on their child that is different from ours. They are much more passionate about their child, and so they should be. They care much more about their own child than they do the others in the group, and so they should. They see themselves reflected in the child's strengths and weaknesses, struggles and triumphs, and so they should. Respect is about letting parents be parents, supporting their role as the most important people in their child's life, and not only accepting but being grateful that they are constantly looking out for their child's interests, even when it is a nuisance to us, even when their requests are impossible to meet.

Respect is perhaps most obvious in its presence or absence when there is diversity of cultures, family structures, and child rearing beliefs.

Respect means accepting, as we do with children, that parents are individuals:

- Some will be friendly and outgoing, some won't.

- Some will be forthcoming with information about the child and the family, some won't.

- Some will be interested in becoming involved in the life of the center, some won't.

- Some will read newsletters avidly, come to meetings, bring extra changes of clothes, pay fees on time, never be late picking their child up, some won't.

- Some will exemplify our own views about exemplary child rearing, some won't.

- Some will be very grateful for the care their child is receiving and will let you know, some won't.

- Some will feel guilty or sad about using child care, some won't.

- Some parents, a few, will be very critical of care, irresponsible about their obligations to the services, and even seemingly neglectful of their child.

Staff need to learn to tolerate difference and, just as is the case with children, to be clear about limits, points beyond which behavior will not be tolerated. Tolerance of parents does not mean that anything goes. Staff need to be clear about *bottom line*s, and staff expectations of parents should be made clear to parents from the beginning, as well as finding out from parents what their expectations are and clarifying what the service can provide.

It may be useful for staff to examine their individual and collective ideas about what constitutes the *ideal parent* and the *annoying parent*, the *typical parent* or the *difficult parent*. Where do these generalizations come from, and how might they affect our relationship with parents?

It may be useful to have an *airing* by staff of their views about parents using child care for their very young child when the reasons for working do not appear to be financial ones.

TRUST

Not something that can be mandated, trust comes as a result of shared communication and experience, as well as parents' observations that their child is receiving good care. Staff, especially those who work in centers with very good reputations, often feel frustrated and even offended that parents don't trust them immediately. Trust is built on honesty, and one of the professional judgments that staff have to make is how honest to be with parents about their child, weighing up the impact of their honesty on parents' attitudes and behavior toward the child.

SENSITIVITY TO THE PERSPECTIVE OF THE OTHER

All partnerships are assisted by partners being able to put themselves in the shoes of the other and to see situations from their perspective. It helps partnerships in child care, for example, when staff can accept the inevitable fact that parents will view the program largely from the perspective of "how does this affect me and my child?"

It is not helpful for staff to operate on the mistaken assumption that all parents who use child care are consumed with guilt; but many parents are ambivalent and unsure, especially at the beginning, and they will be searching for evidence that they have made the right choice.

Parents who use child care have many responsibilities, often competing ones, and operate in a work and community context which may not be particularly *family friendly*. They need our support, not our critical judgment.

ONGOING "BOTH-WAYS" COMMUNICATION

Good will is insufficient to bring about partnership. It is certainly required, but partnership also requires systems and structures to ensure ongoing communication. Primacy must be given to face-to-face communication, with written communication used to *supplement*, not substitute, for interpersonal exchanges. Newsletters, policy documents, brochures, notice board displays, meetings, and scheduled interviews are useful; but they cannot replace informal daily exchanges about the child between caregivers and staff. It is possible for a center to have an impressive array of communication mechanisms and strategies in place and for parents to still feel shut out.

Centers need to find ways to convince parents that they want their input about anything concerning their child. Jim's notion of a "why not" approach is a good one — it does not mean saying yes to everything a parent requests, but it does represent a commitment to take seriously parents' requests and concerns, and when staff have to say **no** to a parent, an understanding that a reasonable and non-defensive justification is necessary.

MUTUALLY AGREED UPON AND UNDERSTOOD GOALS

Respect also means accepting that parents want mostly the same things for their child that professionals want: namely for the child to be successful in school, to have friends, to find a meaningful job, to live a fulfilled life. Where parents and professionals differ often is in ideas about the best way to achieve those outcomes. Staff have to be clear about their *bottom lines*, where they will compromise and where they won't or can't when it comes to parents' requests.

TEAMWORK, ABSENCE OF RIVALRY

Working parents may be forgiven for not appreciating the fact that they are the most important people in a child's life, especially when they use care on a full-time basis. Unfortunately, strong assertions are made, sometimes by people working in child care, that "Children in child care have no family life," or "Today's parents are selfish, they care more about money than they do about their children," or the classic "Why do they bother having them if they aren't prepared to stay home and rear them?" Sometimes staff even assert that they have more influence over children than their parents do. These unfounded and erroneous beliefs not only place a substantial wedge between parents and staff, but parents who feel marginalized in the rearing of their child may become so.

A notion on the part of staff that they are substituting for parents prevents a sense of partnership and teamwork and engenders feelings of competitiveness and rivalry, particularly if staff also harbor a negative view of parents who use child care. These attitudes are often unacknowledged, but serve as a serious impediment.

CONCLUSION

What matters most in the establishment and maintenance of a partnership is the following:

- a genuine commitment to shared decision making, even when staff are capable of making decisions about the child alone

- a willingness to engage in a genuine effort to combine professional expertise and the aspirations of parents for their child, their preferences about their child's experience

- persistent efforts to let parents in on what is happening when their child is in care

- systems in place to solicit parents' views, concerns, and criticisms

- continuous evaluation with the aim of continuous improvement

- determination to share with parents all the good news they can about their child

- acknowledgment that to do all the above is difficult.

Those children's services professionals who genuinely embrace partnerships are rewarded by knowing that they are not only supporting parents now, but also making a lasting difference in the life of the child.

This reflection is adapted from an article by the author titled "Parent-Staff Partnerships in Children's Services; It Would Be Easier If They Weren't So Important," in Rattler, Community Child Care Co-operative Ltd. (NSW), Spring 1996.

Some of the material in this chapter appears in both the Australian and American versions of **Prime Times***, which was co-authored by Anne Stonehouse,*

PLACES FOR CHILDHOODS INCLUDE PARENTS, TOO

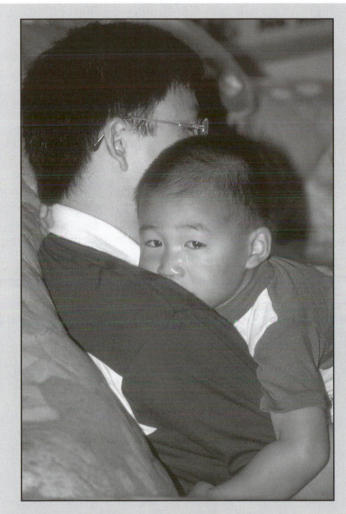

I intended to write about environments that support parent involvement. In the process, I became preoccupied with more basic issues — the emotions and perceptions that guide the reality of parent *involvement*.

"Parents are welcome at any time." In a good child care center, this is the right thing to say, the politically correct policy — valuing parent presence in the center. "We believe in partnerships with parents."

Equally important, equally correct — implying a belief in some parent power. But do we believe it, really? Do we ALL believe it, all the time? And do our practices and environment back up our ideology?

PARENT INVOLVEMENT

Parent involvement is an all-purpose term that encompasses parent boards, volunteering, parent education, fund raising, and the daily exchanges of information. One center's parent involvement places parent action and presence safely on the perimeter — board meetings, special events, and donations; another center has parents intimately involved in center life and decision making around their own child.

What is parent involvement in child care? In discussions with teachers, there is general agreement that it includes much information sharing, parent support by good child rearing and cooperation, some volunteering, special events, donations, and perhaps participation on an advisory board. With some prodding, less so with infant staff, staff may recognize that an important role for parents is advocating for and influencing the care their child receives. Sharing information is one thing, sharing power quite another; and the idea makes many professionals very uneasy.

Confusion over parent roles is understandable because schools, including preschools, rarely accorded the parent a role that incorporated influencing the program's response to their child. The parent's job was to support the professionals. But child care is a different institution. The parent's job is to raise their child, be the expert on their own child, and make sure the child is cared for in accordance with their values and standards.

What is the best child care that money can buy? When Mr. and Mrs. Bigbucks look for child care, they may hire a nanny or seek the specific care they want from programs in their area. They expect control over little Blake's care, not just information about the care Blake receives.

Their purchasing power backs up their parental prerogatives. They may want advice and education from the child care professional(s), but they certainly expect it will be given respectfully with full awareness that it is their choice.

Quality child care is care that is individualized to the child and the family, and education that empowers the child. The best centers work hard to also empower the parents, to help parents feel in control over their child's care. It is a true collaboration that recognizes the prerogatives and constraints of both partners.

Parents approach the parent/staff relationship with some child care guilt and a confusion of messages about what to look for in quality child care. Staff, who often work with children because they feel more confident with children than adults, bring the insecurity that accompanies low pay and status and the same uncertainty about *what is right*. Both groups usually come from an individualistic culture not great about sharing love and intimacy. It's not easy. Often staff feelings and perceptions develop that work against a partnership. Those feelings are a natural outgrowth of the complex relationship and are present in nearly all programs.

"They"

Parents easily become "they" or "the parents," not a collection of individuals. In every population, there are a range of individuals from near saints to clear sinners. We usually use the annoying and problematic behavior of the least agreeable to create our "they" that we rail against or reprove with knowing condescension. The parent who is willing to place their child in care for 60 hours a week — who works part time and pays for facials — defines the "they," along with the chronically late parent, the one who forgets the diapers, the "whiner," and the one who wants her infant toilet trained.

When some staff get together and talk about parents, one wonders whether they are talking about a mutant species. Note, however, the bark is worse than the bite. Many staff who rail against parents actually behave in sensitive and accommodating ways when interacting with parents.

This tendency to create "theys" is certainly not limited to child care workers. It is a natural phenomena that has to be fought, an occupational hazard of service-related professions.

"They Don't Tell Us What Is Happening at Home"

As a consultant, I sat in the teachers' meeting at the small center and listened to staff share about the children and families.

"What about (two year old) James? He's having a hard time and acting out a lot," asked the director.

"I found out through a mutual friend that his parents are struggling and may split up," his teacher, Jane, responded. "It explains a lot. I wish his mom had told us. How can we help their kids if they don't tell us what's happening at home?"

I asked the staff what they would have done if they knew what was going on with James' mom and dad. They replied that they would have tried to give him "more," and they would have understood more.

I asked Jane, "Suppose you were going through a messy divorce and you were under a lot of stress. And suppose you weren't getting along with Alice (the associate teacher) because she was on edge because she's drinking too much. Should we put out a bulletin to the parents — TO ALL PARENTS: The children in Jane's class may behave differently at home because of problems at child care. Jane's divorce and Alice's drinking have resulted in some tension and breaks in the normal routines. But don't worry because care is still good and their on-the-job

performance is acceptable. Just please try and give your child some special attention because he/she may be feeling a little insecure. We thought this information might help explain your child's behavior."

It is tempting to justify knowing all the details of a family's private life because it will help us *understand* or *teach* a child. But we have no RIGHT to know the ins and outs of family life, any more than they have a right to know about our private lives as a means to monitor program quality or better understanding.

For the most part, what we need to know is that a child like James is under some unusual stress and needs us at our most supportive best. Much of the time it makes little difference in our response whether the stress is due to family problems, fitful sleep, mild illness, or all the other sources of children's stress. What we do is try to offer flexibility, warmth, and nurturing. If a child is older, perhaps it may help the child to talk about the situation. But in that case, let the child or parent decide.

Respect for parents demands that, unless the situation is one of abuse or neglect, the parents control what information they wish to share. If we come to know something about the family, as professionals we should ask the parents if they mind, before sharing the information with colleagues or supervisors. In the case of James, discussing his family situation as a staff, based on gossip and without parent permission, is no less unprofessional than a group discussing a teacher's private struggles. When we have a relationship based on mutual respect and confidence, many parents trust us with information about their private struggles.

"They Don't Care"

In child care, we often take OUR institutional limitations as givens, certainly not as signs we care less about the children. Ratios, center size, foods served, the limits of our services, staff turnover — "Sorry, welcome to the real world of today's child care." We usually honestly can say we are doing our best. We'd like to do more — have better ratios, more one to one, more field trips, use fewer substitutes, but the budget gets in the way.

With parents, we are not always so willing to accept their givens. Yet parents' real lives — long work days; the need to find some time for themselves; money problems; a difficulty sorting out what is the right thing to do in a diverse, guilt-inducing, materialistic culture — easily brings out the judgmental in us (particularly if we haven't had to face the world as parents ourselves).

"They don't care" or "they don't care enough" is perhaps the most common hidden thought that lurks in the minds of many child care workers every time they look for extra clothes, cope with a sick child, or regret the poor turnout at an open house. Followed by, "I wish they would get some parent education," as we put together an image of the child's family life based on the child's behavior, our disapproving glimpses of parent-child interactions, and reports from the home front.

As a director, I made sure the parent handbook had a section asking that parents label their children's clothing because "don't they realize how many clothes we have to go through and how alike all the clothing is?" As a parent, I inconsistently labeled my kid's clothing because "don't they realize how many clothes kids go through and what it takes to label each pair of socks?" As a parent, I missed open houses, regretfully, and committed all the parent sins, still caring deeply about my kid.

"They Won't Leave Us Alone"

The flip side to "they don't care" is "they care too much" about some

things. James' mother, Gloria, was a walking negative stereotype of the mother on welfare — high school drop out, overweight, poorly dressed, erratically kept appointments, rarely provided an extra set of clothes for her children, a mother of three, and only 22 years old. More so, she had been reported to the state for suspected child abuse for what looked like a burn on her child's bottom — which turned out to be impetigo. When she got upset with the center about James' care or had questions about his education, one could always sense from the staff an underlying "how dare you challenge us on our care decisions." The more questions, the more staff outrage. Some of her questions/concerns:

- When will James be taught to read?

- Why does he get so dirty?

- How did he get that bruise?

- How could he lose two shirts and a shoe?

- Why do you let James get away with so much?

Gloria was loud and seemed ill at ease and pushy to the staff. Because of this, many staff didn't recognize that her questions and concerns were nearly always appropriate, never frivolous.

Megan's mother, Jane, was nearly the opposite of Gloria — a 42 year old psychologist and Megan was her only child. She was usually late picking up Megan and often was slow responding to staff requests. When she had concerns or asked questions, and she asked many (similar to Gloria's), staff response was less "how dare she" and more "what a typical neurotic older yuppie parent." As with Gloria, Jane's questions and concerns, while numerous and often minor, were never off the wall.

The parents' job is to look out for their child, to monitor their care, and to advocate for quality care and education. Both Gloria and Jane did this, better than many *nicer* parents. When parents are persistent or assertive, they may well be obnoxious (at least to us) and we begin to use stereotypes to discredit them. What staff have to understand is not that parents' concerns or questions are always valid — a parent request or complaint may be ill-founded — but making the request or complaint is a parent acting responsibly.

Mutual Respect: A "Why Not" Approach

One way to characterize the approach is that all requests are met with a non-defensive attitude and "why not" thinking, an approach that grants the parent request legitimacy. When parents asks us for a change in their child's routine, a special activity, or a different way of doing things, we genuinely ask ourselves, "why not?" This is different than a customer-is-always-right approach. It is not an automatic **yes**.

There may be many legitimate "why nots" that lead to a no — for budget reasons, the complexity of group life, we don't know how, staffing, etc. We have no reason to be defensive about our givens that lead to our limitations.

The outcome of a "why not" approach is not unmanageable complexity, but thoughtful care and a foundation of mutual respect and, in most cases, increased trust that we are professionals thinking through good care. The non-defensive "why not" rubs off on the parents and begins to characterize staff relationships as well. Equally important, a "why not" approach leads to innovation and better care.

Looking for High Ground: Balancing Needs of Children, Staff, and Parents

Last year floods of biblical proportions came to my part of the country. Drowned fields bankrupted farmers, and towns were suddenly underwater and families stranded on rooftops. And what terrible hardship befell me, you ask, living as I do near the mighty Mississippi? Only a spring and summer of wet feet and shoes that stank from flooded sidewalks and jogging paths. Not a heavy price to pay for a metaphor — albeit not original, in use from the Bible to pop singers.

It is easy for child care directors to feel they swim in an endless river of needs. The demands of children, parents, and staff are ever-present, always churning together, and more or less met. For most directors, the flow is steady, sometimes leisurely, with occasional rapids. But some-times (and in some programs, much of the time), there are just too many problems, too many needs that flood over, and then we scramble for higher ground, trying to survive. We emerge wet, dirty, and hoping for some respite, knowing that this too will pass (won't it?).

But, at times, high ground isn't enough, and driven by our anger and righteousness, we push further for a seemingly safer perch: the HIGH MORAL GROUND. It is in the scramble for high moral ground that we go shrill, tearing each other apart with sharp aspersions about the character of those who stand in our way. "If THEY only understood (cared about) children (child care, teachers, parents)." "THEY are self-ish (irresponsible, immature, igno-rant)." Sometimes the blows are wrapped in the velvet of condescen-sion — "THEY don't know any bet-ter." There are no more individuals, only "THEY" and our perceptions of what "THEY" do become defined by the worst "THEM," which is unfortunate because there will always be jerks.

Law of the Jerks

Look around you. Isn't it pretty clear that about 1 out of 10 average people are probably jerks? Look closer. Probably 1 out of 20 are seriously deranged.

Now, look again. We can't blame all the jerky and deranged behavior on them. Everyone probably acts like a jerk about a tenth of the time. And, yes, everyone probably acts deranged about one twentieth of the time.

Now, please note: We are part of that everyone. Maybe we should take that into account.

WHAT'S THE HARM? PARENT VERSUS CHILD VERSUS "DEVELOPMENTALLY APPROPRIATE PRACTICE"

A young parent came to her child's lead teacher asking for her to begin toilet training 17 month old Nicole at the center. Barbara saw no evidence that Nicole had the slightest interest in the potty. But she also knew that the family had little money and that Nicole's grandmother believed that family history dictated toilet training should begin at an early age. Barbara said "sure" (despite the protests of her co-workers), she would begin getting Nicole used to the toilet, as long as the parent understood that it might be a while before Nicole developed an interest, and that she wouldn't force Nicole.

It seemed to work. Barbara was gentle and non-oppressive with Nicole, Nicole's mom felt respected and appreciated Barbara's willingness to try; and Nicole seemed to think the whole thing was sort of a harmless lark. Barbara and Nicole's mom began to talk about Nicole and her child care in a new way. But the director got wind of what was going on and, being an ordained member of the Sacred Order of the Perpetually Pure Devoted to Developmentally Appropriate Practice, countermanded the inexperienced teacher and told her that Nicole was too young.

Perhaps. But in this circumstance, what was the harm that counterbalanced the obvious good: a true partnership with a parent, the value of which would serve Nicole far better than a few months respite from the potty? And the teacher's response was developmentally appropriate — appropriate to the development of the parent-teacher relationship and, actually, the development of Nicole within her family and culture. "What's the harm?" is a good principle to keep in mind when needs conflict.

PARENT NEED VERSUS PARENT NEED

Jack's father: "Jack is only seven months old. I worry every time I see Kerry's five year old brother come in with his mother to pick up Kerry. He wants to hug the babies, play with their toys. And he's not the only one. Bobby Jo comes in with her mother and always wants to *help*. Please save us from her help. And those parents don't supervise their children either. Why can't we ban those kids from the infant room? Their parents can pick up the babies before picking up the older children."

Kerry's mother: "If I pick up Kerry first, I have to lug her around in her car seat while I pick up her brother. It makes it difficult for me to have conversations with Bobby's teacher or take the time to see what he wants me to see."

There may not be an easy answer to this issue. Certainly, there are other alternatives to try before banning siblings from the room. But there is no WRONG here, none of the parents or children are doing anything BAD or IRRESPONSIBLE. There is no high moral ground.

FOR THE GOOD OF THE CHILD

In the Child's Garden Child Care, parents are asked to make an effort to spend time in the classroom the first few weeks helping the child to adjust — a reasonable request, very positive for the child. While some parents feel they can take the time, many can't. "I don't understand why they even had this kid if they can't take a few hours off for the good of the child to make her transition easier," said Chris, a teacher frustrated by a child's difficult transition.

Later in the year when Chris's co-worker had just resigned suddenly, Chris was urged (strongly) by the director to delay her vacation because a new child was having a very difficult time adjusting to the center. For the good of the child, a reasonable request. But reasonable for Chris, particularly if she felt pressured to say yes? And what about frequently asking teachers to change their shifts or give up breaks to help this or that child?

There is only so much we — parents and staff — can do *for the good of the child*. Yes, some parents should devote more time and energy to their children. Yes, some teachers should respond more to the individual child's need and worry less about standard routines, schedules, breaks, and even their planned curriculum. But who are we to draw lines and judge who are the self-centered few? It is destructive to use the idea of *the good of the child* as a sword of righteousness to judge the other.

TEACHER SECURITY VERSUS CHILD SECURITY

The new teacher was eager to begin transforming the room, making it hers. It would have a new tone and sensibility — it would be better! The routines would change, the bulletin boards and decor, pieces of the curriculum and the daily rituals. But the director said to go slow, wait for a few weeks, and then change things gradually with the involvement of the kids. The teacher felt like a sprinter, shackled at the starting line, and she was angry.

It was a classic battle — security versus security, a teacher's security versus a child's security. The teacher wouldn't feel secure in the job until she could make the room her own, reflecting her competency, interests, and style. But the children's security depends on a predictable world, which is always called into question when the people who anchor their world leave.

It was also a classic case of egocentrism — on the teacher's part. She told the director, "What's the big deal? The children will be fine." Well, the big deal is that a new teacher is an upheaval who brings a whole new set of expectations and sensations — a different voice, body language, touch, lap (and rules for its use), even a different smell. When the teacher quickly begins to upset all the other pillars of security — the routines, rituals, sense of place, and expectations — that predictable world for the child falls apart. Imagine replacing a lost lover over-night with someone who wants to redo your home — and you get the idea.

PARENT ECONOMICS VERSUS TEACHER ECONOMICS

An angry teacher: "These parents have to understand. We deserve more money. What we do is important. I don't see how these parents can live with themselves, paying us less than dog catchers."

Yes, child care workers deserve more money for an important, demanding job. Yes, many parents by and large should pay more, even though child care is very costly.

But let's take the righteous moral tone out of the argument. The teacher with the fiery rhetoric was wearing a dress made in China, a sweater from eastern Europe, driving a car with parts made in Mexico and Korea, eating fruit picked by migrant labor, and herself using family day care priced less than the center where she is working. Her way of life, all of our lives, are made affordable by cheap labor.

When we act as consumers, very few of us are swayed by moral argument, however sympathetic. We all feel financial pressures and look for affordability in our purchasing. The more effective argument for higher salaries is not moral, it is quality — parents need to understand that child care salaries need to go up to attract and retain good staff.

DOING THE BEST WE CAN

I watched a four year old boy, recently arrived from Vietnam and new to the world of winter, hurriedly struggle into a magnificent new snowmobile suit in a rush to go outside. Hopelessly lost in a tangle of fabric, zippers, and too many holes to choose where to put an arm, leg, or head, he ended up scuttling out the door like a crab, with an apologetic smile that said, "Well, I'm doing the best I can."

Later I saw that same look on the face of a parent guiltily quieting her tired child with a cookie, a teacher listening to a parent complain about a bite mark on her child's face, and a director once again negotiating a truce between two wonderful, but hopelessly incompatible, teachers.

Child care involves complex, intimate, and often intense interactions between people. When we fight for high moral ground, it turns into an emotional swamp — and then we all feel bad. We lose sight of how many children, staff, and parents are making heroic efforts just doing the best they can.

No Surprises:
Reducing Staff-Parent Tension

Much of the tension between staff and parents comes from expectations not being met and from unpleasant surprises. If we can shape parent expectations and avoid disconcerting shocks and surprises, we will improve parent-staff relations.

Depending on the Kindness of Strangers

Alana burst, actually enthusiastically lurched, through the door with a huge smile and stopped — keeled over is more accurate. She and I didn't recognize the woman we both expected to be the much beloved Roxanne.

We looked for Roxanne but only saw another woman in the room who didn't know me but did seem to know Alana. That was a little disconcerting, but somewhat comforting. She was friendly and seemed okay (which to me means a smile and no tattoos or odd body piercing). I did have to ask who she was and then volunteer information about Alana. I like the program and trust the director, but I left feeling like a pretty lousy parent because I had just handed over my 13 month old kid to a stranger.

It goes against every instinct of a good parent to hand their child over to a stranger. But substitutes are a fact of life in the real world of child care — even (though hopefully rarely) multiple substitutes in a room. Obviously, we should try to reduce the chances it will happen by pairing rooms and shifting staff, or using floaters. But assuming we

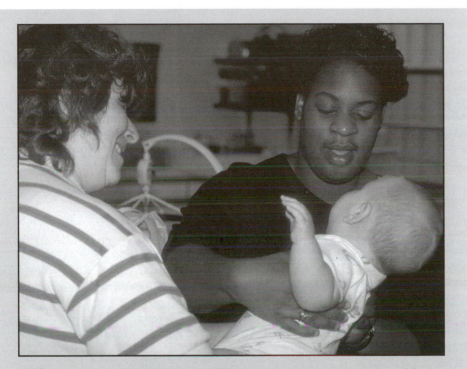

"What do you mean it isn't ready?" My car wasn't ready — I could see that. It was on the lift and the wheels were off. It was nearly 5:00 and they said it would be ready when I talked to them at 2:00. Great. It wasn't ready and I had to pick up my kid at the child care center by 5:30. Another late fee (I think it's up to $100 a minute for me!) and another dirty look from Emma's teacher. I was mad, and what could I do but be surly.

I needed the car to be done, and it was frustrating not to have it. But what was maddening — and did not bring out the kindlier, gentler me — was that I **expected** the car to be done and it wasn't. That expectation raised the stakes.

There are a whole range of unpleasant or frustrating experiences that will happen in child care. Children's clothes will be lost, a child will bite or get bitten, separation will be hard, children will get sick — again and again and again. Parents will no doubt experience staff absences, staff turnover, program changes they do not understand, and teachers making mistakes in judgment. Good programs work hard to minimize all of these experiences, but **they will happen**. Paraphrasing Marianne Moore, there are real toads in our garden.

will never be 100% successful, what can we do to help parents adjust to reality?

Parents will feel a lot better if they know the role that substitutes do play and if they don't find out the room's staffing as their eyes scan the room. We can manage expectations and avoid surprises if we take the following steps in communication:

✔ At the enrollment intake, bring up the substitute issue and discuss your screening, any orientation you give substitutes, and how you ensure adequate supervision of substitutes.

✔ Never assume because a substitute has worked before and you and the staff know her well that all the parents in this room know her

---

SO LONG, IT'S BEEN GOOD TO KNOW YOU

Parents are taught to evaluate a program by its turnover, which is legitimate. But parents need to know that, given the typical workforce in a child care center (many young women during their most transitional period — marriage, pregnancy, career change, and possible relocation), a baseline of 10% to 15% turnover will happen in the best of programs.

Moreover, there is internal classroom turnover as teachers get promoted or make lateral moves, which is simply experienced as turnover to a child or parent.

Centers should shape parents' expectations of what turnover to expect and, of course, they deserve an explanation of how the center manages to cushion the effect on children and parents.

(or even know all the staff in the center).

✔ For every substitute, create a biography sheet with a picture and display on the door with a note for parents to read **before** they walk in (see example on next page).

MOVING ON UP: "IT'S SO DIFFERENT"

We loved the toddler room, and Jake was so attached to his teacher, Bridgett. Now he just seems so lost. There are so many kids in the room when we bring him. Worse, I don't know what goes on during the day, and the teachers don't tell us very much. I don't think it's nearly as good as the toddler room.

Moving from the small, intimate world of toddlers to the big, exuberant world of the preschool is a big change for children and parents. Parents may experience the differences as a loss and a drop in quality. They may view the staff in the room as inferior to the staff they left. Their feelings are based on expectations shaped by their experiences with toddler staff-child ratios, group size, and the resulting caring routines. Here is an excerpt from a two-page center handout to parents designed to forestall concerns:

" . . . you will notice lots of changes — some of which you will welcome — like lower tuition and many new learning opportunities for your child; others will take some time getting used to — like larger group sizes and higher staff-to-child ratios (the reason, of course, for the lower tuition)."

The note goes on to explain issues that predictably will be of concern to parents. For example:

✔ Higher ratios and group size are possible without a drop in quality because the children are developing more self-help and social skills.

✔ Because primary caregivers have responsibility for nearly twice as many children, communication

---

may take on different forms and daily experience sheets will be less extensive. It won't necessarily mean less communication.

✔ Development is usually uneven — both in rate and across developmental areas. "Regression" should not be a cause for concern because it is normal for children to race forward to new heights and fall back to familiar plateaus.

✔ Children benefit from a wider age range.

THE UNKINDEST CUT: "WHY DIDN'T YOU TELL US?"

Nothing is as unpleasant as the unexpected first sight of your *maimed* child — that ugly, red, semi-circular bite mark on the cheek or arm. Any advance notification, even if only told seconds before entering the classroom, is preferable to the visual discovery.

Let parents know all the actions you take to prevent biting and to bring a biting epidemic under control before they experience it.

"HE DOESN'T WANT TO LEAVE AND (SOB) HE LIKES YOU BETTER THAN ME"

Sooner or later, most children will put parents through the ordeal of appearing to not want to leave by acting indifferent or dramatically refusing to leave — or acting up at the sight of parents and creating an awkward situation.

We should know and explain to parents that the least likely explanation is that the child actually has weighed the home/child care settings and elected to stay at the center because he likes the staff so much. We can save parents some guilt and sorrow (that may strain the parent-staff relationship) if we anticipate the occurrence and explain to parents that **it will happen** — and that some of the reasons for the behavior include an assertion of independence or stubbornness, wanting parents to experience their world, or separation emotions that may translate into trying behavior when they see the one person in the world they are closest to.

"How Can We Not Surprise Them If They Don't Read What We Give Them?"

It is the information age. We are bombarded with information "we should read" from all facets of our lives — on the job, child care and schools, instruction manuals for our latest technology, neighborhood associations and politicians, newspapers, magazines, and on and on. Our information for parents is important, but it is only a fraction of what a "good" parent or citizen "should" read. Of course they don't read everything, and neither do we!

Effective communication requires a strategic sense that understands the world of busy parents, the importance of timing, and the uses of multiple communication vehicles — handbooks, notes, signs, and meeting

---

STAFFING CHANGE TODAY

Because _____ is out today,

your substitute is _____.

Photo

Jane has three years experience in child care, is the mother of two, and has been on our substitute list for one year.

---

minutes (the topic of a future column).

"No Surprises" and the Organizational Culture

In "Places for Childhoods Include Parents, Too," I suggested that centers should have a "why not" approach to parents (and staff): all requests or ideas are met with a "why not" attitude. This is not a "customer is always right" approach,

rather an "it's always legitimate to question and suggest" approach. It respects the customer (parent) or employee.

A "no surprises" approach is another key element in a culture of respect that promotes partnership. It is based on an understanding of and empathy for the circumstance of others, and applies equally to the center's relationship to parents and to staff (and, of course, to children).

MANAGING EXPECTATIONS: NOTES TO PARENTS

Where do parents get their crazy ideas? Overheard at a conference workshop on working with parents:

➤ Don't parents know that toddlers bite?

➤ Why do they expect that their child can stay inside?

➤ Do they think that I am getting rich off of this?

➤ Do they expect the same TLC in a 20 kid preschool with 1:10 ratios that they got in the toddler room with 1:5 ratios?

➤ Don't they realize not everyone can have the lead teacher as the primary caregiver?

➤ Do they expect us to be like first grade?

➤ Why do they expect that their sick child can stay and everyone else's should be excluded?

What do parents expect from us anyway? Good question. A lot! But where do their expectations of us come from? From everywhere: media, their experience with child care or the lack of it, *Choosing Child Care* handouts and — most of all — us. It's not just what we say and do, but what we don't say. If we know which issues will devolve into a clash of realities, and we certainly do, we can help to shape expectations and reduce conflict.

PARENT NOTES

We create expectations in all of our materials, from the center brochure to the parent handbook to signs on our walls. Producing written and visual materials is one of our most powerful tools in shaping expectations. Creating a series of "A Note to Parents" on issues is useful for being prepared when issues arise and also for creating a *no surprises* culture. Parent notes do more than provide information. A good parent note:

Anticipates questions and concerns that parents have.

We can anticipate questions because we hear them all the time: about the food program, outdoor policies, male caregivers, biting, transitions, fees. Often the Q & A format lends itself to parent notes because we write what we are so used to saying to parents.

Outlines our thinking.

Parents need to know that our practices are based on experienced expertise, careful thought, and, when appropriate, research. The message is not "We have the truth" but "This is our way."

Refers back to and reinforces other communications.

Notes should always remind parents that we have written policies in a handbook, resource materials, handouts, and the like.

Sets a positive tone.

Notes always set a tone; sometimes negative — defensive, preachy, or condescending ("We are the experts with the truth"). Usually, the right tone is relaxed but takes the issue seriously and is more conversational than formal. The note reads like a note — not a dry pronouncement or stiff, formal handbookese.

Reinforces the center culture.

Notes and other communications reinforce, for good or ill, the center culture. Notes can reinforce a culture of "We (parents and staff) are all in this together" or a "It's our center and we (staff) are the experts." My preference is a culture of "We (parents and staff) are smart people and can work together to figure out the right approach," "We listen and work through issues," and "We try hard to balance a variety of factors."

— Hemingway You Ain't!

So what if you don't write well — it comes out dull, stiff, confused; and where are you supposed to get the time to wax eloquent anyway? You do what we all do: get help, beg, borrow, and steal. It's the director's job to get the communications together, but he or she may not be the best writer. Take advantage of staff who can write, excerpt from articles and books. Good writers also let others read their writing and suggest changes; rarely are we as clear as we think we are.

In the following excerpt from a note on biting, note the empathy for all perspectives, the challenges of balancing needs, and the outline of issues. There is no assertion of truth or surefire solutions. There is a clear "We are all in this together" message.

ON CHILDREN BITING

Periodically, in even the best child care program, outbreaks of biting occur in infant and toddler rooms, and sometimes even among preschoolers — an unavoidable consequence of young children in group care. When it happens, it's pretty scary, very frustrating, and very stressful for children, parents, and teachers. But, however unfortunate, it is a natural phenomena, not something to blame on children, or parents, or teachers — and there are no quick and easy solutions. . . .

Children bite for a variety of reasons: the simple sensory exploration of babies, panic, crowding, seeking to be noticed, or the intense desire for a toy. Repeated biting becomes a pattern of learned behavior that is often hard to extinguish because it does achieve results: the desired toy, excitement, attention.

Dealing With Biting Is a Program Responsibility

The program accepts responsibility for biting and other hurtful acts and for protecting the children. It is our job to provide a safe setting where no child needs to hurt another to achieve his or her ends. . . .

Biting is a horrifying stage some children go through. It is a common phenomena that has virtually no lasting developmental significance. A child who bites is not on a path towards being a discipline problem, a bad person, or a cannibal. There are a number of possible explanations for why some children bite, none of them the fault of a "bad" home, "bad" parents, or "bad" teachers. Most of the time, it is hard to guess what is going on in the child's head. . . .

Here is what we do to try and extinguish the biting behavior. . . .

Balancing Program Commitments to All the Children

Some children become "stuck" for a while in a biting syndrome and it is frustrating for the parents of victims that we are unable to "fix" the child quickly or terminate care. We try and make every effort to extinguish the behavior quickly and balance our commitment to the family of the biting child with that of the other families. Only after we feel we have made every effort to make the program work for the child do we consider asking a family to withdraw the child.

NINE SOURCES OF PARENT/PROGRAM CONFLICT

- Biting and child aggression
- Outdoor policy
- Food
- Health policies
- Staff turnover
- Transitions to an older group
- Multiaging or grouping
- Fees
- My child's education

In the next note on outdoor policies, we share our perspective without being defensive, empathize with the parent's reality, and assert the policy.

THE "OUTS AND INS" OF OUR OUTDOOR POLICY: A Q & A FOR PARENTS

Does my child have to go outside every day?

Here's the policy as written in the Parent Handbook:

"Health experts are unanimous on the importance of fresh air, and the negative health consequences of children spending too much time in closed, indoor settings. If a child is well enough to be in the homebase, the child is generally assumed well enough to go outside. Except in extreme weather, children are expected to go outside every day. The director or assistant director determines whether conditions are acceptable for outdoor play."

What if I ask that my child stays indoors today?

We usually have to say no. While we would like to individualize, staff-child ratios rarely allow us to stay with one or two children while the group goes outside. It is also often difficult for the staff to try and find another home-base that is staying in to care for the child (and may be uncomfortable for the child).

But what about my child's health?

We understand that parents naturally have strong feelings about keeping their children healthy, which we share. But health experts agree that cool or damp weather is rarely harmful to children and going outside is essential (see our handout from Model Health Policies).

Does the center make exceptions?

We never say never. But if we are going to allow a few exceptions, we also need you to accept and respect the more common times we are unable to accommodate your request and have to say no.

What if my child is not dressed properly?

We will try and frequently remind you when your child is lacking something (a hat, rain gear, mittens, etc.). We know that things disappear, so we will also try and keep on hand extras for those inevitable times when items disappear. But the program depends on children arriving with all the requisite clothing for a full, active day, indoors and out.

The final two notes are written to help parents with a situation that almost all parents experience. Just having the notes illustrates sensitivity and understanding of the parent's reality.

END OF THE DAY REUNIONS: THEY DO LOVE YOU BEST!

At the end of the day, staff, parents, and children are all likely to be tired. Children usually have had enough of being in a group; and as other children start going home, they begin to anticipate the arrival of their parents. Parents would no doubt like a warm welcome from the child at the end of the day and a smooth and pleasant exit from the center. Unfortunately, for a variety of reasons, this may not always happen. Sometimes when you arrive to pick up your child, he or she may:

➤ *look up briefly from what he or she is doing when you greet them, and return to the activity; or*

➤ *become distressed; or*

➤ *begin to "act up" and engage in taboo behavior; or*

➤ *that same child who did not want to stay in the morning may actively resist going home.*

However, there are a number of explanations for this behavior, the least likely that "he or she would rather stay here with caregivers":

Children are complex human beings. They often act as social scientists, using their behavior to experiment with how the world works and their place in it. In the process, they will both delight us and cause us concern. In this instance, one thing is certain, you are the ones they love best — they just have a funny way of showing it. . . .

BIG STEPS FOR YOUR CHILD (AND YOU): MOVING ON UP TO PRESCHOOL

Moving up to preschool is a major transition, for your children and for you! You will notice lots of changes, some of which you will welcome — like lower tuition and many new learning opportunities for your child. Others will take time getting used to — like larger group sizes and higher staff-to-child ratios (the reason for lower tuition).

Higher Staff-Child Ratios

As children develop and mature, their dependence on adults begins to diminish and they learn to adjust to group life. Higher ratios and group size are possible without sacrificing quality in care and education. Yet there is a price:

➤ *The amount of one-to-one adult-child attention is reduced slightly, which is generally acceptable because the child's increasing self-help skills and newly acquired social skills and interests take their place.*

➤ *With higher staff-child ratios, the number of primary care children per caregiver goes up and staff-parent communication has to change.*

We expect staff to be creative and find time to communicate with parents — this may involve notes, phone calls, and bulletin boards.

At the same time, it helps greatly if parents make the effort to tell teachers what information they particularly care about, because parents care about different things. If you especially want to know about certain activities, mood or behavior, nap or friendships, let your primary caregiver know.

Program

Expectations for the child's educational experience increase when they enter preschool. And why not? Preschool children are transforming themselves daily.

With the larger group, what you observe may appear confusing, even chaotic, if you are expecting an orderly classroom where teaching is ever-present. But there is an order, a structure based on learning centers and expectations of behavior of both teachers and children in a rich learning environment, and a social context, that allows development to proceed at the child's pace.

FINAL THOUGHT

Much of our success at establishing the kind of program we wish to have and achieving full enrollment depends on customer/parent satisfaction. Customer satisfaction depends on fulfilling or exceeding expectations. Child care is a business in which everyone sort of knows what to expect based on our own experience of schools, moms and babysitting, and word of mouth. Many of those expectations may be far from what child care providers want, or are able to fulfill. If we don't take advantage of every opportunity to shape and inform those expectations based on our vision of quality and our real world of trade-offs, we set ourselves up for conflict or failure.

CHAPTER 8

TRAINING AND CHANGE

- Double your staff development budget — it's probably less than .05 percent of your budget. Encourage staff to take courses, attend workshops; buy training materials. Send more than one person to training and think about which staff might complement each other at training.

PAY ATTENTION TO WHAT MOTIVATES INDIVIDUALS

All of us need recognition. For some, recognition of the impact that we are having is a driving force; for most, the recognition of others is important as well. Recognition will motivate and sustain change, even unwilling changes, if the recognition is of the sort that we value. Understanding the positive effects of our actions on children and parents or other staff; recognition by co-workers and supervisors for the work we do that makes an extra difference; and recognition that travels beyond the confines of the center through a newsletter, community newspaper, or an award that goes home all have an impact. Some ideas:

- Create a slide or videotape presentation for staff that captures staff at their best moments and describes the effects of their actions.

- Develop serious and semi-serious awards and certificates, such as *Caregiver of the month, For continued humor and sensitivity on the single worst day of the program's history, Most interesting activity of the week,* etc.

- Give staff a few hours off to develop a good idea or to present ideas to other staff.

- Extol the virtues of staff when giving tours,

- Use the newsletter to let everyone know you know what they are accomplishing.

CONCLUSION

As I carefully warned, the purpose of this piece was not to prescribe or offer startling new innovations. My goal was to remind directors and trainers, including myself, that to be effective we must take into account the real complexity of change and not let our enthusiasm or heavy workload seduce us into shortcuts that might render our efforts ineffective.

In child care, it is hard to move beyond a concern for the present. The most effective change efforts are not one-shot events but are those planned with an idea of the necessary follow up. The more staff and program development efforts are planned as events in a continuum of efforts, the more likely the success.

REFERENCES

Fuqua, R., and J. Greenman. "Training of Caregivers and Change in Day Care Centers' Environments," *Child Care Quarterly*, V, II, No. 4, 1982.

Greenman, J. "Program Development and Models of Consultation." In J. Greenman and R. Fuqua (editors), *Making Day Care Better: Training, Evaluation, and the Process of Change.* New York: Teachers College Press, 1984.

Jones, E. "Training Individuals: In the Classroom and Out," *Making Day Care Better.*

Pettygrove, W., and J. Greenman. "The Adult World of Day Care," *Making Day Care Better.*

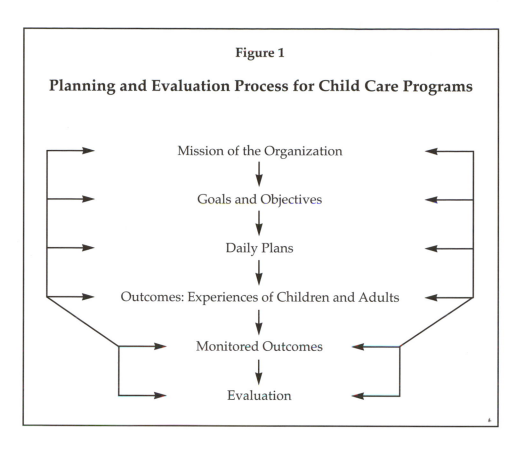

Figure 1

Planning and Evaluation Process for Child Care Programs

Mission of the Organization

Goals and Objectives

Daily Plans

Outcomes: Experiences of Children and Adults

Monitored Outcomes

Evaluation

— more fingerplays, activities, techniques; the most difficult is helping someone to toss out their old bag and begin a new one — for example, replacing how I *teach* that works with kindergartners with how I *teach* that's appropriate with babies.

STAFF ARE NOT ALL THE SAME

At all training sessions, individuals are present, not staff — each with different ideas, learning styles, motivations, and an assortment of bags of tricks. These bag ladies and gentlemen will come out of each session with their own individual understandings and synthesis. The more that we are aware of and understand the differences, the more success we may have (Pettygrove and Greenman, 1984). Who are some of these people?

Mary Lou, a program coordinator with a degree in child development who plans to return to graduate school to study special education: "I consider myself a professional and get very frustrated with people who don't. Training is important. I think a lot of people just babysit, some good babysitting, but they don't really teach and work at providing good learning environments. I am not a caregiver, I am a teacher."

Barbara, a soon-to-be grandmother who teaches in the same program, has a completely different view: "I have been taking care of kids all this time, teaching them and doing just fine. Most of the workshops I have to go to are Mickey Mouse, taught by a guy who never had to take care of kids."

June, a 37 year old single parent of three, has worked with children since the early days of Head Start and at the same child care program for the last three years. After she has completed the course for a CDA credential, she thinks she may take courses at a community college and receive a degree: "I usually like the courses and the workshops if there are other people in them like me. I don't really have the time though."

Add 18 year old Wanda who's waiting for an opening as a key puncher, 22 year old Steve who hasn't decided what he will end up doing but delights in young children and the freedom with which he is allowed to plan his groups, and the other recognizable types that make up the adult world of child care. We, or at least I as a director, want a staff with a range of characteristics that reflect the multidimensional world outside: grandmother types who fuss over children and "nurture them and feed them and scold them and keep them clean and safe and well fed" (Jones, 1984), "Mr. science types," and "Ms. organizations" — people who together will provide the nurturing, socialization, and learning experiences that the children require. Staff may vary in terms of training, experience, ambition, motivation, energy, and free time.

LEARNING ≠ CHANGE

If learning resulted easily in change, we would all be thin, fit, relaxed, active listeners; our parachutes would be packed and we would be generally delightful souls. But doing what we learn is a matter of will, discipline, and an external context that may or may not be supportive. (I know all the time management tools; knowledge isn't the problem, my personality is.)

STAFF DEVELOPMENT ≠ PROGRAM DEVELOPMENT

In 1978, I put together a midwestern conference, *Day Care Environments*, which appeared to be a smashing success. Not only did nearly all conference attendees enjoy the conference (keynoted by Elizabeth Prescott, Thelma Harms, and Fred Osmon), but evaluations commented on the new insights gained and concrete ideas. As part of the conference, Robert Fuqua and I studied 18 programs that participated in the confer-

ence (Fuqua and Greenman, 1982). Some also received preconference preparation to increase the value of the conference. All programs sent the director and at least one other staff.

Using the Harms-Clifford Day Care Environment Rating Scale, we evaluated changes occurring within three months after the conference — change a child or parent might experience. While training may have created important effects due to increased enthusiasm, sense of professionalism, or effects which will show up later, in most of the programs only marginal change occurred. Some of the programs that received the most training changed the least.

WHAT GETS IN THE WAY? ALL THE THINGS THAT MAKE CHANGE DIFFICULT

How many people are involved? How many people have to change their behavior? "In one program, an assistant teacher returned from a workshop eager to try some of the ideas she heard on developing free choice times. She was blocked by the lack of interest or understanding shown by the other staff. After some of the other staff received similar training, some changes were instituted." (Greenman, 1984)

How quickly can change be affected and take hold? Time for adults to think, plan, and work together without children present is the most precious commodity in child care. (How rare this commodity is is often not understood by trainers with background in lab schools and half-day programs.) How much of this time is necessary for change?

Change requires time to consider alternatives, to achieve some understanding and workable consensus, and to work out the inevitable difficulties. "An effort in one center to individualize aspects of toddler schedules by changing certain routines and redoing the room arrangement fell short because the effort required too much time to achieve. From the time the program decided that the individualized schedules were desirable and achievable to the institution of the changes and the working out of the kinks (four months), some staff turnover had occurred, the director's attention was pulled elsewhere, and the consultant who had helped to promote and initiate the change was no longer available. Eight months later, the schedules were no more individualized than before." (Greenman, 1984)

What changes in resources are necessary? Will the change take money, politically delicate redistribution of space or materials between classrooms, increased storage?

Effective Training and Program Change

Where does the above leave us — given that change is a difficult and complex process; the people in child care are an assortment of humanity and motive; and resources, particularly thinking time, are scarce? Here are some suggestions:

Development should be built into the program. The best organizations are thoughtful and creative. There is a sense shared by most members of where the organization is and where it is going — further, where it *might* go if certain things were to happen. There is a sense of potential. It is knowing both what the next incremental level of quality is (perhaps more parent involvement) and a sense of the ideal and the determination to realize it (parent involvement in all aspects of the program). The organization is opportunistic; when an opportunity presents itself, the organization recognizes it and is in a position to take advantage of it. There is strong visionary leadership; the whole organization is striving.

The vision does not have to center around expanding, which is most common, nor be confined to the director or just a few staff. In the best programs, almost anyone in the organization could tell you what the program is about and what it is trying to become — e.g., more individualized, serve a wider age range, a more systematic curriculum. The process outlined in Figure 1 is more evident, more conscious, and spread throughout the organization, although not necessarily more formal or more systematic. One has a sense that the program is thinking all the time.

Building program development into the program is the result of good leadership. Some ideas on how to create the socio-intellectual ambiance necessary:

- By hook or by crook, finding time for meetings is essential. Without the time to think and plan and thrash out new ways of doing things, child care is merely doing babysitting. Think of all potential resources that would allow staff and sub-groups as small as two people to meet. Circulate written outlines, drafts, minutes to generate awareness of what is going on.

- Take program philosophy, goals, ideas, and curriculum out of people's heads and put them in writing everywhere: in handbooks, newsletters, wall posters, self-guided tour instructions for new staff and parents. When you proclaim what you believe and how you are trying to achieve it, it forces you to think it through and provides others a chance to ask about it or to challenge it.

Tailor staff development to your staff. "Competence in child care is learned through education, or experience (including parenting), or through being in touch with the child in oneself. . . . Any training aimed at increasing quality in day care needs to build on caregivers' best instincts, their own values, and their sense of what is right for children and for themselves as adults with children. . . . Learners are not empty vessels waiting to be filled by experts. They are persons with a wealth of meaningful experiences." (Jones, 1984)

Good training respects the people we are trying to reach. All too many training programs operate with the "If we can get the contract, we can do the training" attitude and provides trainers, often graduate students, with little knowledge of the real world of child care — the context that caregivers must operate in — and who are only a step ahead of caregivers, if that, in terms of the content of the training. Here you see training/learning/change, only training equals more training contracts. If the training didn't take hold, "Well, it must be the fault of the caregivers!"

When program development is built in, staff development is based on the logic of individual development and program needs that is generally understood. In a thoughtful aspiring program with strong supportive leadership, staff development is accepted as a matter of course.

Staff development includes anything that encourages your staff to think about what they know and don't know and what they are doing. Some ideas for training:

- Some staff, those who see themselves as professionals and have ambition, can be helped to become trainers and consultants themselves — not experts, but facilitators utilizing their own experience. Encourage them to put together workshops for your staff and local conferences.

- Put together a collection of readings for staff and parents — articles or snippets on development or child care that reflect your program's ideology and practices. Utilize staff and parents as editors.

- Try to utilize parents, interns, and visitors as observers and use staff to interview them.

rationales for the eventual decisions, why this course of action was taken or this equipment purchased, is critical for participants to feel that their participation was taken seriously.

PARTICIPANTS:
ARCHITECTS AND DESIGNERS

The value of good architects and designers is in the way they think and what they know. The knowledge of how built space works as a network of systems and the different alternatives of arranging spaces, managing flows, relating to the outside, creating moods and behavior patterns, and the range of materials available is what they bring to the process.

Directors and teachers are often limited by what they have experienced in the way of child care spaces and program models. They rarely know many alternative ways of developing space. Visiting other programs and reading design resources can help overcome this. What program staff should know and be able to articulate to other participants is what the goals of the program are and how the adults and children in the program behave in the present space. Combining their knowledge with that of architects and designers increases the chances that the space will work with a minimum of the unanticipated side effects that haunt many programs.

"The architect is very well known and has done schools and other children's settings, but I don't know about this," said a worried child care director, indicating the blueprints she was holding. "This" was a site for a downtown child care program for children under five years old with no drop-off parking, a space-consuming library, a mini-amphitheater, and very little meeting or storage space. Luckily, this building wasn't built; but others have been — high sealed windows; tiny play yards; out-of-scale rooms; and intriguing, but unworkable layouts.

Averting disaster requires architects who listen to early childhood professionals and directors who observe and listen to teachers and parents and children and who are not afraid to assert their views. It is when architects *know* and directors *know* or are silent that there are problems. Professional arrogance or arrogance of authority or status, combined with time constraints, leads to problems — problems that may never be openly acknowledged.

When a building, a design, or a bright idea doesn't work the way it was intended, the failure may be blamed on the users — staff and children. This is a common problem in architecture and design (and of course applies to the advice of experts in almost any endeavor). Worse, the users may accept the failure as their own, which has happened

in a number of state-of-the-art child care facilities. Those architects or designers didn't return to assess the outcomes and have gone on to build new versions of flawed designs.

These failings are compounded by the difficulty in balancing form and function, a tension inherent in design. Architects and designers are usually much more sensitive than others to the form of things, the aesthetic affects of designs. This is both necessary and positive; our lives are enriched by beauty and forms that challenge us to think. But there has to be a balance.

The styling director for Ford Motors, George Walker, when criticized for the sleek door frame design that was difficult to cope with in an era of stylish hats, replied: "It's hard to believe anyone would mind getting his hat knocked off for the sake of a clean line." An interior designer's reaction to her stylized graphics being partially covered with storage cabinets in a nursery school echoed Walker's, "Can't they do without a few materials and appreciate the design?"

BUILDERS

Contractors and skilled craftsmen bring to the process specific knowledge. In some cases, it may simply be the skills on how to do the job that you have spelled out, (e.g., build this stairway). Real craftsmen bring an understanding of the craft and join the collaborative design process, helping to determine the best way to accomplish goals ("Have you thought about a ramp or a spiral staircase?"). Success depends on recognizing what they know and don't know.

Not all carpenters can design or adapt plans to ensure structural integrity. Like most architects and designers, it is unwise to assume any builders will have knowledge of children's behavior or child scale or understand the program context. The design criteria for use and safety is the child care professional's responsibility and must be clearly expressed.

WANT A CHANCE TO PLAY GOD?   OR   SIMPLY HELP DO SOMETHING NEAT?

"Sunday in the Park with George"
(and Jim, Bruce, Butch, Rich, Bonnie, Bill, Jan,
and hopefully a host of others)

The Glendale Child Development Center Playground
Sunday, October 19
9:00 to 5:00 (or pieces of that time)

What we will be doing is this: laying stone like a jig saw puzzle to create a splash pool bed and the stream. It will be a fun chance to do something creative and beautiful that we hope will make your child's childhood at Glendale even more special. No special skill is required and not everyone needs a strong back.

SOME THINGS TO KEEP IN MIND WHILE TRYING TO CHANGE THE WORLD, GENERAL MOTORS, OR YOUR CHILD CARE PROGRAM

The temptation to present the truth as we know it to the unenlightened — our model way of doing things — appears irresistible. The literature is engorged with articles like "Principles of Effective Training" by Uriah Heep and "Better Education Through HEEP: Human Early Education Planning." Daily new glossy training brochures cross my desk: "Today's Women Supervisors," "Learning From Mrs. Heep," "Better Management Through Heeping." Well, you get the idea.

Perhaps because the only acronyms left are sacred or profane, I'd like to avoid prescriptions and instead concentrate on those points that need to be taken into account as we try to change individuals and programs. I warn you, the following may be heresy and runs counter to the prevailing sales/evangelical spirit so evident today in everything from "Better Parent Seminars" to "Change Your Thighs and Moral Fiber Through Reggaecize."

The fact is that change is difficult. It is often painful and may be short lived. Changing a relationship or an institution which is a web of relationships is even more difficult. If we hope to *develop* ourselves, our staff, or our programs

and actually improve the experiences of children and parents, we need to understand the whole of what we are trying to do.

All the points discussed here are obvious. But they are notions we — directors and trainers — most often in practice try to short cut or understate in our haste to produce results or because of our faith in the new, improved idea that we are trying to establish.

TRAINING ≠ LEARNING

It is easy to provide training — workshops, books, handouts, videos, and so on. It is not that difficult to make training entertaining, where people leave having enjoyed the experience because of a dynamic speaker, interesting anecdotes, fun hands-on exercises, and ample handouts. Providers of training often have a hard time keeping in focus that having training happen is not an end in itself, only a means; change is the desired end. The reason so many training efforts can claim great success in good conscience is the evaluation of training generally measures only the amount of training, the numbers attending, and how it is received — not the change effected or even the actual learning gained.

Successful training is where those present learn new information or skills, or a new synthesis of ideas and skills. The easiest training is adding new tricks to an existing bag of tricks

CHANGING SPACES, MAKING PLACES

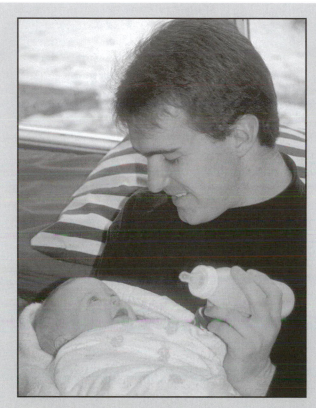

Change seems like it should be so easy. Armed with enthusiasm and good ideas, we can transform the classroom or center into the setting we *now* feel it should be. Unfortunately, beyond minor adjustments, it is rarely so simple. Whatever has been occurring has been happening for a reason.

The status quo — *the way we do things here* — has a logic, however strange it may seem. Child schedules, staff schedules, meal schedules, and carefully worked out scheduled assignments of common space usually molds the structuring of time. The structure of space flows from the allocation of physical resources and the way people and groups have used the resources over time. The physical arrangements and routines that seem self-defeating to an outside observer usually are grounded in the working out of solutions to past or present problems. However, neither rationales nor the results of past decisions may have been reconsidered for a while.

In one program, materials were organized to accommodate a very short staff person and remained that way two years after the staff person left. In another, the daily schedule was designed to facilitate part-time shifts, and much of it remained the same despite a change in staffing patterns that eliminated the part-time routines. In a center where turnover of head teachers was high in three of the five classrooms, the two other classrooms acquired most of the choice furnishings. A casual comment from a licenser, "I think couches have to be fireproof," or a director, "Dramatic play works better by the window, don't you think?" may play a major role in the environment for years to come.

There are three major reasons why change is so difficult. One is that people do what they know how to do, and most of the time they believe in what they do. Second, in an institution, the individual's actions and desires are meshed with the actions of others. There is always a strong pressure to continue present behavior; to do otherwise may alter the daily routines or challenge the benefits or desires of others.

The third block to change is that change takes time, two kinds of time. Time away from children is the most precious resource in child care. Time to think, meet, plan, work through problems, and develop collegial relationships with other staff is scarce or non-existent in many programs. It is easier to continue to do things the way they are done, since there is rarely time to work through any complexities.

The other kind of time is time to sustain change, which often requires stability of people and material resources over time. If staff turnover or fluctuating revenues is a problem, planned change is more difficult.

Understanding that major change is complex and time consuming is important, because often the result of a failed attempt to change is to blame the idea. In a toddler program struggling to develop divided space and individualized learning opportunities, changes in staff and the director's erratic attention due to assorted crises stalled change. When the same ideas came up a year later, the perception of some staff was, "We tried that and it didn't work." Change happens when it is believed in, when the timing is right, and when there are resources to sustain the change.

A Participatory Process

Child care is a group process. Changes always involve others, whether moving a piece of furniture or building an addition. The more extensive the change, the more individuals are involved. There are those who may have to sanction, approve, or ratify change — administrators; funders; fire, safety, health, and licensing regulators; insurers; and others in authority. There are those who have to effect the change — purchasers, builders, staff, and so on. And, finally, there are those who have to live with the change — staff, parents, children, and community. All come to the process with different perspectives, desires, and roles to play.

A participatory process in planning, design, and implementation does not have to mean an endless egalitarian process, culminating in a compromise end product that serves no one well. Nor does involving teachers and parents (and children) in designing or implementing changes necessarily mean having to cater to current desires and interests and skill levels. What is important is that their perspectives and their needs are laid bare. Human experience is the foundation of good design. The more the design process takes into account the blend of roles, attitudes, and behaviors the space will encompass, the better the chance for designs that work.

Involvement in the process can take many forms. Two obvious levels are observation and interviewing. Paying attention to how the adults and children go about their daily lives, using the spaces and materials, adapting or accommodating to the particularities of the space provides critical data to decision makers. Asking them why they do what they do — make the children wait, use or don't use certain spaces, stay inside — and how they feel about the space adds to the information. Going further and asking for their ideas, their wish lists, is useful and may provide surprising information.

An architect, sitting on the floor with a serious looking four year old,

asked the child what she wanted in the room. "Some place to sit with my mom when she comes so we can talk and get my snow pants on and point at my friends" — certainly a reasonable design issue not addressed in many buildings. Asking children questions like where they like to go and where and when they get excited or frustrated or sad helps adults understand their perceptions of space.

In some instances, a decision-making committee or design jury works well. If the goals and design criteria are clearly expressed, asking those who either have a special expertise or a large stake in the result to decide between alternatives is different than having the committee come up with the design.

Participation in the implementation of change invests people in change. It is unsettling for all of us to be moved or to deal with changes. Incorporating a role for children, staff, and parents in the process of planning, building, or moving hastens the settling process. Children can be involved in moving furniture or the contents of a cubby, making pictures or maps of the new and old spaces, adding new decor or dismantling old.

Participation also empowers people. Good teachers, parents, and competent children need to see themselves as environmental designers, capable of adapting environments to accomplish goals.

Change always has allies and obstructionists. A participatory process need not give undue consideration to nay sayers. Clear ground rules about the nature and extent of participation is necessary to avoid misunderstandings.

Brainstorming sessions and wish lists raise unrealistic hopes, unless it is clear that ideas and wants will be winnowed down and competing factors like cost and other needs come into play. Clearly explaining the

TAKING CHARGE OF CHANGE

by Paula Jorde Bloom

Whenever I am with a group of seasoned directors, the conversation invariably turns to how they are coping with a particular change in their programs. While administrating early childhood programs has never been easy, it seems the director's job has become increasingly complex and more difficult in recent years.

Directors point out that the funding and regulatory agencies they work with require more paperwork and documentation of program activities than in years past. They comment that the changing nature of the family has created a host of issues that make meeting the needs of children and their parents more challenging. They report that they now spend considerably more time on attracting and retaining quality staff. In addition, directors report that they must now deal with complex legal issues relating to child abuse, infectious disease control, and insurance liability that they did not confront a decade ago.

In a world of such high-velocity change, it is easy to feel exposed, vulnerable, and out of control. I am convinced, though, that it is possible to navigate the currents of change rather than get caught in the undertow. As Jim Greenman says, change is an integral and necessary ingredient in the administration of early childhood programs. It is not something to be avoided. There are seldom *quick fix* solutions to the complex problems that face early childhood programs. But directors can take charge of change and implement program improvements in healthy and constructive ways.

In many respects, change is an abstraction. It takes on personal meaning only when we can link it to specific examples that have some relevance. When we talk about educational change, for example, we usually refer to changes in policies or practice intended to improve some aspect of programs. For example, we might decide we want to implement new procedures for reporting children's progress or keeping anecdotal notes. The reality is that there are usually multiple kinds of changes going on simultaneously in any program — some major with important consequences; some minor with minimal consequences.

As a starting point, I think it is useful to distinguish between technical change and adaptive change. Technical change usually relates to problems about things. These problems can typically be solved with a straightforward change in procedure such as implementing a flood disaster plan or making changes in the drop-off routine at a center.

Adaptive change, on the other hand, is where there is no clear-cut solution available; even defining the problem is often difficult and fuzzy. Adaptive change often means getting people to tackle tough problems that require painful adjustments in habits, attitudes, or values. For example, lack of participation in staff meetings may be due to any number of factors, not the least of which could be time, teachers' disinterest in the topics, a competitive spirit among staff, or lack of expertise and confidence to be able to contribute in meaningful ways. Improving teachers' participation can't be achieved without sorting through beliefs, values, and underlying tensions that might be reinforcing current behavior.

So how can we take such an abstract concept as change and translate it into some fundamental principles that will serve to guide center improvement efforts? Let me offer six:

Change is a process not an event. Most organizational problems do not fit into the category of being able to be solved in a short period of time. Indeed, most major educational changes take several months, if not years, to implement. Many changes fail, not because they are poorly conceived, but because they are rushed. While we often think of the changes we want to make in a neat, linear, sequential way, no matter how well we plan it, change seldom unfolds in a linear way.

Furthermore, change seldom has a precise beginning or a definitive end — it is a grave mistake to view it as a single event. A director I know wanted to change lunchtime routines and begin implementing family-style serving. Even though the staff all agreed on the merits of the proposed change, getting them to alter actual practice took much longer. For the first week or two, things seemed to go fine, but by the end of the first month, the teachers had reverted back to their old practice of dishing out individual servings. It actually took almost a year to internalize these new procedures.

Change is loaded with uncertainty. As we implement change, there are surprises, there are detours, and there are unpredictable things that happen for better and for worse. Change is a learning process. It often means coming to grips with a new personal meaning about issues, events, the people around us, and *ourselves*. Anxiety, difficulties, and uncertainty are intrinsic to all successful complex change.

What this means is that change is highly personal. We may implement change at the organizational level, but the meaning of change and what determines its success is experienced on an individual level. We can't forget that how individuals react to any given change situation will vary. We need to listen, acknowledge feelings, respond empathically, and provide encouragement and support. If we can tap into people's specific concerns, we can begin to modify the conditions of change to ensure success.

What works well in one setting may not in another. We all know stories of educational innovations that have flopped. Someone goes to a conference and gets all excited about a new approach only to find out that the conditions and circumstances that helped the innovation *take hold* in the first setting didn't exist in the second. There are so many variations among centers, both in people's willingness to adopt new procedures and in their capability to implement new approaches. This does not mean that the innovation or change is not worthwhile, it only means that it may not be equally appropriate for all settings. The most successful educational experiments seem to be those where models have not been adopted wholesale, but rather **adapted** to meet the unique needs of the center.

Success depends on the felt need for change. A director recently shared with me her frustration at her inability to get her teachers to change their behavior on the playground. She characterized their behavior outdoors like that of lifeguards — they sat around and watched the children rather than interacting with them. The director talked to the teachers about the importance of making the outdoor play area an extension of the indoor classroom, but they didn't buy in. From their perspective, there was no problem. They saw the outdoors as an opportunity to socialize. What this director noticed was compliance when she was around; and when she wasn't, they reverted to their old ways. She learned there is a big difference between compliance and commitment. Teachers won't internalize a proposed change unless it is consistent with their value structure and helps solve a problem they experience.

All change isn't necessarily good. The old adage "If it ain't broken, don't fix it" certainly applies to the administration of early childhood programs. Change for the sake of change can be detrimental. It seems to me one of the key functions of the director is discerning what, out of all the choices for improving programs, is worthwhile to pursue. Understanding that any program can only absorb so much change during any period of time, it is incumbent on directors to be very selective about those practices and procedures they elect to change. This means examining some widely held assumptions. One such assumption is *bigger is better*. This may not always be the case.

Change can have a ripple effect. One of the maxims of effective change is *think big, but start small*. Oftentimes, directors who are enthusiastic and excited about a new idea they want to implement get discouraged that everyone doesn't immediately embrace it. A director may not be able to convince her entire staff to try a new curriculum or a new procedure, but it may be possible to get the teachers in one classroom to buy into it. Their success may have the ripple effect of inspiring others. Tom Peters, a management guru, once said, "The most efficient and effective route to bold change is the participation of everyone, every day in incremental change."

The director plays a pivotal role in both assessing the need for change and structuring the conditions that will make the change successful. It is not a haphazard process. Guiding successful change efforts is really a delicate balance of providing direction and suppressing the urge to overmanage. But I believe it is possible to *take charge of change*. This means being purposeful, examining old assumptions, looking critically at what is needed, and then setting out a strategic plan to make it happen.